Money as Sacrament

Money as Sacrament

FINDING THE SACRED IN MONEY

A Book for Women

Adele Azar-Rucquoi

CELESTIAL ARTS
BERKELEY / TORONTO

Celestial Arts
Box 7123
Berkeley, California 94707
www.tenspeed.com

Distributed in Australia by Simon & Schuster Australia, in Canada by Ten Speed Press Canada, in New Zealand by Southern Publishers Group, in South Africa by Real Books, in Southeast Asia by Berkeley Books, and in the United Kingdom and Europe by Airlift Book Company.

The stories and comments of the women profiled in this book are drawn from taped and written interviews conducted over a three-year period and authorized with signed releases. Out of respect for the interviewees, the author has concealed their identities by changing their names, occupations, and, often, hometowns; many of their circumstances have also been altered, and in a few cases, time was collapsed. This said, the essence and truth of their stories remain untouched.

Cover design by Toni Tajima
Book design by Tasha Hall

Quoted materials reprinted with permission from publishers.

Library of Congress Cataloging-in-Publication Data
Azar-Rucquoi, Adele.
Money as sacrament : finding the sacred in money / by Adele Azar-Rucquoi.
p. cm.
ISNB 1-58761-137-6 (pbk).
1. Money—Religious aspects—Christianity. 2. Women—Religious life.
I. Title.
BR115.W4 A93 2002
241'.68—dc21

2002067248

Printed in the United States of America
First printing, 2002
1 2 3 4 5 6 7 8 9 10 — 07 06 05 04 03 02

"The first practical step that an individual can take to free himself from the thrall of money is not to turn away from it, but to take it even more seriously, to study himself in the very midst of the world of money, and to study himself with such diligence and concern that the very act of self-study becomes as vivid and intense as the desires and fears he is studying. "The truth shall set you free," not because it will give you explanations, but because the conscious experience of the truth, even when the truth is hellish, is itself space and light and contact with a higher world.

And what will the individual feel after he begins this work of studying himself in the world of money? If he persists with diligence and guidance and the support of companions, he will experience a feeling more intense than anything the outer world has to offer. With a force and an authority he has until now hardly ever glimpsed in his life, he will directly experience the unbelievable contradiction within himself between the wish for God and the attraction toward material, outer life."

MONEY AND THE MEANING OF LIFE
By Jacob Needleman

Dedication

To you, Mama, who taught me that life is joy. You cried your tears but in the end, released a lifetime of laughter. Your generous and playful way with money is my vision, the very ink for the pages of this book.

Acknowledgments

This book would not be in your hands had it not been for the loving support of my husband, Jim. He was there to jump-start the book, to help edit but mostly to believe in it when I doubted. He helped with language when I couldn't find my own. Thank you, my darling.

Thanks to my friend and editor, Kären Blumenthal, who took on this project, wholeheartedly supporting it with blossoming faith and her own evolving money story. Her thoughts brought new light to my thinking.

Thanks to the women who freely and generously poured their personalities onto these pages.

Thanks to my parents and others in my family, especially my brother Roland, who through the years bounced me away from my many frozen money positions.

Thanks to my convent sisters, The Sisters of St. Joseph of St. Augustine, who shaped my early religious development and blessed it even when it followed some surprising directions.

I can't forget four cheerleaders: Dorothy, Ofe, Renee, and Lynn, whose "yeahs!" brought me to believe the book would someday be published.

Gratitude to my editors at Ten Speed Press, Lorena Jones and Annie Nelson, and then, of course, to all you readers who believed in the book enough to honor it with your money.

Finally and always, thanks to God, best friend of all, Who daily spoke to me through morning pages and lighted candles. I owe You.

Contents

Introduction

I MARRIED A HOMELESS MAN. MY MARRIAGE SHATTERED WHAT I'D LONG considered my common and perfectly sensible money beliefs. However, if the truth be known, I'd been dancing awkwardly with money throughout my life. My new husband was just exiting from an emotional crash that had left him totally without financial resources. When we met, Jim had lived on the streets for about a year. Our marriage brought our mutual monetary fears to a head. Jim challenged every money belief that I ever had, leading me, eventually, to write about the whole matter. Along the way, as I learned to love this man, I entered into a brand-new relationship with money. I felt a deep sense of relief, and at times even fun, as my tangled money roots, having held me fast since childhood, began to loosen. The generous movements of our marriage propelled me finally to accept money as a friend.

"What's money *for*?" Jim asked me. I was surprised by his question. So what *was* it for? For later? When was that? For now? If so, will we have enough later? I turned to face the myriad comfortable and not-so-comfortable financial misconceptions that had blocked my life. Thinking obsessively about money was ingrown, part of my DNA; I'd lived with money doubts all my life, and it was time for corrective surgery. A grocer's daughter, I saw numbers everywhere: markups, price checks, discounts. My father's antique silver cash register was a close childhood friend. In my earliest memories, I could rattle off a customer's change without glancing at the money; I knew how money felt. Jim was quick to notice that after seeing the price of an item only once, I could remember it, down to the penny, weeks later. Everything seemed to have a price for me. He wondered what price or value would I dare put on *him,* with his empty pockets?

After sixteen years as a Catholic nun, I left the comfort of the convent, a place that didn't require me to grapple with the issues of modern life. I had no philosophy about money, other than an unconscious mix of learned attitudes from my immigrant father. Mimicking his anxieties when striking out on my own, I worked compulsively day and night, on three jobs, nearly wrecking my health in the process. I lived not in joy, but in a kind of gasping, spiritual survival mode, a soul-depleting, frantic state. My behavior was irrational, but I had convinced myself that I desperately needed every dime I made. How much was enough? Was there ever enough? I quickly found myself miserable and exhausted, and after a number of years, it became clear that I had to undergo an emotional overhaul in the area of finances.

I sought to unearth the hidden, dark places where I dealt with money, places both mystic and archaic. My relationship to God—my belief that He showered manna on the world and would always provide—ran smack up against lifelong financial insecurities. As I worked through some of my fears, I was shocked to realize, at my parents' death, that I was suddenly heir to a hefty amount of money. While this may sound like an answered prayer to many, the anxieties surrounding my new-found wealth were as overwhelming as when I was poor. I hated money as a poor woman; it confused me even more as a rich one.

In my new role as a wealthy woman, almost a decade since leaving the convent, could I learn to love the gift of money? Church sermons were critical of the rich, as if possessing money made them less spiritual, tainted them, pushed them further away from God than the poor. But I struggled for a different slant on the church doctrine, an integration of my own deeper truths with my affluence. I longed to affirm the flow of money as an extension of human identity, to recognize its creative uses, and to eliminate the burden of judgment on those of us blessed with it.

Painfully and slowly, I came to see that all God really wanted was for me to be myself—a woman deeply shaped, conditioned, and blessed by a unique relationship with money. I didn't need to resist my true self. All the years of my life were pieces in a spiritual puzzle: first in a grocery store, then as a nun in a Florida convent, followed by lean seasons of church service, then receiving my parents' ample inheritance and living off it. I was amazed that my confusion served to shape my very authority on the subject of money.

In these days of intense commerce, as banks speak real time to other banks around the world, as stockbrokers trade money at breakneck speed, and as families are caught up in their own high-powered money circuits, I believe we are desperate to locate the meaning of it all. Especially in this current climate of corporate greed in high places and dishonest accounting practices, we need to recognize the enormous difference between *grace* and *greed* and always ask ourselves: *where is Spirit in all this currency, and what is it saying?*

As I accepted myself more and more, I recognized Spirit had been missing in my relationship with money. Money had come to have that distinctly cold, distant menace of an enemy. How did others perceive money? Was it just tender or something much more? I longed to know whether people struggled with money as much as I did. I wanted to know everything about how people dealt with money, how they'd grown up with it, how they talked about it, and how they shared it with their families and communities. It was my marriage to Jim years later, that enabled me to seek these answers. He and I set out to examine other women's relationships with money. Our investigations took many years. Curiously, we found people eager to relate their struggles on this characteristically shrouded, even forbidden, subject. It was as though they were saying, "What took you so long to ask?" Still, of all those people that we interviewed, few could attest that they loved money and the freedom it gave them.

Many interviewees, particularly those in their middle years, reported evolving from an uneasy alliance with money when young to a decidedly more comfortable relationship with it as time passed. One middle-aged woman put into words a thought that represents my own these days: "I see money as an energy, which, if I manage it well, will assist me in creating my destiny, a *comfortable* destiny. I'm not interested in status symbols, designer jeans, name-brand items, or becoming a compulsive consumer." I couldn't have said it better!

I have come to write about money, in part, because I discovered that I liked the journey. I enjoyed meeting women and freeing them to explore their stories. Was I also helping to free some women from the familiar guilt of having money? I have seen that money conflicts exist in each of us, both from having it and from not having it. This book is about making peace with money.

Sacred or Profane?

I SELDOM WALK OUT MY FRONT DOOR WITHOUT THINKING, "WHOA, have I got my purse?" Then I'll feel the familiar tug of the shoulder strap. I'll stop a moment to rummage, checking for my wallet, my checkbook, feeling the edges of a plastic card tucked within. I don't feel right going out without a few twenties or a fifty hiding in my wallet's folds. These are the forms of money that I "need" to have with me even if I don't plan to shop. I'm not the only one. Rarely do you find a woman without cash on her, no matter how paltry the sum. "Ah, it's there; I'm safe," she thinks. We might touch the bills, for reassurance. It's that comforting feel of cash, the miraculous commodity that keeps life moving—pays the grocer, the postal clerk, tips a waitress. But it's more than that. You don't think money can buy happiness? Maybe it can't, but it certainly seems to stand for it. Fixed in my worn wallet are limitless possibilities for nurturing my soul. No longer is money a source of shame and ambiguity in my life. Nowadays, whether I drive my car, pick up a birthday present, or splurge on another orchid, I celebrate this gift we call money.

What we do with our money is an outward manifestation of our inner truth. Money is not just a worldly possession; rather, it's a synthesis of matter, spirit, and exchange. Like the cathedrals built in great cities, paper bills and metal coins build vital signposts of God's whereabouts. Life happens, like it or not, when money is exchanged. God's presence, if we look closely, shimmers in each transaction. Just watch the cash register connections when kindness springs between clerks and customers. Check the smiles, the satisfied faces, the joy of interchange, the last thank-you. The God I know trusts us to juggle this very ordinary stuff of life, while being fair, honest, and generous with it. It takes two to exchange money. This spiritual faith in money, however mysterious, energizes me, energizes my belief in God. I don't leave home without it.

Seeing Money as Sacrament

AT THE DAWN OF THE NEW MILLENNIUM, TRADITIONAL BELIEFS ARE being challenged, mulled over, or discarded as we seek new meaning and happiness in our daily lives. Charged with a fresh and invigorated spirituality, people are looking at the ordinary in original ways. People tend to reject what does not work, and the old ways are coming to an end. Survival fears, greed, and consumerism are fading, and they are slowly being replaced with richer, deeper values. Bookstore shelves are brimming with spiritual titles. People are hungry for meaning. Consequently, it is time that the fundamental symbol of human exchange, this ubiquitous thing we call money, be considered in a new light—not just as a necessity, but as a holy, living, dynamic stream available to us like daily bread that nourishes us or the water that slakes our thirst. Simply said, it is time to think of money as sacrament.

The word "sacrament" means more than celebrated Christian rites. It is also anything possessing a sacred character or mysterious significance, such as a sign, token, or symbol. *The New Catholic Catechism* says a sacrament is a mystery "as being at once body and spirit, [wherein] the human person expresses and perceives spiritual realities through physical signs and symbols" (no. 1146). The old *Baltimore Catechism,* which many of us Catholics were reared on, declared, in a strict sense, that there are seven sacraments and that each one is "an outward sign instituted by Christ to give grace." In the modern spirit of expanding on that venerable definition, I propose that we admit, at last, that there are surely many more than just seven sacraments. And let's also broaden that limited tenet to make the word "Christ" interchangeable with "God."

Money is certainly a sign, token, or symbol, and, through the centuries, it has been imbued with mystery, power, energy, and terror. But rarely is it thought of as a genuflection of divine love, beauty, and gift. I've thought a lot about this, and I've come to the conclusion that, for many reasons, money and sacrament can be one and the same.

In our mindless, crazed drive for money, something closer to our roots strives to surface, something much more fundamental and authentic, something clearly of spirit. Who among us would go to the lengths we go to for the sake of acquiring mere *stuff*? Our hunger is for well-being, and our money symbolizes that pursuit.

Money endeavors enable us to rise above the ordinary, connecting us to the divine. All money is manna. Strictly speaking, it is in no way earned, as we like to believe, but it is given to us as world citizens, necessary for our nourishment.

Like ourselves, American money is imprinted with divine possibilities, found not only in the familiar yet rarely considered motto "In God We Trust," but also in the two Latin phrases appearing on each one-dollar bill: *Annuit Coeptis* (God has favored our undertaking) and *Novus Ordo Seclorum* (a new order has begun). Inside the capstone of the pyramid on the one-dollar bill, we have the all-seeing eye, an ancient symbol for divinity.

Like prayer, money is everywhere, linking us with one another and bringing something new. Money breeds oneness, togetherness. Commerce and community spring from the same root. I give you something, you give me back a little something. In the exchange, something new is created, something that wasn't there before. Economists have names for this mystery, such as "marginal value added." Business people talk about the "bottom line." I call it "sacrament."

Like grace, money is an essential life energy, a current flowing from above, nourishing and lubricating as it washes in and out of our lives. Is it only coincidence that we call our medium of exchange *currency?*

Contemporary language, always a signpost, points us toward the sacred in money. Consider other expressions for money: "bread," "dough," "pennies from heaven," or "the almighty dollar." Money is also the exchange of *goods*—referring to the "goodness" of it.

Money takes its place alongside other earthly tangible realities that Jesus used to point us upward: "Let's have a meal together," "Bring me the water" (at Cana), "Consider the lilies," and my personal favorite, "Show me the coin of tribute." Typically, charmingly, the God of the Bible used the clay of life to transform the ordinary into sacred truth.

When outwitting his attackers, Jesus also said something compelling about money. What *does* it mean to "render to Caesar the things that are Caesar's *and* to God what is God's?" His use of that conjunction, *and,* rather than *but* has deep meaning for me; instead of splitting the two choices, Jesus connected them. In some liberated, holy sense, rendering to our contemporary world *is* to render to God. By paying taxes and by supporting the needs of our daily lives fairly, generously, and gratefully, we reaffirm that everything is given by God for order and purpose.

I also see money as sacrament because, as the Jesuit scientist Teilhard de Chardin says, "Nothing is profane for those who have eyes to see." When my faith is present to me in the very coinage I handle—in my bank accounts, stocks, bonds, and accounts—I create the possibility of miracles in these commonplace realities. In formal Catholic theology it is questionable whether a sacrament can be fully efficacious without a person's awareness of the grace offered. Certainly, as the gospel of Mark points out, Jesus could not work miracles in his hometown because of the people's lack of faith. We possess the ability to choose, and every money transaction carries the potential to lift us above the mundane, to give our choice spiritual meaning. We must have the eyes to see. It's up to us to make the choice "holy."

Key Findings

When I started this book, I searched library shelves hoping to find a history of women and money. I wanted to place my interviews within a historical context, to trace women's financial progress throughout the centuries. I found no such reference. The shelves hold few books about women and money and next to none that link money with spirituality. Only in recent history are some women beginning to control their finances and refusing to depend on men for survival. In this free-for-all era of dot-com start-ups and fall-downs, this dependency on males is rapidly disappearing. While there have been women of wealth throughout the ages, few earned their fortunes by their own skills, intellect, or sweat of their brow. The wealth, in most cases, as in my own, was created by and inherited from fathers and husbands. My interest in the subject was deepened by the lack of available information about it.

I do not pretend to be an expert on the subject of women and money. I am not a psychologist, but a seasoned observer of human nature. I draw on many years of counseling women privately about money in their lives and conducting workshops about the female psyche with regard to the nature of money. Perhaps because I have been a nun, people feel particularly free to discuss their most private feelings with me; certainly I feel honored that these women have opened their hearts to me, making me privy to this private, complex compartment of their souls. If money is life energy, the "stuff of life," those who have access to it should enjoy a power and advantage that is unimaginable to those who don't. This truth is a deep concern of the women that I interviewed. All agreed that we are at a turning point, a new phenomenon unheard of by our mothers. How are these working women faring in their recent relationships with money? Have they been delivered from yesterday's money and angst? Now the number of women working outside the home greatly outnumbers the women who do not.

The majority of the women interviewed for this book believe that money and spirituality are indeed entwined in deep and mysterious ways. Some could articulate this thought better than others. One woman said, "Money can buy trouble, or it can buy security; it all depends on me." She implied that money is an objective materialization of underlying attitudes, that the condition of our heart determines the health of our financial life. Some women admitted to trying to buy love, a sense of well-being, or affection—all attempts, usually foiled, at creating security through the dollar. Some matured, they said, when they realized that happiness is an inside job, and nothing outside themselves could bring satisfaction. But if I learned anything from writing this book, it is that, while strictly speaking, money can't buy happiness, earning even a small amount of money can pay the first installment on self-respect for many women.

After years of counseling and interviewing women, I unearthed a number of key findings that are essential to the discussion of women and their relationship to money. The first and most obvious, of course, is that a woman's identity is profoundly strengthened when she begins earning money. This is particularly true in the case of divorced women who have become entrepreneurs. However, many married women do not realize this power. A married woman who earns money may not be allowed to make decisions about how to spend it, compromising her self-esteem. One woman in this book, a successful marriage and family counselor, did not realize her full power as an individual until, after twenty-six years of marriage, she stopped turning her checks over to her husband and opened her own accounts.

The taste of financial independence, no matter how meager the paycheck, is sweet indeed. It has a transforming power. One very happy unmarried woman told me, "Never again do I want a man to tell me what I can or cannot do with my money, nor do I ever want to ask for money from a man, or anyone else." This same forty-something woman, after assessing her life situation, cashed in a hefty retirement account and bought herself a now fully-paid-for dream home. "I simply can't wait for someone else to buy it for me, can I?" she said.

Another of my findings, one that surprised me, is that a great Rule of Silence exists in American homes, not just in past generations, but in the current generation, around financial matters. Outright discussion of salary, spending habits, mortgage payments, credit card debt, prices paid for objects and activities, even among the most intimate of friends, and in some cases family members, is taboo. Children are often excluded from family money discussions. Yet, oddly, I found women anxious, excited actually, to share their money secrets. I sensed a feeling of relief when they started talking. It was, without exception, a burning issue for each woman. "No one has ever asked me to discuss my feelings about money" was a line I heard over and over.

I also found that, like personality traits or acquired tastes, each woman is highly individual in her approach to money. Internalized money attitudes accumulate through the years, slowly building a vast part of a woman's identity. No two "money identities" are the same. A woman brought up with painful money experiences will probably suffer feelings of financial inadequacy as an adult. Conversely, a healthy acceptance of and a sense of joy about money, taught in childhood, creates an adult woman with an optimistic, hopeful, and realistic attitude toward her financial life. Not surprisingly, women who grew up in households where parents quarreled about money tend to be in marriages that draw them into money quarrels.

But these are generalities. Many of the women in this book worked hard to overcome childhood privations. As a child, one woman was denied meat at each evening meal. In her family, the men were served meat by women who sacrificed their pleasures and needs for the men in their lives. This woman now makes it a point to serve herself a meat entrée at her evening meal, usually a lovely filet mignon or a nice lamb chop.

One of my most interesting observations was that, whether they are rich or poor, all women experience anxiety about money. Do I have enough? Where will I find more? What do I do with what I have? Affluent women, I found, struggled with questions of guilt. How does it feel to be a "have" in a world of mostly "have-nots?" One woman in this book, a socialite ex-wife of a prominent physician, described her feelings as "separation anxiety" from those who don't have money. This distress does not keep her from living a free-spending lifestyle, but she pays an emotional price for her indulgences. All interviewees were asked, "How much is enough?" Few could answer.

I discovered that some women who have lived in poverty have, surprisingly, experienced an "emotional vaccine" that creates a sort of immunity to fear around survival issues. After decades of doing without, except for basic survival needs, one of the women in this book talks of coming to a place of new peace around money. "I know it will come," she told me. "I know I'll make it." Another woman, who recently experienced a small windfall and could begin to enjoy some of life's small luxuries, says she never thinks about money, she is so unaccustomed to having any. Unlike the affluent socialite, this woman experiences little confusion about money. "You have it or you don't," she says without bitterness. "I normally don't." I am convinced, after interviewing many poor women, that poverty is not good for the soul. The inability to reward oneself with life's small pleasures—a simple dinner in a restaurant, a new piece of clothing, a bottle of cologne—diminishes the spirit and invites depression.

Women who have been dealt financial blows have an uncanny ability to be creative and somehow right themselves in the face of overwhelming odds. This may have something to do with the feminine nature—attributes such as patience, intuitiveness, and inventiveness—coming to our aid in times of crisis. I was particularly impressed by the women who live with little in the midst of mind-numbing materialism and affluence in our society. I was reminded by many women that Lady Poverty, as St. Francis describes the condition, teaches us to live with little, and joy does come from friendships, flower gardens, and the silence of the woods. One woman, who knows how it feels not to be able to pay her bills, said she finds refuge in books. "Treasures in the public library bring the outside world into my limited one," she said.

Not surprisingly, I found that money and anger seem to reside side by side in the female psyche. Perhaps the anger stems from too many years of bondage to men and the powerlessness that women often feel in a society that pays only lip service to female financial independence. I saw anger in the eyes of some of the older women—those over sixty who depend on social security checks or have been forced by divorce or death to leave their homes and enter an unwelcoming labor force where, because they were unprepared or untrained, they work at demeaning jobs for servants' wages. Moreover, I found that many women came out on the short end of the stick in divorce, the quality of their lives greatly diminished by the fracture of their families. Despite women's growing independence, a great number of women over fifty, those who grew up believing that marriage would take care of the money, are tragically unprepared to take care of themselves financially.

One of my clearest findings was that a marriage in which money goals and issues are discussed openly is a marriage that works. One family therapist that I consulted noted that she can gauge the health of a marriage by a couple's shared attitude toward money. "It is when they drop the 'mine' and 'yours' stuff around money, and it becomes 'ours,' that I know they are in good shape." One interviewee, who was in a thirty-five-year-long marriage, said that both she and her husband "mind the money." "Minding," she explained, means they pool paychecks into a joint checking account, and when either needs cash, it is withdrawn without question. All major buying decisions are mutual, and when it comes to large expenditures, the one who vetoes wins. When either one has a financial bonus, they treat themselves to hot fudge sundaes.

Along with the interviewees' stories, I have incorporated family histories and dialogues. While holding to the spirit of their accounts, all names, occupations, and locations of the women interviewed for this book have been fully disguised to protect their privacy. This book carves out a fascinating slice of truth about women's souls and their relationships with money, whether single or married, rich or poor. As I wrote about other women, I learned much about myself and my own relationship with money.

Please note that throughout the book, when I refer to God, I have chosen to use the proverbial "He." Use of "He/She," which more accurately reflects my beliefs, was too awkward for my purposes here.

AZAR'S MA

Chapter One

Counting the Coins—Fledgling Women

I CAN MARK THE DAY WHEN THE PRESENCE OF MONEY TURNED SERIOUS; my father asked me to help run our tiny grocery store. I was a fourth-grader and proud that I had never missed a day of school, but Dad was alone in the store that day. A baby brother was on the way, and Mom was in the hospital giving birth. This request was so strange to me, so unlike my father, that I can still hear his words. They weren't exactly a command, but his request ran counter to his oft-stated conviction that education, and only education, could break us from the shackles of Old World existence.

"Will you work the cash register for me, honey?" He was standing in his stained apron, hands on hips, a short, stocky man with an olive complexion and worried eyes. His pride was revealed by the shakiness in his voice. Daddy never liked asking for help, especially from his children. I was already out the storefront door, off to the world of classroom and playground and school friends. School was freedom, away from the endless, grinding chores. I reluctantly put my books down and, with a sigh, joined my father at the counter.

That day I entered my father's world of money. With Mama absent, her wifely post at the cash register abandoned for motherhood, my father was desperate, saddled with working the front register while slicing sides of beef in the back. The work was hard on Dad, but on rare occasions like this he did recognize his limits. Hire someone to help? He wouldn't hear of it. He had hired two employees in the past year and fired them just as quickly, or they up and quit; I never knew which. So it was up to me that day. My first job at nine years old!

Finding my way around that register was my earliest real dialogue with money. The excitement got to me. My heart beat wildly. I stood still while Dad leaned over to accommodate my height. He spoke kindly, pointing out the meaning of one color-coded oval key after another. I learned which ones to press—none went down easily for tiny fingers—and when the cash drawer released, how to slip bills into the drawer's black slots and pull out the right change. I practiced counting aloud over and over, carefully pulling out the green bills. When the store's front doors opened, the first patrons of the day could barely see me, the little girl with long black curls and wide eyes peeking from behind the ornate register. But they handed me their payment just the same. The sale completed and groceries bagged, I carefully placed exact change into outstretched adult palms and slammed the drawer shut, hearing the register ring as if sounding the signal of a signed contract. Here I was, Dad's ally in business. I savored the money exchange for the feelings of wonder it brought. My father's gentle head pat was more thrilling than report cards brimming with As and perfect attendance.

What's more, those four days surely taught me more about math than a year of classroom exercises. During my first foray in this business, my father patiently taught me, spent time with me, and affirmed my worth. In no time, it felt as if the register were my very own, grown-up plaything and I was full grown. And this stuff called money—my hands recognized it; I could master it. And I could reach others with it, especially Dad. *I could be trusted.* Why *wouldn't* a little girl love handling money?

Those days alone with Dad were all sunshine and closeness, magical days where I was the star attraction at the check-out counter. I must have absorbed all of my father's passions: his hope to succeed, his strong faith, his hard-driving work ethic, and his love of the gamble. Dad, me, and the money. We were a triangle. In that special time of ours, my own money consciousness was born.

Azar's Market

AT THAT TIME ORLANDO WAS A SMALL CITY OF ORANGE BLOSSOMS, with crystal lakes and cattle ranches on the surrounding flatlands. World War II was the town's main concern. A huge billboard on the courthouse grounds touted the names of local men serving in distant lands. A sleepy city then, only two department stores faced each other at the corners of Orange and Central avenues. I remember the first time an Orlando-made cigar hit the market. Our friend, Mr. Curry, introduced Santa Granada brand cigars and sold them in my father's market by the box.

Divinity dwells in the everyday, in the penny we throw across the sales counter.

—Renee T.

Whenever I travel to small Florida towns and hear the ring of an ancient cash register, I'm a child again, getting that approving pat on the head, chit-chatting over the counter with customers like an adult, recognizing when half-crazy Mrs. Smith was stealing tomatoes under her sweater, or when Mr. Anderson had had too many beers and shouldn't be giving me money for more.

I recently read about the poet Adrienne Rich describing how her father, intent on helping her improve her handwriting, had placed pages of poetry before her every day. Adrienne meticulously copied and recopied the imaginative words while a love of language grew in her soul. A poet was born. That story hit home; without knowing it, I had gradually absorbed the art and genius of commercial exchange. A sense of bartering, fixing values, and assigning prices—money's language—took root in me in those formative years. As I look back, I can't remember playing with a single doll, but I do remember raking the money in from those hotels on Boardwalk and Park Place.

As far back as I can remember, sounds of commerce flooded my young ears: meat cooler doors skidding open and shut, the whine of the meat slicer as it cut perfect, thick, pink pork chops with "just a slim rim of fat, Mr. Azar, please," and serious debate drifting from the back about the best price for Dad's choicest cut. Popping Coke bottle tops off on the soda machine and coins clinking and spilling into the cash register over the voice of my grateful young mother. "Thank you, Mrs. Laughlin," she'd smile, pushing sweat and dark hair out of her eyes.

Our market was about the size of an average convenience store, lit by white fluorescent lights and cooled by wooden ceiling fans whirling the Florida heat out the door. A sturdy, white, cement-block building, the store rose in the middle of a giant citrus grove. In orange blossom season, a galloping sweetness invaded the store, reminding us of the goodness and abundance of Florida living. From the time I was four, I spent my childhood playing, barefoot and dirty, in that small world of furious enterprise. I took in my parents' whispered prayers that we succeed. Mama's morning sign of the cross was as constant as the very air that I breathed in the richly scented Azar's Market.

Our grocery on Mills Avenue was nothing less than a bustling community center. People read the colorful signs that Mama plastered on the wide windows and were lured by her specials, but often they wandered in just to talk. In the back of the store, Arab men gathered in dark clutches, wielding tiny cups of steaming, dark Turkish coffee, gabbing on and on. Housewives flocked in to buy, but also to spend some time and share a good word. They lingered over pyramids of cucumbers and eggplants and yellow squash, clucking back and forth with my father about finding just the right tomatoes for the evening's tossed salad. "Take that one!" he would command. When Dad proclaimed a tomato good, the wives knew that *that* was a jewel of a tomato. With an infectious smile and banter reserved only for them, he'd convince them to buy a few more.

Sunday in the grocery was the big day, compliments of the Lord. He sent congregations to Azar's Market, an extension of the church community. We enjoyed twelve hours straight of explosive earning, blessed by the fact that every other grocery in town was closed. And we surely did bow our heads and utter heartfelt gratitude for that! Every Sunday night, after clearing the dishes, we counted the collection right there on the dining room table. It would not be exaggerating to call it a sacred ritual. Mom carefully laid three gray canvas money bags on the table, then shook them upside down. Oh, the sight, the awe of all those coins streaming out. Mom's nimble fingers separated the coins, pushing them into piles: quarters, dimes, nickels, and pennies. She quickly dressed them, like rolled cigars, in brown bank wrappers. Dad fussed over the bills, eyebrows furrowed, smoothing out each one, pulling the corners even, then pressing the pile flat with his forearm. We four kids were the congregation on our knees around that table, wide-eyed, watching these venerated cocelebrants blessing the manna of their labors. No one spoke. The air tingled with something nameless and holy. This closing of our week marked the Azar Sabbath.

And so I was caught in the whirl of Dad's dreams and anxieties with no turning back. Like other immigrants, I felt that the push to succeed meant putting shoulder to grindstone day in and day out. Work was an everyday martyrdom. The business of business was paramount. In the scriptures, St. Paul was pretty fired up about the subject: "He who does not work, does not eat." Dad knew his Arabic bible. So trained, I easily fell into my father's overblown work ethic and was trapped there for most of my adult life: part-time college jobs, nonstop convent chores, and then, decked out in new miniskirt, three jobs at once. Like the typical immigrant, I never thought not to work. It made me feel alive, secure, and purposeful. But something was always missing. The future was unceasingly somewhere else; the present was never good enough. As early as my teens, I was convinced that an obsession with money was dangerous. But my father never wavered from his fixation on finance, eclipsing his wife, his children, even his own well-being.

Early on I came to see that I had two fathers: the smiling daytime gentleman displayed for customers and the dour nighttime patriarch, reserved for Mama and us. I learned that work was an act of faith. If I completed my tasks, I'd be safe from Dad's glares. Recently in an old scrapbook, I discovered a sepia photo of me, leaning against a giant oak, looking away from the camera. I wore a simple flowered print dress, probably one that Mama had sewn from scraps. There were the long black curls that Mama loved so, delighting in her own Shirley Temple. (I remember how she cried the day I cut them off.) I wanted to hug this little girl, twirl her curls once more, bestow on her the attentiveness of a dad far removed from an unrelenting passion for money.

Swishing the old broom across the cold cement aisle and emptying burlap bags of their bouncing potato contents, dust and all, into the lower bins were my regular after school assigned chores. Then there was the giant popcorn machine that I fed each morning. It greeted customers at the market's entrance, a colorful yellow-and-white model like in the movie theaters. When Dad lugged customers' groceries to their cars, they'd have to pass me and the heavenly, buttery scent of freshly popped corn. I'd thrust a fresh popped bag under their noses. If that didn't do it, I'd add my widest smile and "go right for their heart" (my father's words). I was never far from this circus of activity: "Honey, have you shelved those Heinz cans yet?" Mama would yell. "Hey, close that cooler door!"

My favorite spot: the candy counter. I carefully stacked Baby Ruth and Black Cow candy bars, always hoping that Mama would notice and say, "Take one honey!" And sometimes she did.

That property where Azar's Market once stood is now a thriving nest of stores with Korean and Vietnamese immigrants working their own mom-and-pop businesses along the same stretch of Orlando commerce. As I drive past, it's easy to imagine these new immigrants enduring backbreaking hours, pushing register keys, counting flat green bills in ceremonies like ours, extracting a future from each of those small stores. Tucked somewhere in the back rooms of these family enterprises are wide-eyed children, eyeing the bustling exchange, watching plastic credit cards do the work of the old cash registers, catching their parents' dreams just as I once did.

Limited global wealth is a fallacy. There is more than enough to go around and there are always new ways to create wealth.
—Anna D.

A Driven Man

Rejected at Ellis Island at the age of nine, my father was sent back to Syria alone. Luckily, he got a second chance; an uncle was found to escort him back to America across the Canadian border. Like most immigrants, his pockets were empty when he arrived. A string of menial jobs awaited. As with many another immigrant, he labored at these until he connected with something deeper; his strong Middle Eastern sensibilities helped Dad discover his earning potential as a grocer and a remarkable talent for risk-taking and his major culinary gifts.

Predating the printed recipe cards and booklets available in today's supermarkets, Dad would bark out classic Arabic recipes to our shoppers: "You put the lamb in the bottom of the pot with the onions, cook until brown, pour in a can of tomatoes and enough water to cover the top. Add crushed garlic, salt, and allspice after it's cooked." They were spellbound. Traditional Syrian dishes like tabouli, savory spinach pies, *laban* (homemade yogurt), and piping hot Syrian bread (now dubbed pita), which Mama baked weekly, were mainstays on our table, and preparing these dishes in the back of the store were some of my father's happiest moments. Those wafting smells never failed to relax him. He would sing old Arabic songs while simmering peas. And when a customer accepted his invitation to join him at the tiny table in the rear to sample his uniquely seasoned black-eyed peas, his smile lit up the room.

Yet most of the time, Charles Azar was an untethered driven man. In Syria, as a child of hunger and bitter denial, my father had foraged the open fields for wild greens to augment the family's single meal of soup. "I'd pick anything I thought would fix hunger, weeds too," he told me. Now, like the proverbial early bird, he was up and out at day-break, rain or shine. He drove into the Orlando Farmer's Market, compelled to gather the best pick of tomatoes, squash, Bing cherries, and Georgia peaches, roaring back in our brown '33 Plymouth in time to unbolt the store's door, hoping his customers would want what he just bought. And they usually did.

Fresh-faced and smiling, my parents welcomed business at seven sharp. Azar's Market foreshadowed the "convenience" concept of eternally staying open, and what a success that was. If a customer asked Dad his closing time, he'd smile and respond, "I'll stay open as long as you like." It was as if his customers owned the store and he was happy to work for them. I don't think they suspected that the promise of a filled cash register kept those doors open. Dad loved to stand at the curb, in his stained apron, gaze transfixed at the remarkable combination of words emblazoned in black letters across the store's marquee: Azar's Market. He'd earned it! When life was closing in on him as his first Orlando business attempt failed, family lore says, he'd spent the dead of night in prayer. God took his petition seriously, and the rest is history. With nothing more than the equivalent of a sixth-grade education and no collateral, my father, a diminutive man in baggy pants, approached the local bank for a loan to build a store. And he got it, delivering us from the Old World into the New.

Like my father, my mother also had two personas. The first was youthful and often hidden and is hard to remember. As a child, I always knew where to find her: standing behind that check-out counter. But I could never quite touch her inner core, obscured as it always was by Dad. Like all Arab women of her time, bending low to please their husbands, my dark-haired mother dutifully followed Dad at a distance, nearly buckling under the weight of his orders. Yet I hold dear two dynamic portraits of her while still a young woman. One expresses her deep-seated anger.

It was after dark, after the store had closed. She was reading a letter from her older brother. Suddenly she dropped to her knees and let out such a scream that the whole neighborhood must have heard. I froze. This was a different mother, one who needed help. I ran over to her and picked up the letter, proud that I could read. *Blinded by a snow storm, a hit-and-run driver left Mama's body dead in the snow. We didn't know where to look for her, and found her hours later. We'll hold her funeral up if you could come.*

I'd often heard Mama tell my father of her long-held dream of returning to her original home in Paterson, New Jersey, to visit her mother. But like many of her dreams, she had laid it in an old drawer, hoping to open it some later day. Life had slammed that drawer shut. My mother didn't go to the funeral because Dad said the store needed her. I can still hear her heaving sobs and see the moon bathing her face. I could only lay beside her quaking figure and rub her back, hearing her mumbled words. After a while, she turned and played idly with my curls, a curiously comforting gesture for both of us. Dad's greed couldn't spare her, and I don't think she ever forgave him for it. Money, as it so often did, dictated Dad's choices.

> ***I wasn't really clear about what my father did to "make" money, and I was never informed about my parents' financial status.***
> ***—Sharon W.***

I brag about another vivid memory of this young Mama to friends. It occurred one late afternoon. I must have been around twelve when Dad, sitting on the living room sofa, suddenly let loose one of his unstoppable harangues. His rage filled the living room, addressed to no one in particular and everyone at once. It started with simple complaints, then rose to a raging tirade over a salesman who had flirted with Mama, and ended, as usual, with Dad's red face and booming voice blasting everyone in sight. I sat across from him, frozen, wanting to slip out at the next pause. Mama was in the kitchen furiously chopping scallions when she suddenly burst from the tiny kitchen like a rocket going off and flew right at him, brandishing a long blade. She stood over him, eyes aflame, and shoved the sharp knife right up to his throat: "Not another goddamned word!" Dad's eyes bulged out of his sockets, as did ours. None of us had ever heard this voice or seen this person. The knife didn't move and we didn't either, sitting stone still. I fell absolutely in love with my mother that day; she appeared as fearsome as any Amazon in mythology. Sadly, her standoff was good for just that once; Dad's stream of verbal abuse continued unabated through the years, and Mama settled more deeply into her well-worn, shadowy role. The Arabic culture rooted in Mama was too strong while Mama's liberated genius—what I like to think of as her true self—appeared only after my father passed away.

As for her proficiency, Mama had no equal. Dad knew that she was the solid-gold base for his venturous undertakings. Without her people skills, her ability to read contracts, initiate telephone calls, and her records of all taxable income, he might have remained in that humble grocery forever notwithstanding all his considerable talents and charm. The gifted and brainy woman voted top of her New Jersey class deftly juggled business, husband, and the four of us. She was the center of our existence. Mom kept supplies filled and handled sales reps better than Dad ever could. An efficient accountant, she knew which invoices to pay and when. She was our policewoman who caught thieves hiding cuts of meat or cans of Spam under oversized jackets. With four kids running wild in the grocery that we called our playground, she was undaunted. She provided the opening song at the doorway, the cheery "Good morning!" followed invariably by a sly joke she'd gathered from a salesman, as likely as not off-color. Between customers, she lit the fire under pots of stuffed grape leaves she'd rolled that morning. Patrons warmed to Mama, and she appreciated that, given the rigors and coldness of a life with my domineering Arab father. If she had only known her power!

I thought a lot about my childhood and money lessons, but in vain. I mean you could never even tell the price of a shirt.
—Libby M.

Over steaming dishes of lamb, stuffed grape leaves, and *laban,* Dad officiated at the table. Sometimes his laughter easily spread over dinner and just as easily he could descend into sudden tirades while the rest of us did the best we could to eat under the onslaught; it was difficult for me to stay angry at Dad. I didn't have to look hard to see the internal demons pulling at him. "You're a nobody with no education, no verbal skills, and only five feet tall."

But Dad the businessman was not to be stopped. First, he grabbed up the empty lot beside the grocery, then bought the wider lot on the other side, uprooting dozens of orange trees. Savings from the register grew until he built stores that launched major real estate dealings and continued a dizzy ascent all the way to Wall Street. I am ever inspired by the memory of the dark, once-destitute Syrian slamming the full register shut and joyfully crying to God in Arabic, *"Nuschur Allah!"* (Thanks be to God!)

Dad's biggest and most mysterious gamble early on was the purchase of a small, working orange grove just outside Winter Garden on a crooked dirt road. To drive out there was like traveling to another country. And what did Dad know about orange groves anyway? Somehow, someone or something rapidly doubled the eight thousand-dollar investment. You can be sure there was steak on our table that night. How he bragged about his good fortune as he gathered Arab friends, store owners like himself, around a table at the all-night poker feasts. This was not the kind of poker men played in salons. Here, friendship and competition mixed with loud joking and jostling past midnight. Cigarettes dangled from the sides of mouths. Ashtrays, bottles of golden ouzo, and a couple of decks of cards spilled out on the plastic tablecloth to create a friendly gambling ritual. In my nightgown, I'd sneak behind the door and listen to the moans or laughter when one man successfully called another's hand. Whoever got the pot here got it fair and square, and the date for the next game was set before anyone left. Poker always seemed to me the outpouring of the spirit of Arab men doing what Arab men do—throwing the dice, celebrating their victories, eating enthusiastically, sipping from their ever-present shot glasses. I surmised early that throwing dice and taking chances with money is neither bad nor sinful.

Money talk was normal at home. Money was the way you got things done, the way people faced life. Dad taught that money discussions were as natural as teaching me how to lace shoes or ride a bike. "What's your best price?" was as familiar to me as "Our Father" might be to someone else. After all, the Arab who had participated, had spoken up, had played the game, was the Arab who could sleep at night. Salesmen sauntered through our grocery's front doors, briefcases bulging with ads promising my folks fortunes if they'd invest in this or that. Then the money talk got serious, louder—always friendly, but with an exciting edge as two conflicting interests drew sparks. The haggling! Dad loved haggling at the grocery store. After we sold the market, Dad went on to hustle big land deals, agonizing over what appeared to me to be insignificant issues. I longed to yell at him: "What earthly difference could five hundred dollars make on a deal when you're forking over fifty thousand?"

Years later, a friend of mine, listening to my childhood stories, aptly explained the psychology behind Dad's bargaining. "You give yourself an edge, mental insurance. If you're not willing to settle for a stated price, you feel that nobody will ever get the best of you." Something like this lives in me too.

I like to think that for all his dogged determination and financial resourcefulness, Dad finally, at the end of his life, recognized the value of a love that cost him nothing, a love that was right under his nose all along. A sudden brain clot sent Dad to the hospital and in just a few weeks, he welcomed death. Only the night before he died, I had sat close, spoon-feeding him a cold dish of vanilla ice cream. He was seventy-seven years old. Twenty-four years after leaving home, I stood before a crowded room to deliver my most heartfelt farewell. Dad had paid dearly for his family crimes: all four of his kids abandoned home immediately after graduation. According to Mama, my parents sat alone at the dinner table many nights immersed in doubt. *"Didn't I do all that I was supposed to do? I provided for them. What did I leave out?"* Our poor father was rich now, but facing empty chairs. Indeed, what is our profit when we construct a life from nothing and in doing so lose something that makes it all worthwhile?

One night, long after Dad had died, I sat with Mama on her condo deck. I brought up Dad's behavior as she painted bright red polish on her long, oval nails. Mama wasn't afraid to let loose now. The inner power my mother had discovered since Dad's death was remarkable. She was, in truth, a different woman. The moon was queen over us that evening, reflecting light on the two of us now safe from that stifling male domination that had so gagged our honesty, our behavior, our thoughts. I watched Mama sip from her cup. Her brow was no longer wrinkled in anxiety and a new softer expression beamed from her eyes.

"Sometimes, Mom, I forget how revolutionary Dad's way was and how he was

Something so common as money must be a blessing.
—Shirley G.

caught between waves of the old and the new. And yet, look at us now! If he hadn't pushed so hard would we both have this carefree life to relish? It's sure nice to see you so well protected." My words surprised me. After his death, I was beginning to alter my view of Dad; my anger was receding.

By this time, Mama had fully roared into her own person, powered by a love of life that she'd stored somewhere in another old drawer. After Dad's death, it didn't take her long to tap into the pure fun of spending his money. And why not? Wasn't the wealth just as much hers from all those years working behind that counter? And the new Mama believed that abundance was a true gift. She received it surprisingly guilt free. What a mentor she became for me!

I had one other money mentor as a child: Mama's brother, Uncle John. He was an expert, not in the ways of making money, but in how to spend it. Smiling, he would stride into our home and paint it with welcome bright laughter. A traveling man, Uncle John toured the carnival routes hawking cotton candy and popcorn, toting a carnival atmosphere into our too-serious lives. He threw dollars around simply for pleasure. Money was like some magical essence that deeply amused him. Unheard of! Plugging a coin into my ear and finding a silver piece there, he would laugh at our find as much as I did. Then there were the dollar bills magically appearing on an ice cream counter to pay for second helpings. Naturally, we couldn't get enough of Uncle, and he couldn't get enough of giving.

Unlike my father, his dollars were vital, selfless, fun. And he refused to let Daddy corner him into a more responsible role; he had no paychecks, no savings, and no anticipated, ideal future. One day, while the brothers-in-law played backgammon, Dad mentioned that Uncle John should make a will. "Your girlfriends might be around," Dad joked. Uncle John leaned back, and guffawed: "I don't need a will, Charlie. Tell them that being of sound mind and body, I spent it all!" Dad couldn't handle this free spirit, but Uncle John didn't let it bother him. He kept coming to visit us, this flying saucer of a soul.

Decades later, when Uncle John suffered his first heart attack shortly after visiting me, in my new role as Sister Adele and with all my new-found religious zeal, I quickly grabbed my prayer book and beads to assist him, right through the gates of Paradise if need be. I found him lying on a hospital gurney, quiet and peaceful, eyes closed, arms across his chest, smiling. But I was all business. After all, according to my mindset then, Uncle John had never done penance for his four-letter words, his alliances with dozens of women, and other assorted church-condemned practices. But I loved him. I simply had to get him heavenly passage. "Uncle John," I entreated, "Say the Our Father with me." He lay still, then raised his head slightly, opened his eyes wide, and studied me intensely. As he eyed the beads in my hand, he quietly proclaimed: "Honey, I don't need your prayers. Life doesn't owe me a damn thing."

I always pick up a lost penny. It's a signal that more is on its way.

—Carla M.

Uncle John lived many more years, and his words of faith will stay with me forever. Sure, he wasn't a practicing Christian, never had been. He never uttered God's name except in jest. Yet the divine spark that lives in all of us crackled and leapt to an amazing brightness in Uncle John, illuminating an innocence that never got sucked into anything like "upward mobility." For me, he was one of God's mystical money spenders. God would send it, and Uncle John would spend it.

Fledgling Women

By my teens, for good or bad, I had forged a definite money-oriented personality. During my interviews, I've discovered that too few young women recognize the value of becoming comfortable with money early on. They deal with money, play with it, sometimes fight with it, but they rarely observe what's behind all that charged behavior. Most arrive at adulthood lugging baggage from their parents. From the money talk I've heard, they admit that, all too often, their monetary behavior reflects their parents' attitudes.

In financial matters, most young women are filled with anxiety. "Money is the scariest word I know," blurted twenty-four-year-old Maggie when we talked. Money causes her to suffer, to doubt herself, doubt her parents, doubt society. Maggie's lack of education about money management—not the kind offered by professional financial planners, but the attendant emotional juggling—was apparent. She insisted that money is "evil." Maggie, like so many other women, is the victim of a malady afflicting the best of families—money silence. While I revere the rule of silence that exists in convents and monasteries, the wall of silence that surrounds money and blindsides families about finances is worrisome. One young woman revealed, "In my childhood, money just wasn't discussed. I was trained not to talk about income. Not talking about money was quite silly. There it was, right in front of us, and we were mum about it."

At a recent money workshop that my husband and I hosted, a young lawyer named Sharon admitted, "Money did not exist in my family. It was absolutely ignored. I find that I'm extremely curious now about the number of parents who retard their children by remaining closemouthed about finances. That's a major childhood influence in itself."

When asked about their family's money habits, most of the women in the workshop looked blank, then described a prevailing silence. As children, these young women did not know their parents' income, net worth, or economic status. Poor girls thought they were rich. Rich girls thought they were average, even poor. All of these young women, as if from the same family, loudly complained about their parents' woefully inadequate financial disclosures.

I felt encouraged when I learned that a young librarian in attendance, discouraged and fed up with her parents' silence, had sought and found a money mentor in a competent and open parishioner at her church. His advice shifted her thinking enough that she had actually purchased her first home under his watchful eye. Another woman had sought financial counsel from one of her church members, and as a result, had cut up her credit cards and was able to sleep through the night in peace.

Mentors like these are available everywhere, they are everyday folks who have faced the issue of money and vowed to understand its power. Any woman contemplating marriage and/or children must pledge to do the same, refusing to drag old money behavior into a fresh, new relationship. Women must insist that they and their partners discuss money in detail, laying all their financial hopes and fears on the table. If necessary, couples should get a money mentor to work with them long before they're married. It could determine the marriage's long-term health.

Little Pia: *Early Imprinting*

Morgan comes from a family where the mention of money was not just taboo, it incited survivalist responses. She was determined, however, not to repeat that pattern. Mother of eight-year-old Pia, Morgan launched an intelligent money program when Pia was just five. This is how she, with the help of a psychologist's guidance, designed it.

Pia's allowance is the number of dollars per week that she is years old. At eight, for example, she receives eight dollars a week, or thirty-two dollars per month. While this may seem like a bundle, one-fourth of it is placed into a savings account that Pia cannot touch, and one-fourth of the amount is whisked into a college fund. Morgan supervises both accounts. Another fourth of Pia's allowance is reserved for any special or large purchase, such as a bicycle. The last fourth, perhaps the most important, is Pia's weekly spending money, and she is allowed to spend it whenever and wherever she wishes.

Morgan is amazed by how carefully Pia handles her money. Pia saves diligently, regularly requests statements from her mother, and often wants to know how much is in her college fund. Before she is ten, Pia will be taught to read debit and credit columns. She will know how to track her money. She will learn how to think critically and pragmatically and how to negotiate. She will know the thrill of saving and spending, and, most important, she won't fear money. Morgan is offering Pia more than a financial education. Using this money program, she is introducing her daughter to money's purpose, instilling a sense of financial astuteness and security. The eight-dollar paycheck always arrives on schedule. (Morgan vowed that she would respect her daughter's worth as an individual, which means the check is never late.) More important, Morgan ritualized the custom of granting an allowance, moving it to a level of mother-daughter bonding. Sure, money conflicts between mom and child will emerge, but the resolution will tighten their relationship. Pia's growing money philosophy flows from a safe and open place.

> ***No doubt my sense of self-worth has been wrapped around this money stuff for years.***
> ***—Mona G.***

Maggie: *Money Curse*

Young Pia could certainly model a healthy money relationship for Maggie, a college student caught in a tangled web of money misjudgment. "Maybe it's good for me to talk about money, because I don't like it. I'm untrained. If I could do without it, God, I'd be so much happier." Maggie is a bundle of energy, albeit troubled. "Look at it all! My apartment rent, my car payments, food, clothing! I couldn't make it!" she said. Maggie, like many of today's youth, was forced to return to her parents' home after college. Even with a job, she couldn't make ends meet. She felt like she had made a U-turn in life. At home, the old family chores, family rules, and even family food flooded back. Maggie was angry and frustrated by the way life had seemingly turned on her.

Her approach to money seemed cursed from the start. As I listened to her laments, the lyrics of Bob Dylan's folk song played in my mind:

"Money doesn't talk, it swears." The small Vermont college that she had attended hadn't prepared her for the next world of economics, she wailed. "I've become so one-track on making money that I don't have fun. It's all paycheck to paycheck! What the hell good was my scholarship?" Now in a masters' program, Maggie was agonizing over dollars and cents: "It's a losing war. I feel strapped, defeated a thousand times." Academically educated but untutored about money, Maggie faced a world that demanded that she get smart, and fast. But right now she wanted to change the subject.

"Let's have lunch? Peanut butter sandwich?"

She rose and I followed her. In the sunny kitchen, I noted all manner of modern appliances on the countertops. Cable, Maggie's tabby, played with my feet. Maggie glanced over her shoulder as she spread peanut butter on slices of wheat bread. "I ate peanut butter and jelly sandwiches during an entire college summer," she announced proudly. "Peanut butter was considered a treat in convent days," I assured her as I accepted a lovely tray of cut-up veggies, fruit, and slices of cheese.

As we munched, I searched the youthful face, noting that her money woes weren't about to leave her anytime soon. "Tell me more about your college life," I urged. Her face brightened. "Compared to other students, my peanut butter dinners did pay off. I'm out of college debt free, while some friends still make payments." Then her eyes darkened, and she put down her sandwich. "I'm going to be brutally honest about my folks," she said.

Maggie was close to her father, and that's where she began, revealing pent-up frustration over her father's emotional knots around money. "I feel like a victim of Dad's pattern of silence. He doesn't want to talk about money. He just wants to spend it. Both of my parents are terrible models when it comes to controlling their spending. I know they feel guilty by the way their eyes dart when they drag stuff into the house." We were silent a moment, both shocked by the energy behind her outburst.

She went on, pointing to a glass shelf balancing dozens of objects—sculptures, ceramics, figurines, and pots. "Unnecessary junk," she said. Leaning back, Maggie pulled Cable onto her lap to quiet herself.

"Dad's excuse is that he grew up poor. But to get rich, he spends too much time working. The money buys him another car, or a top-of-the-line stereo system, and then he's back in the vicious cycle again and takes on more work to stay ahead." She looked at me angrily. "I told him so once, but he said he feels *entitled."*

Her tone shifted. "Maybe it's not their fault, maybe it's not even money's fault. All I know is that bills control my life just like they control theirs." Maggie slipped the cat to the floor. "Isn't it the role of parents to teach children the realities of money?" she asked.

"Maybe when money's so close, so available," I offered, "we don't want any reins on it, or even want to talk about it. Perhaps your parents are simply uncomfortable exposing their deepest feelings where money is concerned." I said, "Honest money discussion can open doors to our inner lives."

From the way Maggie jumped up, I knew I had struck a chord and entered an area she was not prepared to deal with. "I've got to get to class," she announced, glancing at her watch. She grabbed her purse and books, saying, "I'm just trying to find my way."

I gathered my things and made my way to my car. Could someone with baggage like Maggie ever find a comfortable relationship with money? At home, I pulled a jar of peanut butter from the pantry and stood it by my perpetually burning prayer candle, thinking of Maggie.

Sarah: *Money Love*

No two young women could feel more differently about money than Maggie and Sarah. Sarah Thomas had a prayerful girlhood, and, at four, her reverence for God's word and things spiritual took root. With candles and altar lights, Mass and Holy Communion planted seeds deep in her heart. She merited a coveted prize for reciting twelve psalms from memory in Sunday school. For an already alert, conscious soul, grade school was a time of reading scripture, talking things over with God, and attempting to follow, like young Joan of Arc, divine direction.

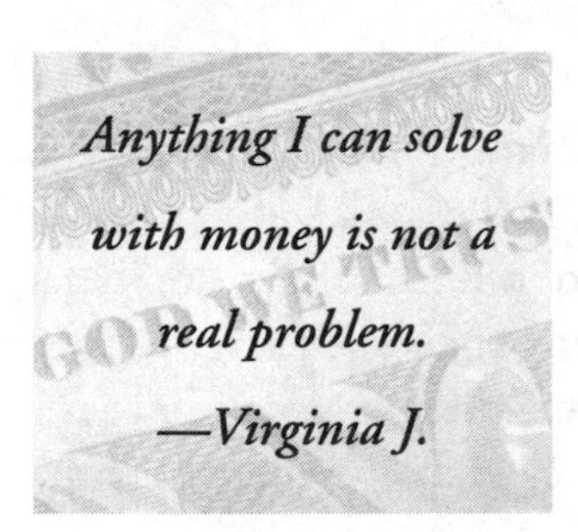

With her fresh face, no one would believe that Sarah is over twenty. I delighted in her sparkle and relished hearing her weave money talk with talk of her faith in God's abundance.

Sitting at a table in a restaurant, Sarah described her feelings with gusto: "Money is the determiner that coaches my choices. I pray for guidance, and most of the time, I get it." In contrast to most of the young women I'd interviewed, Sarah reflected no distress, didn't whine, and didn't blame her parents for the money education that she didn't get. "I believe God is neutral about our having money. His concern is that we be happy, and I believe that 'Truly He doth supply all our needs,'" she said. Sarah quoted scripture: "Consider the lilies of the field, your heavenly Father knows their need and feeds them."

The sheer breadth of her scripture understanding, so positive and so real, was moving. Not Bible pounding, her faith stood as a companion, and God was especially present in her day-to-day choices. "I find passages that praise riches, that say God's abundance is land, house, food, wine, and pets, all life supports. Then I ask myself whether these things reflect the sacramental aspects of money."

Hearing her, I knew she had come to her understanding early, and, unlike many who believe Jesus wants us to give all our goods to the poor, Sarah is adamant: "I don't give all my goods away! I treat myself."

Whoa! My spoon stopped in mid-air. She dabbed at her salad, then waved her fork in the air, as if imitating some young preacher before a congregation: "What about the story of the Good Samaritan? He was no dumb-head. He knew he needed money to do good."

I picked at my salad. The food was secondary to the nourishment of Sarah's energy. Her life experiences had been beautifully shaped by God, leading her away from a New York Carmelite convent to a divine pathway of her own arranging. Unlike before, it was precisely her paycheck that helped shape her spiritual contentment. I had never encountered a broader money perspective from such a young soul, nor a clearer example of the spiritual vigor of a healthy attitude about money.

"Look at Solomon," she continued, "and his wealth that gave him the ability to accomplish great works." Clearly, to Sarah, money and spirituality had never been, as they are to so many of us, mutually exclusive. And the Bible backed her up. Sarah had woven money and faith into a tapestry that satisfied her basic need to serve God and the world: "When I spend my money, I feel that I provide jobs for others," she said, sipping her coffee and smiling at me.

Such dogmatism might have turned me off once, but the quality in Sarah's voice, her charm, her youth, her earnest eyes left me a captivated novice. I felt like Jesus, who once had said of the Centurion: "I haven't seen faith like this in all of Israel!"

Ann: ***Paralyzed by the Past***

I thought of Sarah and how her money personality differed from a young woman I read about who had inherited half a million dollars. Her inheritance had scared her, and she tucked it into savings and aimed to completely banish it from her mind. Avoiding money is one way to sidestep a great life opportunity.

Ann was plagued with avoidance issues. She acknowledged to me that she allowed financial decisions to linger to the point of tangling up her life. Ann had accompanied me to a friend's getaway beach home for a weekend. Balmy Florida weather, a radiant sky, and a warm sun greeted us. Ann sprawled next to me on the wooden deck, a baseball cap smartly perched on her head, eyes watching the surging waves. But I could feel the tension building.

"What can I say?" she finally blurted. "I'm just a horrible procrastinator. It's not that I don't pay my bills. But I always pay late. Nobody jails me or tows my car away. It's just that I don't want to look at my money problems."

I turned to face her, giving her my full attention, but didn't say anything. "The truth is that I'm a compulsive spender. I bounce checks, and I'm late with my payments. I figure that if I don't look, the mess disappears," she said. "Sure," she continued, "I'm kidding myself. My bills spiral out of control."

I looked toward the horizon, hearing her confession over the ocean's roar. "I was finally approved for a new car, but I had to pay a huge penalty for all my former late charges. And guess what? I'm still late with car payments," she said. She paused, whether to take a breath or to quarrel with herself about revealing more, I wasn't sure. The green ocean lapped the dunes, then slid back again. Children, free of money worries, built sand castles on the beach in front of us.

Ann reminded me of a child, anxiously disclosing sins. She began to speak rapidly, saying, "I haven't a clue as to how much money I have in the bank right now or probably more to the point how I got this way." She knitted her fingers tightly, playing nervously with her rings. Ann's honesty is the characteristic I find most appealing about her, but frankly, I was astonished at her bungled money practices. Despite her stature in the business world—she commands an excellent salary as an executive with a prestigious law firm—she had to scramble to get a car loan. It had been humiliating, as the credit check had revealed her glaring lack of responsibility.

Was it past fear that paralyzed this young executive? Her parents' fears? Hardworking middle-class people, unlike Ann, they paid their bills reliably, always on time. Yet a disaster had struck them during Ann's high school years. And, like most children, she absorbed their quiet alarm. For long periods, the family was forced to live from payday to payday because her father's business suffered.

"Dad always paid his employees before paying himself. He'd come home with a reduced paycheck, or sometimes without one at all." She was silent for a long while.

I broke the quiet, "Fear can be a useful, even wonderful protection against losing all one's money, whether it's an investment in the stock market or placing an entire paycheck on a long-shot horse. I believe that kind of fear is healthy. But when we are consistently defensive about money, always retreating, never stepping forward to deal with it, the fear becomes self-defeating." She nodded mutely.

At this time in her life, Ann requires a larger apartment, yet she has shoved that move to the back burner in fear of exposing her poor credit rating again. She holds her head aloft with a lie. "I tell my friends that I just don't want to move."

Revealing lingering grief, Ann connected money to her mother's death. "Money doesn't save anyone from dying," she said ruefully. Once again, I watched fear and the common tendency to dwell on the past block her clear thinking. At this rate, she'll always have money troubles.

Ann and I fell into a thoughtful silence. I knew we had gone as far as we could in our money discussion. I felt sad that I couldn't help Ann fix her quandary. But as I had resolved in the beginning only to interview not to interfere, I had to let go any desire to step in.

I slipped off my sandals, adjusted my beach chair, and watched the sun sink into the ocean. Nonetheless, I had a niggling feeling that Ann might never enjoy a monetary metamorphosis. It was up to God.

Amy: *Old Money, Old Fears*

I couldn't shake Ann from my mind during a trip to Boston for a conflict resolution workshop, a gathering of socially conscious activists who wanted to do something about America's racial divisions. While at the conference, I met twenty-five-year-old Amy, a brainy young woman who proved again that having money doesn't mean happiness. Amy had a slight figure that seemed even smaller under oversized denim overalls. I was captivated by the maturity in her voice. Amy agreed to an interview over our lunch break. We ordered sandwiches and found a place in the corner of a small grill.

She poured out her story quickly, between bites. "I come from a privileged Boston family," she said, eyeing me for a reaction. When she didn't get one, she went on. "My family has enjoyed old money for generations. So I'm stuck with it. That's why I'm at this workshop. I hoped that by talking, the shame I carry might vanish."

She paused, looking directly at me for the encouragement to continue. "Growing up in financial wealth is the biggest life challenge I had to face," she said, her eyes sad. She described a life fraught with emotional obstacles. Being born upper class is not necessarily easier than being born poor. It's emotional scarring of another color. Unlike Maggie, or Ann, or even Sarah, Amy wrestled with the problem of excessive money. She was a poor little rich girl. Painful incidents at school taught Amy that existence in a world of haves and have-nots would be eternally brittle. Barely out of college, her family bestowed her with the power to direct enormous amounts of money to charitable institutions. Yet each time Amy met a new person, she was faced with the nagging question, "Do they love me or my money?"

> *Some people are tested by having money, while others are tested by having none. But the vast majority of people sort of flounder around in the middle.*
>
> *—Pat G.*

Several workshop participants ambled by carrying trays. They greeted Amy amicably, and she seemed relaxed speaking with them. The sessions we had just left dealt with our individual prejudices about the rich and the poor. Amy had admitted to all of us that she was wealthy. One of the participants had asked Amy, "Did you think we wouldn't like you?" And Amy had answered, "I didn't know. But I do know that this kind of honest talk about money is new to me."

She had confessed that belonging to the "owning class" left her feeling blessed and confused. So what else is new? I thought to myself. We all experience those feelings. But I didn't realize just how ugly it could be to be considered a "have" by an angry and deprived "have-not," that it could hobble a life.

Choosing to attend a public high school, Amy had hoped to be like everybody else, but she stood out. For the most part, she enjoyed a few friends but was always aware that she was economically, and somehow socially, different. "Early on, I realized that wealth breeds isolation. The kids just didn't trust me."

A close friend of mine, whose childhood poverty contrasts Amy's economic abundance, came to mind. She had recently married a professional who works with the wealthy. Her husband is an antiques appraiser who regularly hobnobs with powerful people. He zeroed in on his wife's bias. "You'll have to get over your prejudice toward people with money. Some can't help it. Some earned it. Others inherited it, and from what I observe, most are trying to be good stewards."

I asked Amy whether, as an adult, she finds that people still don't trust her because of her wealth. She nodded her head vigorously. "It's true; they still don't," she agreed. I was aware of a sadness in her. She had few friends and a part of her still yearned to join the "ordinary" world. That Sunday evening, Amy gave our workshop group a burning truth to be reckoned with. Her presence was a sober reminder that, too often, we tend to isolate, marginalize, and judge not only the poor, but also the rich. Neither can be God's way any more than the other.

Kari: *Legacy of Pain*

Contrast Kari Diaz, a nouveau riche girl, to Amy, our old-world money girl. The challenges are the same. Old friends of mine, Kari's free-spending parents had separated many times. Kari and her brother were forced to live with one parent or the other. Now eighteen, I saw her to be mature beyond her years, the culmination of playing mother to her own immature mother. I hoped, without prying, to warm her to the subject of her parents' money issues, certain that the discussion would shed light on Kari's own money ideas.

Kari's parents had played a dangerous union of political games with their family. Theirs is a chess match of his and hers, of winner take all after outrageous deceptions. Kari was persecuted as a child, her parents pulling her in opposite directions, unaware of the harm they inflicted on her young soul. On the surface, the family squabbles were always about money, but there was a hidden need for something more, perhaps power, surely control, always recognition. Kari's parents allowed their money spats, even before they acquired lots of it, to rule their marriage, baffling their children with this eternal tension.

Kari's words tumbled out: "Despite the fact that Dad gives me a good monthly allowance when I'm away at college, I feel insecure. I want to buy clothes, but buying them means I end up broke, so I just wait till I come home to buy them."

I was curious. "Is spending money on clothes a cause for conflict?" I asked.

"Absolutely," she said. "I bounced three checks last year." Not looking at me, she continued, "Dad had to pay twenty dollars for each bounced check. He was furious, and he closed my checking account, making me furious too. That checking account gave me a sense of worth, a feeling of security. I miss it."

One glorious Florida morning, we sat on the veranda of her parents' condo on Jacksonville Beach. The only sound was that of Kari's voice against the wind, waves, and squawking gulls. She added a spoonful of sugar to her coffee and smiled. She seemed anxious to talk. I scanned her luxurious clothing. We zeroed in on a familiar subject: How does a young person spend money and feel good about it?

"Do your parents object to your spending?" I asked. It was startling that her parents, ignoring their own rampant consumerism, would judge their daughter harshly for hers.

"Well, yes, I always hear about it, so I don't always tell them," she admitted, adding that she sometimes spends foolishly and sabotages budget plans. Because she's tight-lipped with her mother and father about being broke, she searches out friends for short-term loans.

I was amused and saddened at Kari's deceptive twists and turns, evidence of her early money conditioning.

As for the family's sudden wealth when Kari turned sixteen, she explained that she had no idea where it came from. Her dad's whirlwind financial success was apparent after her sixteenth birthday. "He surprised me with a new white BMW convertible. I was stunned," she said.

Kari's father was raised poor. She wondered if the effects of the hard knocks her father experienced as a child were manifested in his bizarre behavior. "Dad actually walks around saying, 'I'm the powerful one!'" Kari added. "He's so obviously trying to fill a huge void, thinking that money makes him powerful."

"Talk about your Mom," I said, as I flipped the tape on my recorder.

"Well, she's totally extravagant," Kari answered. "When she shops, she buys anything she picks up. Once, she carried this glass windmill up to the counter and never asked the price. Dad and she had at it when he found the thousand-dollar credit card charge."

> ***Money is the great mystery of exchange.***
> ***—Michelle R.***

Warming to her topic, Kari explained, "You won't believe what happened last week!" Despite a traffic snarl, her mother was determined to return a video before 5 P.M., before taking Kari to a 6 P.M. class. Justifying her choice, her mother shouted, "Your dad will explode if I have to pay the two-dollar late charge!" As the time disappeared, Kari screamed back, "All of this over two lousy dollars!" Sounding like a battered woman, her mom yelled back, "Whatever it takes, Kari. I'll do anything to avoid a blowup."

There was nothing I could say. Kari turned to the ocean and stared a long while. She finally turned to me and said something I will always take with me: "God doesn't intend that money be this crazy!" I nodded agreement. After a bit, we gathered our cups and went inside.

Naomi: *Cleaning Up Her Money Act*

"Debt was our demon," twenty-six-year-old Naomi confessed bluntly. "I used the credit card nonstop like a drug, until finally, I felt hooked, seduced." Details of her disastrous credit card addiction filled our conversation one afternoon as we lounged by my pool.

Married only four years, Naomi and her husband had had to face their demons. It was the familiar story of credit cards flowing into their mailbox, unsolicited, tantalizing them with how much more joy they could experience by charging it.

"When Peter and I picked out our engagement and wedding rings, I didn't want a flashy diamond. But we got one anyway, and we financed it," she said as she twirled the rings on her finger, holding out her hand, giving the rings a long appraisal. "That silly decision," she added, "began our downfall; we just kept financing more and more and got into a routine, one signature after another. We were always eating out, taking trips, buying expensive name-brand presents—all on credit cards—until we were in over our heads. I'd find myself inviting a girlfriend out, and rather than feeling silly about charging a five-dollar lunch, I'd eat more than I wanted and tell her to do the same!"

It took a while for Naomi to grasp that she and Peter were seduced by the oh-so-easy idolatry of plastic cards. Finally, they hit bottom. She had been reading C. S. Lewis's book *Mere Christianity* and quoted me a line: "Every time you make a choice, you are turning the central part of you, the part that chooses, into something a little different from what it was before."

The growing pile of bills drove Naomi and Peter to meet their demon head on. "I broke a few bones in the process," she explained, "but something deep inside finally believed what I'd heard in church: 'Debt is not practicing the perfect will of God, and certainly isn't the smartest way to use money.'"

I understood this couple's failure. Young people, growing up and beset with constant new demands—including, most notably, their children—can easily be caught in the credit card trap. But understanding that we are creating debt eludes all of us in some measure, no matter our age. It's insidious. To fiercely reject the subtle lies of an unlimited credit card culture takes gargantuan effort and matching courage. I eyed Naomi with respect.

Each of us has a different money struggle because each of us is different.
—Amy C.

I told Naomi about a teacher friend who had asked me long ago, "I wonder whether young people see the acquisition of possessions as their passage into adulthood? When their exterior life is filled with 'toys,' do they look in the mirror and see 'grown up?'" Whatever the reasons behind excessive acquiring, Naomi and Peter successfully reversed their pattern. They signed up with a church program. I liked hearing Naomi's take on the healthy use of money, for here was a truth I too had come to believe. The church program attempts to redress the money education most young couples have been denied almost universally. It fills in family silences and creates a safe platform where couples can be honest and examine old attitudes about money.

After an entire summer of money sessions, the church group celebrated by cutting up all of their credit cards! Naomi threw her hands up in mock surrender. Within a few months, she and Peter managed to pay off the last of their accumulated debt of ten thousand dollars. Naomi was proud of Peter, who had deeply absorbed the program's teachings. She recalled a phone call from her father-in-law, when he said, "Son, the lottery has climbed to fifty-five million dollars! You've got to buy a lottery ticket." Peter wasn't buying. "Dad," he answered, "what would I do with fifty-five million dollars?"

Gail: *A Holy Yuppie*

Gail also seemed, at least on the surface, to have come to terms with money, but if you gaze at anything long enough a surprising revelation can take place, shifting one's perspective about that reality. Gail, a brilliant and successful attorney, took time to revisit her youth with me, particularly her parents' divorce. During our talk, and in our silences, she acknowledged more than ever her father's deep caring for her. Now twenty-nine, Gail called her parents' breakup the "season of fury," a time that nearly bankrupted her father. "Money was scarce, and Dad had to work even harder," she reported sadly. Even more devastating, the presence of a stay-at-home mother vanished from her young life.

We sat in her wide-windowed office on the twelfth floor of her office building. Gail's view took in the peace of Orlando's Lake Eola, an expanse of blue sky, and a canopy of green oaks that circled the lake. She hardly appeared a person raised in poverty. I took in her snappy suit, the shiny blonde hair, the alligator shoes. She leaned back in an oversized desk chair as she related a passionate account of a grim world made poetic by love.

In looking back, Gail grasped another, and perhaps more profound, significance of her parents' divorce. "Maybe I was given something many young women are denied. Dad's bank account was damaged, and he had to work harder, but that didn't stop him from getting custody of me. We bonded in a rare kind of father-daughter relationship, and to this day we're the greatest of friends," she said.

Scarcity called for creative efforts to house, clothe, and feed the tiny family of two. They found an apartment. Gail sewed her own clothes. They built furniture together. Resourceful beyond her years, Gail found a creative outlet in building chairs and tables and even constructed a queen-sized waterbed. The first summer that the two were alone was filled not only with the sound of hammers and saws but also with a deepening love between father and daughter. "It was one of the happiest seasons of my life. Dad and I made the most of what we had, and we had fun doing it," she said wistfully.

Others may have thought the family deprived. Her father was away most of the day, working long hours. No designer jeans were in store for Gail, no car after high school, no great haircuts. But what the two possessed was more treasure than any big home or four cars in the driveway. They had, as the Bible calls it, a "love that passeth all understanding."

Gail stared out her window. "Money, in my early girlhood, consisted of thoughtful gifts that Dad brought me each night. I'd lie awake, usually waiting until eleven P.M. or even midnight for him to walk through the door. In his hand was always some silly, inexpensive toy, or perfume, or cassette tape," she said, smiling in remembrance. "Dad never disappointed me. Always something, and he never forgot a warm hug and a kiss before he left me." She paused, then said: "I slept comfortably in the knowledge of being loved." She had the deepest respect for the man, and it showed in her eyes when she spoke of him.

"Only after graduation from law school did I realize the price Dad paid to keep us afloat. He had tried to make a go of it, fighting to pay off the bills that our postman left. Sweating under the pressure, he recklessly worked three exhausting jobs."

When it came time for college, the reality that no bank account existed for that purpose hit Gail. She scrambled and won, not one, but three scholarships. "And I figured out," she laughingly reported, "something I'd learned from my mother. I could survive on canned soup and crackers."

In some way, Gail was shaped by scarcity. Awful? I'm not so sure. A line from Theodore Dreiser's *Sister Carrie* declares: "The true meaning of money yet remains to be popularly explained and comprehended." Whether reared in scarcity or abundance, I believe that we are all shaped by our money histories, which can be a source of personal education.

I headed toward my car, feeling the cool spray of Lake Eola's fountain and paused to watch the waters froth and spin. All of these young women have their lives stretched out ahead of them with so many choices yet to be made.

. . . . .

Dear God, help these fledglings make good choices. Let Your grace in them work! Let money flow through their hands and somehow, always lead them to You. Amen.

Chapter Two

Denying the Gold—Wise Mentors

The first time I noticed them I was seven years old. A pair of Catholic nuns were on a vigorous walk up Robinson Avenue as my father and I were driving past. The duet paid no attention to the tiny finger pointing at them, "What are those, Daddy?" I asked, mesmerized. He glanced over and mumbled something about women who love God, no doubt thinking that was the end of that. It wasn't. They were two of the strangest creatures I'd ever seen—giant black birds in formation. I peered out the back window until they disappeared from sight. Why were their eyes pinned to the ground? Why were they dressed so wonderfully odd?

Spotting those marvelous enigmas that day thrust me toward a new chapter of my life. But it would be a long journey from that moment to advanced degrees in religion and music and, finally, to becoming a director of adult religious education. I would have to become a Catholic first.

It all began quite simply, with a feeble attempt at humor to relieve a tense moment around the dinner table one night when my father lashed out like a pit bull. City commissioners had repossessed a parcel of his land for unpaid back taxes, which he swore that he had paid. Even Mama, ever the peacemaker, put her head down and silently let tension rule the table.

I wondered how I could rescue Dad and give everybody a break. On a bet with myself, I repeated a wisecrack I had learned on the playground. I don't remember what it was, just that it was off-color. Dad slammed his fist on the table, his fork stabbing up in the air, eyes dark and angry. *Yi'll ann abuk!* he yelled his favorite curse. (To this day I don't know the exact meaning of that Arabic invective.) I took a bite, but it refused to go down. How could my little joke merit all this hostility? I stared at my father, dumbfounded.

That indiscretion dramatically altered my comfortable childhood and set me on my life's journey. Where my father got the idea, I haven't a clue, but he thundered that I was to be shipped off to a Catholic boarding school immediately. There I would acquire a proper set of "religious values," despite the fact that we were Greek Orthodox and that Dad often railed that the Roman Catholic Church was "the archenemy of the Greek Orthodox religion."

It was one of my father's most curious and, I believe, telling decisions. Of all the possibilities open to this man, banishing his favorite daughter to a Catholic boarding school for telling a silly, sexually oriented joke probably said as much about his own growing terror of my sexual blossoming. I was his star—the family knew it—and, he had always wanted me as his partner in business. Even Mama knew it. "You're the firstborn, the one he made time to play with," she'd tell me. My father took a huge, uncalculated risk with my future. Who could know the consequences of his choice? For me, a world of spiritual awakening and self-discovery was about to begin.

The September day of my final good-byes remains vivid in my mind. Dad packed the whole family in the car, drove us to Saint Augustine, and deposited me at my new home. After our farewells, my brothers and sister and mother and father slammed the Plymouth doors and drove off without me for the first time, many arms waving from each window. Dad turned to look back once more. He appeared small as he wheeled toward the highway, taking with him all that was familiar—and difficult—in my life. I perched on the white railing and waved. I thought I should feel sad; why was I filled with something closer to joy? I've never been able to explain the enormous breath of relief that swept over my 11-year-old soul that day, bringing a new sense of freedom that I could nearly touch. Yes, there had been the magical days at the register, the treasured thanks from both Mom and Dad. Yet what a relief to be out from Dad's obsessive barking and business and those tedious, endless grocery chores after school. I'd been shipped out, but even in those first hours, I was already loving it, pure alleluia! I surveyed my new kingdom. This was everything that the home built above Azar's Market wasn't. Here was space—wide open and airy.

The wraparound porch was welcoming and the lawn was expansive. I couldn't wait to meet the nuns.

Spiritual Greenhouse

SAINT JOSEPH'S ACADEMY, NESTLED IN THE HEART OF HISTORIC SAINT Augustine, boarded over one hundred young girls back in the late thirties and early forties. A bold, wooden, three-story structure built in 1860, this school was and still is an architectural fixture in the tree-shrouded Spanish colonial seacoast town. Daily, tourists flocked there to take countless photographs. As in an impressionist painting, the nuns sat in their flowing black habits on the wide white porches. There they rocked away after-school fatigue in painted and repainted green rockers as old as the building itself.

I danced easily in my crisp, navy blue uniform, to the tune of academy life. Studies were a breeze, and the nuns were kind. Assignments were completed in the massive wooden study area, where an elderly sister monitored the whispering, quick to clang her golden bell. Chatter, gaiety, and giggles rang out nonetheless, especially from white-veiled novices as they swept the floorboards of the ancient porch.

Unlike the older nuns who furiously fanned themselves in the heat, the younger ones held to a stricter, unwritten rule and allowed the sweat to drain off their fresh faces like badges of hard work. Sweat was part of Florida and part of a nun's life. Sometimes I'd catch a strong whiff from their drenched black serge habits as they glided past. I didn't care. To an impressionable child, the strange smells, wild chatter, and infectious giggles all proclaimed a family enjoying life enormously.

> ***We are Dominican Sisters who invested money in a number of colleges and universities. We have lucked out financially.***
> ***—Sister Joanna***

On free days, I peeked around the walls to watch Saint Augustine's horse-drawn carriages clatter lazily past on the Spanish cobbles. One carriage in particular always captured my attention, in which a finely dressed black gentleman sat high in front, reins in one hand, the other hand gesturing toward us. "This is the oldest Catholic institution," he would say, or "Please note that that historic boarding school is run by the best sisters in Florida." Nuns smiled at his familiar, smooth flow of hyperbole washing over the tourists lounging behind him. I was less interested in the driver's rich monologue than in the music of that voice. I also loved the way he politely tipped his hat to the assembled rows of holy penguins and gracefully bowed his weathered head. I imagined that carriage driver to be as fascinated as any tourist with these somber-clad women who owned nothing, always wore mournful black, and moved about mysteriously. How could any of these strangers fathom that the nuns freely chose all their deprivations? The tourists weren't the only ones; my father, to whom money translated into self-esteem, had to be puzzled too, though he never admitted it to the young daughter he would one day lose to the convent.

At meal times I relished the safety and orderliness at the wide tables. There was no thunder if I upset my glass of water. The quiet clinking of dishes was as nourishing to me as the delicious scrambled eggs and crisp bacon. I easily adapted to the no-talking structure during meals, with tall, red-faced Sister Mary Thomas, her beady eyes on patrol, standing sentinel. Without question, she'd send someone upstairs if they broke the silence rule. Sometimes she jingled a bell if her disapproving look didn't quell any chatter. Other times, on a saint's feast day, her jingle meant that we could talk. The ensuing girlish giggles warmed me with welcome, overdue nonsense.

I won the starring role that year in the academy's musical. I played a clown, a green-and-white bouncy haloed saint who spouted riddles and laughs. How the nuns giggled when I leapt into the middle of the stage, arms outstretched, embracing the entire audience. Their laughter and their applause touched the fledging thespian in me, and I felt my heart nearly burst. Here, I was somebody. I could make grown-ups laugh! Bold and bubbling, I surprised myself most of all.

Thank God you've got the money. Sure it's not what makes happiness, Adele, but it's a great foundation for happiness.
—Sister Toby

Meanwhile, Azar's Market was underwriting this blessed new life, and Mama never missed a tuition payment. But the nuns, unlike my father, rarely commented on that silent, steady bounty called cash-on-hand. When it came to money, I never saw a nun raise her eyes to heaven and proclaim, as Dad would, *"Nuschur Allah!"* Thanks be to God!"

The academy chapel was a spiritual greenhouse. And like a young seedling, I responded to its consecrated nourishment—the kneelers under long seats of dark wood, the brilliant stained glass, the tall saints of cool marble staring down on me. I greeted their gazes unafraid, curious, and comforted. I was fed, too, by all the calm. Silence, not shouting, was the norm at the convent, an uncultured thing that brought with it a sense of sanity and protection. I tried to obey the sisters' suggestions: "Honey, open and close a door quietly so no one knows you've entered the room. Put your kneeler down without any bumps or skidding noises. Be aware of even the click of your purse opening and closing."

Two of the academy's sisters especially left God's imprint on me. Sister Jerome, a gentle woman who treated me like a daughter, made a point of tucking me in at night. Together, we gazed out the window at a radio antenna's beacons sparkling red in the darkness. She said they reminded her of Jesus's presence on the altar. To this day, the sight of an antenna's flashing beacon in the night over an empty field brings back the calm voice of dear Sister Jerome.

Sister Eucharia introduced me to a new best friend, the piano. Sister Eucharia, as small, fat, and wrinkled as Sister Jerome was thin, elegant, and fair, was fiercely intimidating. She rapped my fingers if I missed a note or lost the rhythm and with a crackly voice would command, "Sit up straight!" She jabbed her fist into my back to make sure that I did so and shot out more orders: "Count out loud! Didn't you practice? Your father isn't paying good money for you to miss practice time." Curiously, I responded to her hard-line style. In just two years, Sister Eucharia advanced me to the fourth year of *John Thompson's Instruction Book,* and at the school recital, to my delight, I won top scores. How apt that Sister Eucharia often trumpeted the words "good money" to me as a child. Did she know something that most of us don't know? Here was a woman of God echoing the very sacramental blessing conferred by money.

Despite the horror stories circulating these days about the nuns of old and how they mistreated their charges, I have nothing but warm memories of Saint Joseph's Academy. In those two years, thanks to the nuns' nurturing, God's love rapidly grew in me. It's fair to say that they crafted my faith.

After two years, the sunny days ended abruptly; my parents insisted that they needed me at home. I don't remember crying as I waved good-bye, but my heart was heavy. I knew that I would miss the ordered life, the nightly strolls over the ancient Saint Augustine bridge two by two, and all the merriment. As Mama drove us away, I turned for one last look and saw young Sister Jane waving from the porch. I can still hear her infectious laugh and remember how once she had dubbed me "God's girl."

The passage from puberty to teens, a wise person wrote, is the start of a war that nobody wants to fight. After I got home, Dad and I ignited easily. I was a different child, zealously tracking what, after two years of convent school, I supposed to be the things of God. I found myself looking at life in terms of black and white, good versus evil, God versus mammon. Meanwhile, Dad had been gravitating toward maximizing his stock market and real estate speculations, drifting in precisely the opposite direction from me, or so I supposed. The more Dad pursued his feverish wheeling and dealing, the more I righteously faulted him.

Dad's investment success propelled a family move to Winter Park, a small, upscale Florida city brimming with palatial, oak-shaded Mediterranean mansions built in the twenties during one of the state's early booms. Though our one-story house was far from palatial, I was now rubbing elbows with rich schoolmates who drove their own cars. By the end of high school, I was a smug seventeen-year-old Jeremiah waving my Bible, calling my father to task for his evil ways and my classmates for their material loves. My brother chided me for my insensitivity. "You don't get it. That immigrant inside Dad can't help himself any more than a wounded vet can forget his war. Dad's just making damn sure he's not going back."

My youthful arrogance collapsed one Sunday afternoon as I listened to the radio. The familiar words caught my attention: "Lord make me an instrument of Thy peace. Where there is hatred, let me sow love . . ." The prayer of Saint Francis flooded my ears as if for the first time. The goodness of the academy came back. "For it is in giving that we are given, it is in pardoning that we are pardoned, and it is in dying that we are born to eternal life." I flicked off the radio and walked into our recreation room, sat down, and cried my fiercest tears. *Dad was Dad. Dad would always be Dad. I am the one who needs forgiveness,* I thought. I made my way to the piano and suddenly and forcefully belted out the old Catholic hymn "Make Me a Channel of Your Peace." I played it over and over until something good warmed my judgmental soul.

The years passed, and I could not ignore the calling: I had to be a Catholic. I could no longer attend Mass without making my connection formal and public. One summer, to avoid my father's fury should he find me out, I snuck out every Thursday night to attend convert classes at the Catholic church down the street. I left each week with a banging heart that threatened to give me away, but he never found out. The classes were wonderful. No topic was off limits under the guidance of flamboyant Father Bremner, an off-the-wall, turned-on priest who made Catholicism dance. Dr. Freud, the beauty of penance, and the value of smoking cigars were all valid topics for discussion. I was slowly shifting into a new world of ideas, awestruck at the varied approaches to God. I privately confessed to the priest my dream of becoming a nun. He studied my face. "Wonderful," he said, "but you'll have to give up the idea of having children." He stared hard and waited, but whatever disappointment he anticipated was nowhere to be found on my face. Then he got up, went to the door, and turned back with an enormous grin, saying, "But never doubt it, you'll be mother to hundreds of kids."

> *This contradiction of money abounds. Few realize its powerful intensity.*
> *—Amy C.*

On September 11, 1953, baptismal waters wet my hair and mingled with my tears. I was a brand-new Catholic! Unable to get enough of church, whenever I could, I'd slip down to Saint James Cathedral to sit alone and pray in the dim, comforting light, just like the old days at the academy. The words "Whoever leaves mother, father, brothers, and sisters for my sake" reverberated loud and clear. Part of me was horrified at the idea of becoming a nun; give up clothes, movies, and friends? Glimpses of convent life dogged me, nonetheless; I couldn't brush my teeth without seeing my face framed in black cloth. It wasn't long before I knew what I had to do. I confided my secret to my sister. She went pale. "They've done a lobotomy on you!" After a few weeks, she convinced me to confess the truth to my parents.

Dad's outburst was predictable. The entire house shook from the blast. "That's what you want? A place where you don't work, where they feed you, a place of no worries?" (Worrying to Dad was a *responsibility;* the Arabic way to honor God is to fret. Some men wear out whole strings of beads by worrying, a sign that they really care.) "Is *this* what I raised my daughter for?" he ranted.

In the summer of 1954 at twenty-one, before my final year of college, I wrote the Mother General of the Sisters of Saint Joseph of Saint Augustine, requesting permission to enter the community. On September 8, the feast of Mary's birth, having abandoned my linen dresses and suede purses, high-heeled pumps, and graduation watch, I was ready to take the plunge. But there was no preparing for the tears, the shaking, the lack of certainty that clawed and clutched at me at the last moment. My Aunt Margaret offered to drive me because Dad had barked his refusal to do so, but as I stepped into her car, he tried a goodbye hug. But just as quickly, he stepped back. His bottom lip quivered; he was embarrassed by his tears. I felt my own coming on. My sisters and brothers had disappeared into the house. Mama, in the bedroom, shut away the scene. The car revved up; Dad grew wild. He yelled after us: "Don't be fooled! You think you're leaving the world of money? You'll see! Those nuns have to have money, too! Nobody lives without it!" As Aunt Margaret pulled out onto the street, his message roared across the lawn and, eventually, across the years of my life.

Lady Poverty

People ask, "What was it like living in the convent? Did you get enough to eat? Didn't you get bored wearing the same old clothes?" And, of course, "Didn't you miss the company of men?" No two former nuns agree on what the convent gave them and what it didn't. Some shrug it off, saying it was simply a time to abandon the world. Some regret having stayed so long. One of the saddest replies to such questions gave me pause: "I stopped singing the day I entered the novitiate."

Yet there were some, like Maria as portrayed in *Sound of Music*—a story I never get enough of—who believed that convent time was a magical time of adoration and order. I count myself fortunate to be in this company. In the convent I matured as a woman, maneuvering through trials as well as relishing moments of deep joy, all the while feeling God's ever-present love. Still, for all that, convent life was ordinary, not so different in its day-to-day demands from those of any sincere army private or dedicated CEO, all hoping to walk through life with integrity.

That day, Aunt Margaret drove rapidly toward my unplanned future. No one talked. Then we arrived: the novitiate grounds sprawled lazily on the banks of the wide Saint Lucie River, exuding the charm of some bygone grandeur. The surroundings evoked fabulous croquet and lawn parties and dancing till dawn—scenes from an F. Scott Fitzgerald novel. Formerly the residence of a Coca-Cola magnate, the estate had been willed to the sisters on his death. The stately main building, perched on a hilltop, could have been Tara of *Gone with the Wind.* I was stunned by its beauty.

I bid a hasty good-bye to Aunt Margaret and ambled down to the end of the riverside pier before presenting myself at the door. A wave of terror rolled over me. I was about to make a commitment, like marriage vows, but what a marriage! This was a four-hundred-year-old practice. I gazed at the radiant blue skies, the lush palms, the lavish river whispering by me, all so brilliantly perfect. What's to worry? Not a dark cloud in the sky! Could this be for real? *O God take my hand.* I loped back up the hill to the front door and knocked. Heavy double doors opened, and there she was, draped in her black-and-white religious habit, covering everything except her hands and face. The laughing blue eyes pierced me. Mother Mary Louis, Mistress of Novices, extended her hand then covered mine with both of hers.

I stepped inside, unsteady and wide-eyed and shaky as a lost rabbit. Mother wasted no time and led me to a small room of complete serenity. Off came my green silk blouse and white linen skirt and on slipped the plain postulant's black skirt and blouse. A small black veil hid my curls. I smiled at myself in the long mirror, one of the few remaining vanities in this erstwhile opulent household. "Can you do it?" I asked myself.

Cloistered for two years! Only that morning I'd been living as I chose, kicking off my shoes in my informal, cluttered, fast-track world. Now, as Mother put it to all of the novices, "You're out of the world. You are here to save your soul, to learn the rules, and to follow them. God wants nothing less."

One of those early days, in the novitiate library where mahogany shelves brimmed with hundreds of Christian classics, I read through my assignment: Alphonso Rodriguez's spiritual treatise, *The Way of Perfection.* It was pretty severe stuff: hair shirts, fasting, even ritual flagellation. Occasionally, my gaze wandered out the window to acres of surrounding tropical beauty, even an olympic-sized swimming pool. Everything so manicured. Suddenly, a sharp pang: can all of this material luxury be *holy?* The question plagued me.

I loved the free time when I could run to the dock's edge, the wind blowing the thin veil away from my face. White egrets soared above me, now and then honing in and settling on an unsuspecting fish. Wind and water, sun and blue sky, spiritual bounty surrounded me. One day an undeniable inner voice put it to me straight: *You are meant to be right here, to take vows, and in the meantime, to claim this scenic abundance for your own.* My heart burst. I threw up my arms and shouted to those egrets, *"Deo gratias!"* I lay back on the dock, my black-laced granny shoes dangling just above the water, I mouthed the sentiments of a transported Saint Peter to Jesus on Mount Tabor, "God, it's so good to be here."

> *Money is the last thing Sister Jodie will worry about. If something comes up that we need, she'll say, "Go ahead and get it. Don't worry."*
> *—Sister L.*

I mused over the three ancient vows one by one. *Obedience.* Superiors's orders couldn't be any worse than Dad's orders. *Chastity.* That would be the easiest. I'd never been with a man, so what was there to miss? But what about *Poverty?* Sure, I'd given a closet full of clothes to my supportive friend, Angela, and felt no regret. But *Lady Poverty* would become my fiercest wrestling partner. Almost immediately, this demanding Lady began to extract from me not so much the denial of goods, as their *acceptance.* In a topsy-turvy sense, this vow seemed created just for me.

My first lesson of poverty occurred a few weeks after my arrival, and I had discovered that I wasn't anywhere near as detached from the outside as I thought. It was Dad's first visit to the convent, and he presented me with a small portable radio in a compact, beige leather case. I felt warmed. Dad hadn't given up on me. Mother Mary Louis, however, had different ideas about the matter. "You must turn in that radio," she said gently. "Think again, Mother. I'm not about to turn in this radio," I growled internally, surprising myself at the intensity of my feeling. Fortunately, that wasn't what Mother Mary Louis heard.

"Yes, Sister," I said, avoiding her eyes. After a ferocious inner fight, I put the radio into her hands that evening.

Over time, I found new meaning in the word "possession." I discovered inner possessions that no vow of sacrifice could take away. Mother Mary Louis uncovered my piano skills and stretched them to organ techniques good enough to accompany the novitiate choir. She noticed other "possessions" too; having entered at the advanced age of twenty-one, I had, she said, "worldly skills," which absolutely delighted her. "You can drive! You can type!" she exclaimed. I prepared lengthy documents for her. In this place of traditional self-deprecation, my self-esteem was curiously nourished as it had been by the nuns of my youth. And, like them, my soul took off like a kite in a fresh, cool wind.

I don't define our Catholic vow of poverty as destitution, but rather stewardship and using our money for the service of others. The vows free us up for ministry and mission.
—Sister Mary D.

Time passed. After two idyllic years of living high on God, I had to leave the serenity of the convent. God's will now, according to the rules, was to ship me from this magnificent cloister to the plain walls of a classroom. There, thirty high-spirited fourth graders in a thriving West Palm Beach parish school awaited me. I didn't care who saw my tears as I stepped into the convent station wagon. Mother did, and whispered, "Surrender your will, Sister Adele, and you'll do fine." I felt a stab of fear. *Surrender my will?* Being dumped suddenly into the din of traffic jams and mind-numbing secular busyness, among people who had no idea who I was, felt, at that moment, like relinquishing the true meaning of what it was to be a nun.

In the classroom, battle lines were drawn quickly. Fourth graders manifestly did not want what I had to give—namely, how to learn lessons noiselessly. So it took a while to fall in love with my lively charges, but we soon connected, especially on the volleyball court, and some of those ties endure to this day. A greater challenge confronted me in the parish convent. My old nemesis, abundance of material goods, stared me in the face. To the average person, a bedroom, a closet, and a desk of one's own are common fixtures. Add to that a wide recreation room offering steady entertainment such as television and a collection of records greater than I'd ever seen before. On one table sat a box of Russell Stover chocolates, free for the picking! Coming from the affluent mansion on the hill, such luxuries should not have seemed opulent, but they did. Again, I questioned how I was to be, before God, the humble ascetic I desired to be.

I did as I was told and waited for something holier to happen. I taught piano lessons after school, directed a stage production of Gilbert and Sullivan's *Mikado* one year, and wowed the parish with Humperdink's *Hansel and Gretel* the next year with a tally of five thousand dollars in gate receipts. Pride reared its unwelcome head as parents' continued praise despite my prayers for humility. I noted that fellow nuns who tutored kids for extra income for the convent breezed in and out of their classrooms without choking on money angst like I did.

One day, Sister Saint Ann requested that I buy the groceries that week. She pulled out the grocery list and, to our horror, a hidden five-dollar bill floated to the floor. I gasped, my hand covering my mouth. No sister was ever supposed to carry cash. Embarrassed, she quickly stuffed it into her bodice. I hustled out the back door. Guiding the blue sedan out of the driveway, a sudden rain pelting the windows, my thoughts spun out of control. Even Sister Saint Ann! Our community's jewel, who laughed so warmly with her class, scooping the tiny ones into her arms. Later I voiced my bursting confusion to venerable Sister Evangelista. "Where's the cross of Jesus we're supposed to carry? We have it all: a comfortable home, furniture, television. There's nothing else to pray for!" I wailed, pitching my anger at her as if it were *her* fault. Sister looked me up and down. She gently brushed a fleck from my sleeve and said, "My dear, you'll find your cross, and soon enough, I reckon."

In the following years, I moved from one assignment to another, drawing new songs out of new children, growing, I hoped, like Jesus in wisdom and knowledge, mellowing in the grace of my vocation. But one night, long after Sister Evangelista's gentle upbraid, I noticed that every nun at our dinner table who was speaking was voicing a litany of complaints about petty matters. I felt tears collecting and wondered, *God, what's going on here?* I looked away, out the window toward the calm lake, the last rays of pale sunlight shimmering on its surface. I was at a crossroads, questions hammering at me, and there was no one with whom I could engage in an honest exchange. I flashed on Sister Evangelista *(My dear, you'll find your cross . . .).* My heart quickened; I needed time alone. Leaving the table, I excused myself and sped up the stairs to my room. I sat on my patio and stared at the water. Muddled by angry feelings, I finally received a clear message: "Anyone can give up a car or a house, but to give up joy, laughter, and rich conversation at the dinner table—that's life depleting." A night of exploration brought eventual understanding. The evidence was clear. Poverty wasn't just about making peace with the material world; there was a whole menu of impoverishment that spread itself before me, including loneliness, confusion, and intellectual dryness. This was not the sort of poverty I had chosen, and an internal emptiness brought me to my knees. *God, I'll go crazy listening to these complaining nuns! Help!* Then I heard a quiet voice: *If you try—just smile at the table—that might be the only virtue I require of you now.*

Lady Plenty

MUCH WORK REMAINED IN MY INTIMATE STRUGGLE TO BALANCE poverty with abundance. As hard as it was to accept Lady Poverty in all her unexpected guises, it was always Lady Plenty who took me by surprise. It took the soul of a child to reach out and gleefully accept the goods put into one's hands; that sort of innocence eluded me.

One of my final assignments brought me to Orlando's Bishop Moore High School. My brother, Roland, visited me at the newly constructed convent, adjacent to the school, an architectural showplace, hardly the picture of convent austerity. Proudly, I showed him around the expansive grounds where our home rose on the shores of a breathtaking body of water. Each nun's room had a private lakefront balcony. Roland and I ogled the view, pointing out ducklings paddling in and out of waving reeds. I bubbled about how I loved praying the psalms here on my balcony, as if it were an outdoor chapel. "God gets real close when I gaze out on this lake," I gushed. Roland nodded, visibly impressed by it all. Then, suddenly, he shook his head, and said, "So what's the difference between being a millionaire and living like one?"

In one single stroke, that query crumbled my understanding of centuries of Christian teaching on poverty. He was on to something.

We lived richer here than half the world's population! I was thrown into confusion. Again, my heart ached, and soon I sought the counsel of wise Father Caulfield, the high school's president. This kind man, beloved by students and nuns alike, was both a man of prayer and the rugged boss who commanded respect from tough senior boys. Father listened over coffee, as I spewed out my concerns. "Sister Adele," he finally said, taking my hand, "let's try to look at this differently. Doesn't faith accept whatever God can offer? So you're confused. And your brother's comment hurt. It's all part of the package." He took away his hand, sipped his coffee, and added, "As for me, when it comes to poverty, count me out! I *like* owning my car and the feel of money in my wallet. But, should someone need my car, I'd hand over the keys in a second."

We know God loves the generous giver as it reflects His own infinite generosity. I believe money given is God's love in action.
—Diane M.

Out on my balcony that night, a full moon skimmed the lake's ripples and flooded my raw soul like a balm. Suddenly, Dad's familiar Arabic utterance, *"Nuschur Allah!"* sounded in my ears. I bowed my head, praying, "So what if I'm a millionaire! Lady Plenty, you and I can be friends. *"Nuschur Allah!"* It was another step toward accepting God's abundance in whatever form it might come.

As the liberating winds of Vatican II exploded through the church in the sixties, my convent journal records my own loosening up: *Came to the convent to find myself, away from traffic and the business of money. Came to find my place in God's plan. The prayers have illuminated, the penance has cleansed, the silence has revealed a new voice. But most of all, close living with diverse personalities has become my claim to victory. That is the hardest part. And if anybody asks, let me make it perfectly clear: the interior life is a life of hidden poverties and, quite possibly at times, open warfare.*

My work as a sister bloomed over the years and at a certain point I felt it was complete. I had gone full circle. I had taken a risk long ago, stepping into a blessed black habit that set me apart from the world. Now, that world beckoned me again. I felt another risk needed to be confronted, requiring another leap of faith. *"Do I still belong here, God?"* I dared to ask.

Wise Mentors

I was terrified to be just plain Adele again. I liked being Sister Adele. The title recognized my role in the order of things. As I contemplated leaving the security of everything that meant "God" to me, I gradually grew confident that somehow this risk of walking out would be for God too. It would force me to find my own way, to find His presence on my own, to battle this money question in unfamiliar settings. I began my good-byes. I trusted God to send me the witnesses that I needed to stay aware of His presence out there in that enterprising world.

When I left, I took a dog-eared, thin, black booklet, *Confidence in God.* Now in my purse, this prayer aid had lived in my new habit's giant pockets while I scrubbed clothes in the basement laundry, swept chapel dust, or dried my not-quite-shaven hair under a beaming sun on the porch. Hungry to read every word, I would randomly flip the pages and trust God to speak, praying that I could accept the lesson. Even at twenty-one, I had recognized that confidence in God was another way of affirming confidence in myself. The two aspects were inseparable.

Now, I was out on my own and far from the mini sermons in my little book and from my black-robed mentors. I prayed for new teachers. Whether in books or in a live person, it didn't matter; I sought women with confidence in themselves, especially concerning worldly entanglements like money, love, and sex. I hoped to find wise souls who believed that money was part of the divine expression, even if that meant living in material splendor. The women in the following section, the ones I call "Wise Mentors," are the answers to those prayers.

I bless these steadfast sages whose respect for, and even love of, money never seduced them into making it number one in their lives.

Their stories encompass many challenges, but, as you will see, it was confidence in themselves that kept them on the straight and narrow and led them to expanses of sunny possibility. The dollars that passed through their hands and supported their intentional journeys were, and continue to be, filled with Spirit.

Rachel: *Shining Through*

My friend Rachel describes the process of manifesting choices, including money choices, as Bad Face/Good Face. Put on Bad Face, recalling a hurt, clutching onto an injustice, and we proceed to act from that place. Over time, such choices can close in on us and eventually squeeze the life out of us. Or slip on Good Face and we act as if every piece of our past contributes to a future good action. Every Good Face action opens a door to unimaginable abundance.

"Where do you get your phenomenal energy?" I asked Rachel one day.

"I simply can't help it! I wake up feeling grateful, excited about being alive," she replied.

Rachel's aliveness spilled over into shopping sprees. She took me shopping one day, and I spent more money on clothes that afternoon than I'd ever spent at one time, never understanding how money could cause such behavior. In the weeks that followed, I realized that the afternoon with Rachel was another "coming out" for me, stepping into a whole new world of fashion, femininity, and sensuality. Unexpectedly, I came alive while spending all that money!

"The truth about money," Rachel said grinning as we sat in the Belgian Godiva Chocolate Shop, "is that I always feel like a little girl when I handle it. I used to walk around with a little pocketbook, and inside it I carried a change purse filled with coins. I'd line up my dolls and stand before them like a teacher, with that little pocketbook strap over my arm. Through the years, I've acted as if I'm still playing with that money purse. Money never meant more than make-believe paper dollars and shiny metal buttons. Well, even now, I've no relationship with money," she admitted, shrugging.

I found it fascinating that Rachel, who enjoys deep relationships with people on many levels, claims to have no relationship with money.

"When a client pays me in cash, I'll do this funny thing. I'll waltz into Sam's office and laughingly throw the cash on his desk. He loves the stuff. 'Oh, goody!' he'll shout." Rachel threw up her hands, mocking her husband's glee. "Truth is, I've never attached much importance to money, even when I made bundles of it. I felt free to buy myself an outfit without ever feeling naughty." But Rachel insists she uses her money "to make love," as she describes it.

"My little purse had accumulated thirteen thousand dollars in savings. For Sam's sixtieth birthday, I planned to surprise him—blow it all, give us a week at a new Avatar workshop in California. The next day, I enrolled us in the three thousand dollar-per-person workshop and felt free, even though Sam was traumatized by all that spending! But he allowed me to do even more! I took him to the Fairmont in San Francisco, the most elegant place I could find. We spent the whole birthday weekend there. And I blew all that money." She smiled at the memory.

I took a deep breath. "You never cease to amaze me," I said. "Did you ever regret that spending spree?"

"Never. When the money is flowing, I'll do it again. But now, the tables are turned. My new therapy practice is not generating money." She sipped her coffee, utterly unconcerned with a revelation that would make a lesser woman cringe. Talk about a Good Face!

I couldn't help but feel uplifted. Rachel believes that there is unity in all behavior, so when she takes money risks, she knows that the payout will spread out across all her undertakings. Let me give you an example of just how confident Rachel is about taking risks. One day, Rachel and I persuaded my pastor to let us jointly address the congregation about our work together for Middle East peace. That Sunday, the very Jewish Rachel grabbed my hand and held it high as she exclaimed, "Adele represents my double enemy! She is a Catholic. As a child growing up in Belgium, I ran from Catholics because they threw stones and called me a 'dirty Jew.'" She paused, looking from one side of the congregation to the other. Still holding my arm high she continued: "Adele represents another enemy. She is an Arab. My people and hers have yet to make lasting peace." Then it was my turn. I took a long breath, then my words of peace and love came easily. When we finished, you could hear a pin drop. Suddenly, a deafening applause flooded over us, prompting a standing ovation. We took it in, the smiles, the hands clapping, the warm sight of smiling friends. How people long for peace! And the lesson was clear: Whether in the wallet or at the pulpit, whatever is worth having is worth taking risks for. And our holiness lies in the stretch.

Impressed by Rachel's ability to energize people, I asked, "Rachel, why did you let go of your old practice? You were making lots of money then."

"To work with couples," she answered. "Marriages need both partners to work, not just one partner, and I wanted to help them.

"Learning to be a marriage therapist required sacrifice, though; it sucked up thousands of dollars. And suddenly, all the fun around money vanished. It was no longer a game. I found myself tight for the first time. I asked myself: 'Who is this creature called money? We've yet to be introduced!' It was the first time I couldn't see profits. At the same time, I wanted to replenish the loan from my father's account, and to pay back my husband for all his financial support."

"Rachel," I interrupted. "Surely Sam doesn't expect you to pay him back?"

"Of course not. But I feel I have a debt. If I don't pay them back, I feel as if I'm still playing with my little money purse, not really honoring what I owe.

"I've come to a new awareness about men. We call them breadwinners. On a daily basis, they are forced to face survival issues—food, clothing, water, heat. Here I am, free to worry about matching income and expenses in my new business with cushions on both sides of me: Dad's nest egg and Sam's thriving business. Most breadwinners haven't even one cushion."

Money Accounting

"Let's wrap up our talk with my three money incarnations," Rachel offered. What followed was one of the clearest accountings of a woman's money evolution I'd ever heard.

"When we moved to Orlando, Sam's work supported us. But a major heart attack jolted our income structure, and Sam had to find other work. We talked seriously. I had a successful, ten-year career making my own money. The amount didn't really matter. So at that stage, I volunteered to take over all household expenses so Sam was free to create a new business. It was a golden opportunity to enter a new challenge with Sam and with money." Rachel described how their marriage took on an even deeper dimension, bonding them as never before.

Sam was relieved; she was elated. She ticked off her responsibilities with her many-ringed fingers:

"I began paying the bills—the mortgage, insurance, and car payments. And all the while I tried to move away from that little girl with the purse. I wanted to be grown-up about money. I wanted to balance a checkbook, but my pencil couldn't make the numbers work; I'd always have to check with Sam. Eventually, my determination began to pay off in self-worth. I was not only making money, but paying the bills."

Rachel affirmed that women experience a new sense of self-identity when, like men, they engage in money-producing labor. She assumed responsibility as head of her household. I felt a thrill at her words. I looked at all the women shoppers passing by us, bundles under their arms. Who paid for those purchases?

"Well, you've told me how you learned to balance a checkbook. How are you with credit cards?" I was curious.

"Aha!" she laughed. "That's another old cloud. When I started using a credit card, I enjoyed myself to the hilt. I found a money method that conformed with my lifestyle—minimal entanglement, spending without fuss. When the bills came, amounting to four or five thousand dollars, I'd pay a little here and there, thinking that would hold them for a while!"

It was hard to believe that this disciplined woman could run up credit cards so irresponsibly. My mouth gaped. Rachel laughed openly at herself. "Yes, and Sam eventually sat me down one day: 'Rachel,' he said, 'this is serious. You cannot spend more than you can pay!' Like a little girl, I was shocked into growing up once more. Sam paid off the cards, but I had behaved childishly. I had been playing and still had a lot to learn."

I wondered whether, in some mysterious way, this Rachel's "little girl" is not actually a freedom song that most women long to sing. She might need to sing with less reckless abandon, but I felt sure that the little girl inside Rachael had urged her to spend money freely, playfully, and to feel secure in her spending.

"The second phase of my maturing—I call it an apprenticeship—was when Sam tried to teach me to read my monthly business report. I'd look hard at the numbers, but they were Greek to me. Eventually, we decided that someone else could handle it, but I did learn one simple equation: I knew how much money we took in and paid out."

"Victory in small chunks!" I laughed.

"And now, in my third phase of money maturity, I became a financial participant with Sam. He said, 'Rachel, you don't know what we own or what I've saved. You don't know about our IRA or what it takes to put our boys through college. I want you to know it all.'

"For several days, the alarm got us up an hour early. We dressed, had breakfast before our staff arrived, and hit the books. My ignorance was obvious. By facing my own debt aversion, I suddenly came to realize how extraordinarily Sam had been maneuvering our money to get the boys to college. Sam answered every silly question of mine, and I learned about money firsthand from a patient partner."

People who know how to acquire money have a relationship with money that is very different from mine. I often feel on the outside of some secret society that seems to be "in the know."
—Lilia S.

Rachel shook her head and smiled ruefully. "In those early morning hours, Sam taught me that his money consciousness had cushioned us; had allowed me, still holding on to my little purse, to ask him to be a little bank for me while I figured out how I could shuffle accounts. He always said yes to me."

"Rachel, give me a last word!" I laughed, as I gathered my purse.

"Let's see." She paused. "I will never allow money to stop me from taking risks. I need to know at all times that I'll be free to do what I need to do, even if that means I'll have to confront the horrible feeling of poverty and indebtedness again."

Jackie: *A Tree Grows in Chicago*

Rachel's good friend, Jackie, had heard about our meeting and volunteered to tell her money story to me. I had been curious about Jackie's history ever since I met her. One bright October day, she knocked timidly at my front door.

Jackie's early encounter—at nine years old—with sudden enormous wealth must have been a defining event in her relationship with money. "Money can bring misery and torment, and without love, it's a negative force," she began. "I know this up close. I lived in the shadow of fabulous wealth."

"How on earth," I wondered aloud, "did your poor family, the neighborhood have-nots, manage to move so close to the haves?" I had to know.

Jackie grew up in one of America's fabulously wealthy suburbs, with friends who had unimaginable lifestyles, unlimited pocketbooks, lavish wardrobes, and chauffeurs. "Dad was a miracle worker!" she laughed and launched into a glowing tribute to her father. "He built our house with his own hands on one of the city's most beautiful streets. He put love into every brick."

Originally, Jackie's parents were forced to reside with her mother's parents in a row house. That arrangement might have fueled a plan to simply get away; in fact, it created a mini-war at the dinner table one night when her father announced: "I want my own home! I want some grass for a garden, a water fountain. I need nature close by." Young Jackie held her breath as her mother exploded: "You're stark, raving mad!" She raged on while Jackie watched the verbal tennis match, back and forth, between her parents. Jackie's mother didn't care about grass, or planting, or anything of the kind. Fear informed her whine, heard through the years, "We can't afford it!"

"So how *did* you afford it?" I prodded.

"Dad found a piece of property, and with the help of my grandfather, a plumber friend, and an electrician, he forged a dream from scratch."

Jackie recounted how, as a young girl from a simple family, she ended up residing smack in the middle of a quarry of Italian millionaires. Another second grader, her close friend Claudia, became an unsuspecting tutor, introducing Jackie to the difficult and often tragic lifestyles of the rich and famous.

"While Claudia's family had every imaginable thing a person could ever want, they were the most unhappy people I've ever known. If I went to play at Claudia's home, a chauffeur picked me up. I wandered the grounds, their stables, sat by their lake, which was complete with swans. The servants' quarters were bigger than our home. As for Claudia's mom, she was breathtaking, looked like Lana Turner. But I quickly saw Claudia's dilemma: her parents stayed drunk all the time."

Jackie paused, before explaining that her childhood friend would eventually commit suicide. Roots of Jackie's wisdom and self-discovery lay in her association with this spiritually impoverished family, yet another twist of God's strange ways to open our eyes to reality. "Even as a nine-year-old, I knew that something was wrong there, very wrong. They had everything and yet nothing. Claudia was a *victim* of wealth!" As Jackie talked, she folded and refolded her napkin into small squares.

I grew up in a household in which money was not a topic of polite conversation. I never heard my parents discuss money.
—Ellen H.

"Once, Claudia's mom was about to go on a trip. She was nattily dressed and smelled terrific and looked so beautiful. But she strode right past us, wouldn't take time to talk with her pleading child who was dreading another separation. Later, Claudia cried in the kitchen. There, the maid consoled her employer's child." Jackie looked squarely at me and said, "That incident shaped my life with money more than anything else."

How did Jackie fare now in the company of the wealthy people surrounding her high-profile husband, I wondered aloud?

She laughed. "I often think about it! I'd say my childhood equipped me to blend easily with rich folks. Maybe they're not all as depressed as I once thought. And maybe I have fewer judgments."

Unlike many of my interviewees, Jackie spoke freely about her experiences. "No matter how alert we may be," she once told me, "we are always in danger of falling into uncharted money waters."

I walked her to her car, and as I closed the door, I felt a rush of admiration for her: "No wishing you had more money. You, lady, are blissfully happy." She smiled and nodded. I watched her pull out of the drive, wave, and then disappear around the curve.

Candy: *Daughter of a Cash Man*

"Perhaps having no money at all is required for happiness." Candy surprised me with that statement. In a paint-smudged T-shirt that hung down to her knees, Candace St. Claire, with her wild, raven-black hair, looked younger than her forty-odd years.

"I wouldn't have missed living four miles from the nearest road, with no heat and only an outdoor toilet, for all the tea in China. Those particular kinds of ups and downs were wonderfully enlightening. They taught me something that I never realized about my stuffy background."

"And what was that?" I asked.

"During my first thirty years, I'd never spoken to anyone without an Oxford accent and a university education to match. Imagine!"

Candy's recent adventure into marriage was nothing short of a miracle. Jason, a recent divorcé, flew to England to renew his friendship with Candy, a childhood sweetheart now divorced herself. Their love affair had commenced back in their teens, when Jay's family lived in England, where his father's Navy command was located. Eventually, time and circumstances separated them. Without the daily fuel required to maintain a romance, they married other partners. Yet they kept up a twenty-year correspondence.

A professional artist and recent émigré, Candy speaks with a bright, clipped accent, a refreshing sound to my Southern ear. I glanced about her loft and took in the brilliant shades of color splattered on generous pieces of fabric. In one corner, squares of newsprint and canvas clothes were pinned to a line. Cans of paint, neatly stacked, lined the space by the stairway. To my left, a swath of sunlight beamed through the wide skylight. I loved the immaculate clutter of this busy environment. Things got done here; this was no artist's dalliance.

Candy joined me on pillows on the floor, pulling her knees to her chin like a youngster. She could hardly wait to talk, she admitted, her voice sounding like ringing chimes. I thought the English can read a menu and make it sound like scripture.

"My daddy was my greatest money teacher. When he knew I was moving to the States, he advised me, 'Honey,' he kept repeating, as if I couldn't get it, 'God forbid that you'll start using credit. Don't fall headlong into Americana!' He meant

You can learn to shift uninvited, conflicted feelings about money into rewarding, pleasurable ones . . . for example, I light a fragrance candle as I prepare to pay my monthly bills.
—Gini C.

don't start that plastic card business! Credit cards were an invitation to 'drop into hell.' Dad was an absolute cash man and would die if he knew that I'd ever use credit." But how did Candy create this gorgeous environment without credit?

"In England, we simply never used it," she replied. "It just wasn't done. We were cash people." Candy jumped up and ran to her desk, rummaging to locate her purse. She brought it back down to her spot on the floor. "If you want to know how cash operates in my life, here it is. I know, for example, exactly how much I have in this purse. I've known what's in my purse ever since I was on my own with two children to raise. It's a twenty-two-year habit; it's robotic. I don't think about it; I just know."

Candy extended her tidy and ordered life to her wallet: no loose change, loose bills, or loose accounts. I looked at her neat wallet and purse. Bills were lined up carefully. Change was zipped away. Candy St. Claire acquaints herself with every penny she possesses! She snapped the purse shut and stood it between us on the floor.

"For emergencies, I've always kept ten pounds on me wherever I go. It's a matter of discipline. For some it might be upside-down logic, making the mind keep track of every penny, but not for me. Not only do I know what I carry around, but I know exactly what my husband has on his person," she continued with a laugh.

In another person, such behavior might suggest an unhealthy obsession, but for Candy, these were the ingredients of a well-examined, carefully weighed life.

"I've always found money a fascinating subject. In England, I admit that we were terribly class conscious, the whole society was. Public embarrassment was the worst that could happen, and it was always alive somewhere. In our schools, being poor was a disgrace."

She toyed with her coffee, stirring thoughtfully. In clear chronological sequence, she began recounting the financial setbacks that destroyed her secure childhood.

"At fifteen I had absolutely no intimacy with money. I was just happy in a plain family with good financial resources. I mixed with those of equal means and kept apart from those less fortunate. At twenty-one, I married a partner whose background was similar to mine. We lived comfortably, but on a simple budget." She peered closely at me as she spoke, eyes seeking connection to assure my attention. "At thirty-three, my life did a complete turnabout. I was alone and forced to live without any hope of income. Unquestionably, my children suffered: no heat, no playthings, no yard to play in." Candy paused, adding, "And we didn't eat meat for six years." She shivered, rubbing her arms in memory of those chilly years, then stood up and headed to the kitchen to refill our cups.

"You've really known some hard times, haven't you?" I said.

"I've always double-checked my motives and my behavior. There's a lot of murkiness around money, but like all crazy parts of life, I work it out like an artist. I like my palette filled with wild colors and my CDs with a mix of classic and rock and roll. I comingle with a bevy of birds frolicking in fields. It costs me nothing."

"Candy, you lift songs into holy lyrics," I laughed in amazement.

"Thanks. I feel that way. Listen, the first time I took a jet, I was thirty-something. I'll never forget it. Electricity ran through my body. The view was breathtaking: God outside and close. 'Yippee!' I shouted right there in my seat. That plane ride unearthed my joyous self, and taught me that if I could say 'yippee' every day, I was definitely traveling on the right cloud."

We chatted for a while longer. Suddenly, Candy said, "I almost forgot. I had a reading done the other day. My astrological chart determines that I'll end life here exactly as I began: with less."

The prophecy made Candy sparkle; she didn't fear the future, and she really did believe "less is more."

Nora: *Let It Flow*

Nora, a therapist, had hinted on occasion about a turbulent past giving way to a wonderful present. Like Candy, Nora has an attentiveness to her spirit, and she allows the future to take care of itself. I lingered outside Nora's office, gazing at the abundance of trees and the flowers beneath them, bright orange and purple impatiens mixed with red geraniums. Nora's office was a restored clapboard home. "I like to think of my office as a healing lodge," she told me once. Few would disagree.

This day, Nora flung open the door, laughing in her strong, unapologetic way. At thirty-four, she stood tall, a solid woman with powerful shoulders and a wide grin.

I entered the tiny hallway and glanced at a mobile floating high in the ceiling, with two angels swinging from it. Raggedy Ann dolls nestled on her office sofa between splashy cushions.

I'd heard that Nora and her partner, Josie, managed their financial housekeeping better than many married couples. They shared trust, respect, and honor—all the emotional stuff that makes for lasting contracts.

"We've never, and I mean never, had a money conflict," Nora said. "We combine paychecks into one joint account. Nobody gives a hoot who puts in more. If I'm short this month, Josie pays the bills. Major decisions bring us to the dining room table to lay out the issue. She's open, and I try to be too. If one wants what the other vetoes, like a major purchase, we wait." Nora grinned. "But usually we create a way to get what we want."

When Nora decided to switch professions, Josie took on extra work to finance Nora's graduate education. Josie was instrumental in launching Nora's therapy business, something that Nora never forgets. They pool their money, decide budgets in tandem, and see each other through life's unexpected side roads.

"Know what?" Nora grinned again. "I wake up happy."

"Now tell me what inspired you to be so cooperative," I suggested.

She thought for a moment. "I had a dad who loved spending and sitting at the other end of the table and a mother who never spent a dime, strangled by her insecurity. I think God placed me somewhere in the middle.

"Dad was a naval officer. He poured money into the family. Games, outings, outrageous presents. When I asked for something, I never heard him suggest, 'We can't afford it.' Mom couldn't get enough strictness. She was always hard on herself and saving for a distant future. Of the two of them, I hate to admit that Mom never learned how to live." Nora paused.

"They squabbled over money as if fighting a civil war, as if our freedom depended on who won. There were explosions in the night, long after we were in bed. Economics were tight despite my father's free-flowing attitude," she said, frowning.

As she spoke, it was clear that her parents' wars figured in Nora's decision to go into family counseling. "Yet I think Dad exhibited the most selfishness when it came to spending money: he lugged home whatever suited *him*. Once, he mortgaged the house to buy a boat, a second mortgage at that! I remember Mom's frightened condemnation: 'Who do you think is supposed to support this family?'"

I asked Nora, "When they divorced, and you didn't have to listen to that stuff anymore, was it a relief?"

"I don't know." Nora shook her head. "I think more than their screams was the unexpected hurt that came from Dad. In my senior year, he axed my long-standing college plans by telling me I had to pay for it."

So what was an aspiring student to do? In Nora's case, she used her anger as fuel. "I went and got a scholarship. I damn well completed my education," she stressed, her cheeks flushed at the memory.

In return for her scholarship from the state, Nora taught in Florida schools for four years after graduation. Despite an artistic temperament not suited to classroom life, she completed her requirement and walked away debt free. It was a time of growth and of heightened self-esteem as Nora uncovered talents, especially "the talent for caring for myself when no one else was willing to do so." Teaching paved the way into the world of regular paychecks.

> *My father brought in the money, and my mother spent it, never once seeking his counsel about how to spend it. Subservience to the male was never part of my mother's personality.*
> *—Barbara S.*

"On the class's last day, I came home to tell it straight to Mother: 'I'm going to travel, even if my bank account is empty. I won't let money, stop *me* from doing what I want to do.'

"After I pay bills, I may be down to as little as one hundred dollars in savings and probably two hundred dollars in checking. But I rarely check the price of any item I buy. Take the grocery store for example: I step up to a Winn-Dixie cash register with open checkbook, write whatever numbers the cash register reports. I do not, and will not, spend time focusing on grocery prices. I need it? I get it!"

I saw on the shelves directly behind her a naval officer framed in silver. The dad who spent money on himself. How much had he fueled Nora's spending habits? I suggested this.

"Maybe I am being like Dad, in pleasing myself, but there's more to it. I had a near-death experience, a car accident. That car crash yelled a louder truth than my folks ever could." She whispered somberly:

"I could be dead right now. Death gives us authority to risk. So accumulating debt doesn't nag at me. I'll pay it off someday." She shrugged. "I've seen too many folks save endlessly for a future that never came. That's where Mom let me down."

Nora grabbed her purse, rummaged, then held up her credit card. "This is my passport to living in the present," she grinned. Was she worried about a large balance? Not a trace of it showed on her beaming face. "I'll eventually restore this card's balance to zero," she said confidently.

To illustrate her free-wheeling plastic lifestyle, she described how she and Josie took the trip of a lifetime on credit. "Friends had asked us to travel to Paris. My savings book read one hundred dollars. My inner 'savings' spoke up: 'Nora, you could be dead tomorrow. Go!' Josie agreed, after all, she's a refugee to this country and recognizes the one freedom no one can take—her initiative! So our credit cards were our passports—and Paris was magnificent!"

Some might agree with Nora's spending style. Others might shrink at the tightness that debt winds around us, as one woman put it, "like a belt that's hooked too tight." Nora delights in life with a credit card.

Nora put her hands together as though in prayer and looked up. "Sure, I'm still paying for that trip. But it was worth every moment. I'm not the greatest money manager, but I've come to believe that only fools judge anyone else's money habits. Some women are credit ladies, some are cash ladies. Why should we care? I don't think it matters a hill of beans to God."

Out of the corner of my eye I spotted a picture of a modern-day Christ hanging on her wall. Don't Sweat the Small Stuff was inscribed under his striking laughing likeness.

Nora caught my eye. "Jesus was poor, lived poor because of his particular *choice.* His style of life is not a role model for me," she said firmly.

It took a long while for me to fully understand Nora's approach to Jesus as a role model. Her boldness impressed me. I could be poor or not. I could have money in the bank, but not fret that I didn't give it all away! It was a matter of choice, I realized, as we lived in the circumstances in which God placed us. I recited an ode of thanks to Nora as I walked to my car.

Angel: *Blooming in the Desert*

Angel and I met as young nuns during our summer college days at Manhattanville, and despite the many intervening years, we have remained friends ever since. Angel also left her community. Once out of the convent, Angel taught high school in New York's suburbs and then, weary of city life, moved to California's public schools. Later, she married and settled down in a home in the Arizona desert. Her life is breathtakingly rich there; the desert inspires prayer.

Cross-country letters and phone calls have kept us in touch. Recently I reread some of her letters. In small, neat handwriting, she had professed: *I've never wanted much and haven't demanded a lot.* Another letter revealed much about Angel's current choice of seclusion. *I'm just now learning to be with the desert. It's taking time. Each week, I follow animal trails, sometimes with Jacob, sometimes just with God. I listen to the quiet of all living things, to the serenity amid this dry terrain. No hurry, no highways and shopping malls. Only the smallest and most potent, the deadliest life forms move this silently, as if they resist being alive. Something in this environment evokes my deepest nature.*

In phone calls we recalled our young nun days. I liked what she believed about our early flowering; Angel savored the disciplines of our religious pasts. During one late-night call, she confided, "The vow of poverty nourished my mind and body. Actually, money was nonexistent for me in those days. What mattered was my spirit, and I knew it. I lived the Rule, yes, but more, it was the time of laughter, of friends, of healthy food that I found there. I liked living with people who loved the monastic tradition. We learned to give up self from the beginning."

"So what was it like for you when you left, Angel?" I asked. Her answer surprised me. "Frightening, mainly because I had become severely institutionalized, to the point of feeling like a released prisoner. Though my heart was no longer there, convent structure had formed my center. Stepping into a strange world at thirty-three required a lot of counseling. I had to determine my own way of living."

Angel's faith was tested when she took on New York's public school system. Teaching a roomful of forty high schoolers paid off in sleepless nights and a slim paycheck! Her "free" life proved far more ascetic than convent days: cold dinners, hot summers, and bouts of loneliness. But

Angel was stalwart, and when her well-established brother offered a loan, she insisted that she had to make it on her own.

Angel eventually earned a Ph.D., and moved up to a yearly salary of fifty thousand dollars teaching high school in Santa Barbara. Her progress, she insisted, was not in terms of money, but in self-esteem. Years passed, then Angel married Jacob, a stockbroker whom she met in an adult night class. They purchased a home, and a few years later they took on another residence, a winter home in Mesa, Arizona.

After years of Angel's coaxing, my husband, Jim, and I flew to Mesa for a visit. What fun, I thought, as we nestled under a backyard canopy on a still Saturday afternoon as a pair of doves cooed. Nature was dry out here; drip hoses were required to turn parched terra firma green, I noticed.

"I think of the desert saints," Angel leaned back, savoring the view, "especially St. Anthony who insisted that his 'books' sprang from daily nature sights, and anytime he wanted to read the works of God, every book was open!" She chuckled.

In her surrender to desert life, Angel felt herself changing. "I fine-tuned my definition of detachment, never sure I was making it. Perhaps I'm becoming too secure in this desert. I'm linked to its flowers, its dryness, its emptiness. But once you think you've found God, watch out. You're back to square one."

Her infectious giggle evoked novice memories, as if everything wonderful was still ahead and we were at the brink of self-discovery, despite our gray hairs. I regarded her blooming citrus trees, with their ripe oranges, fat grapefruits, and bright lemons. Above them, hills of burnt reddish-orange extended to the desert horizon. The beauty was staggering.

"I really can't separate this house from my faith. It's the home that Jacob wanted, his idea of the American dream. And I've learned to see more in it than simply a house." Angel's eyes roamed to the cloud cover. "I think God led me here. Believe me, if anyone goes out into the desert, they will be changed. The desert brings you down, strips you away, leaves you raw. Sometimes I feel like somebody primordial, empty. Strange as it may seem, I love it when I feel empty."

Angel's tone shifted. I heard shadowy currents beneath her words: "It's not a perfect world. Once in a while, fear comes. 'What if Jacob dies?' Those 'what ifs' deplete my soul." Angel has to remind herself that she took care of herself before and could do it again. "I refuse to listen to the tremors, and I just find a cake to bake or go for a run, something to keep me in alignment."

Years ago, Angel had been a kind of guru to me and others. Nuns sought her counsel, and I realized that the years had only deepened her wisdom. We heard a thud. A bright lemon fell to the ground. "Hey, how about some lemonade," I grinned.

"Sure," Angel got up as the back door opened. Jacob walked in, his face pink from a vigorous session on the tennis court.

He waved and headed for the shower. Angel's eyes followed him admiringly, and then she turned to me. "You know that Jacob is my greatest wealth," she said. We raised frosty glasses of lemonade to toast the gifts of our husbands.

Later, amid promises to return, Jim and I drove back down the long desert road as I regaled him with convent stories about Angel and me and how since then she had moved up to a high-paying position. Money never controlled her, not even while banking bigger bucks than she'd ever dreamed of earning.

Dresda: *Living the Dream*

The party was a huge success. The brightly decorated living and dining area had been converted into a ballroom. Vaulted ceilings held clusters of blue and red balloons that mingled with paper streamers. Two small children, blowing transparent bubbles from the top landing, squealed in delight. Baked hams and roast beef platters were stacked along with steaming vegetable dishes on a long table. A smaller table, covered with sweets that Dresda had baked, stood nearby. She had prepared this celebration for her husband's fortieth birthday.

A band of African-American men flowed in through the garden's double doors, their drumbeats embracing, rhythmic. Soon, every toe tapped to the ancient drumbeats. In the midst of the hand clapping and foot-stomping, Dresda found me.

"You wanted to talk to me about money," she whispered in my ear. "I've lots to say," she said, raising her eyebrows mysteriously. We made a date to canoe down the Wekiva River, one of my favorite Florida spots.

Julian and Dresda's love for the outdoors was obvious. Their backyard, a patch of semi-maintained woods, featured a two-tiered treehouse built in a giant tree. Dresda, with skin so young it appears time has passed her by, has but one cross. Her eyes are impaired, forcing her to rely on others for transportation.

I was Dresda's cabbie on our date with the Wekiva River. I loved the river, with its endless shores of rich, damp soil, its Florida scrub, and its ancient oaks. The trees leaned every which way, and the wind moaned a comforting sound in their tops.

Dresda, also a Florida native, was far more familiar with canoes than I was. We set off on the river, allowing the silence to enfold us. After a while, Dresda plunged into her story. "I'm from a Jewish background," she began. "I know that making money, in the tradition of American Jewry, signals a better education, a higher profession. To Jews, money symbolizes achievement."

She paused, settling her paddle across her lap. Her eyes were serious. "As a child, I saw psychic destruction that unnerved me. Maids, cooks—I call them slaves because they were treated as lesser people. I'd hear things like: 'Oh, my girl will do this or that for me.' It was a time of overheard conversation," she said, brows knitted.

Dresda seemed relieved to unburden herself. She gazed at a bright yellow butterfly as it zig-zagged near the riverbank. "We employed a black housekeeper who literally anchored me, who was my second mother. I spilled my little soul to her. Mary was deep into religion, that kind of simple street spirituality that believes God always rewards the good. Most of my spiritual values came from her as I watched her, all the while, absorb my mother's terrible insults."

Generosity, or the lack of it, is a direct reflection of heart, and is not dependent on the size of one's bank account.

—Susan D.

Dresda's voice broke as she recalled a call from Mary's daughter telling of Mary's death. "Do you want to hear poetic justice? Mary was one of those little old ladies who secretly squirreled away her salary under her mattress. Sixty-five thousand dollars! And my mother, all wealth vanished, is now aging, bitter, and living on social security! She can't dine with her well-off friends unless they pick up the check." Dresda wiped her eyes.

Abruptly she shifted back to the past: "You know, I grew up anti-money, and oddly, that may be the reason that I'm so responsible today!"

We drifted down river, the breeze soothing our faces, lost in thoughts of Mary's remarkable fortitude.

"I knew we treated Mary unjustly," Dresda said, softly. "It was then I recognized that life is not fair. It's not fair for the rich to squander their money while others starve. How can anyone believe people can be beneath us because they don't have as much money!"

Dresda described her Miami Beach childhood, crowded with her parents' wealthy friends. "Some of my mother's friends are among the world's top millionaires. These are the people she wants to hang out with, but she's proud and ashamed at the same time. She refuses to tell them that she barely exists on social security. Julian and I give mother a monthly check. She probably feels it's not enough. Somewhere along the road to wealth, some of these people's spirituality crashed," she said.

"What was your dad like Dresda? About money, I mean?"

Her voice lit up. "He was a marvelous, self-made attorney and never bought stuff for himself, just for his kids. He was generous to a fault. Sad to say, his practice left Mom with no life or health insurance. God, she was bitter!"

We paddled to a wide place in the river where the sun enveloped us. Nature's awesome beauty silenced both of us. Dresda spoke, as if inspired. "For me, it's simple, Adele. I use money to create beauty."

Dresda spends her money, quite conservatively she insists, on works of art and crafts, creating a landscape of loveliness in her home. Suggesting that her house, with its circular staircase and gleaming grand piano, appeared "nouveau riche," she said not so, it was "nouveau deal!"

"Actually, the house was a foreclosure, and we got a marvelous buy. But what really matters to us is that it has become a home for others as well." Dresda and Julian formed a circle of friends, who gather to hear speakers, listen to tapes, and take part in small discussion groups. They placed ferns, azaleas, and tall bamboo palms alongside piles of colorfully designed pillows scattered on their floor. It's the kind of classroom that God Himself might create.

As idyllic as their lives are now, this couple's money problems once threatened to erode their marriage. When Julian returned to law school, they knew slim pickings on just five thousand dollars a year. Credit cards became master in their house.

"We couldn't make our monthly payments. Collectors hounded us as if we had done something terrible, like common criminals," she said, frowning.

When she thought she had hit an emotional bottom, Dresda found strength in detachment. "I started selling personal stuff—Oriental rugs, my rings. I got inventive. I wanted my integrity back."

"Were you sorry about what you had to do?" I asked, my voice betraying my admiration.

"I learned that I had control and that Julian and I could do anything together. In a funny way, Adele, I felt like the U.S. Treasury. I created money.

"My problem," she revealed, "is that I squirm when I know someone else is suffering economically." Any hints that Dresda has money, she confessed, make her uncomfortable. If someone compliments her on an outfit, she discounts them with a quick, "Oh, I got this old thing in the bargain basement."

Soon, we found ourselves back at the dock. It's a hard call for some people to learn how to be comfortable with a privileged economic status. Dresda's early impressions of insensitive wealthy people haunt her, and if she lets them, they shame her too.

Back in my car, we drove in near silence, sated by the river's beauty and the flush of our exchange. When I dropped Dresda off, she stood by the door. "Julian and I talked last night about this very issue. We know that money makes our lives more fun, especially when everything else is flowing well. But when they aren't, money won't help. Money is an empty thing, really."

Suzanne: *Rags to Riches*

In contrast to Dresda is Suzanne, who lived her girlhood on the wrong side of the tracks, the daughter of an alcoholic father incapable of holding a job. Suzanne and I sat under the backyard awning of her newly remodeled home, facing her pool's blue waters. To the pool's left stood a bright red set of swings and slides, signaling that youngsters were close by. Suzanne is energized by her grandchildren as she pursues a homegrown experiment she calls "intergenerational living."

In the expansive spirit of the afternoon and the subject in question, Suzanne had poured two glasses of champagne. We raised our glasses and clicked them, giggling like adolescents.

Suzanne's story was of fairy-tale caliber. Despite humble beginnings, she was a true winner. Her riches sprang from overcoming her painful childhood experiences. Her abusive father battered her mother, and he rained a terrifying stream of verbal and physical violence on his children. "Had there been a battered women's center in those days, or even an AA chapter for my dad, things might have been radically different," she said.

Sipping her champagne, Suzanne launched into a tribute to her mother. "When spring came, my mother turned pro at gardening. Together, we planted potatoes, tomatoes, spinach, broccoli, lettuce, cabbage, corn, and string beans. We dieted on fresh vegetables all summer and canned enough to get us through winter. Mom made sauerkraut, dill pickles, and watermelon rind relish. Nothing, and I mean nothing, was wasted." Suzanne learned survival from pure, practical genius.

"Mom had few professional skills, but made use of her uncommon common sense. If life forced her to have children and be denied a profession, then she'd do homemaking professionally. So she sewed, cooked, cleaned beautifully, and sometimes did it for neighbors, too."

Pride in her mother's backbone echoed in Suzanne's tone, and in one episode after another of her challenging narrative. "The church and other neighbors delivered bundles of clothes to us from rummage sales. Mom changed the looks of many of them since I was terrified that I might wear a winter coat belonging to someone's older sister. We chopped wood in winters, and picked the coke ashes at the town dump for our wood-burning stove. But I wanted to die when school friends drove by." Suzanne's eyes were distant.

With the ease of a natural storyteller, Suzanne turned back the clock, recounting a mix of spiritual riches and terrible deprivations. "I lived with so little. And yet we were happy. Joy came from walking in wildflower gardens and just loving the silence. The woods taught me a lot. And I found library books that brought an imaginative world into my dreary one," she smiled.

Suzanne remembers how folks in her small town were shocked when she, now the senior valedictorian, walked off with a coveted four-year scholarship. Later came Jeff, whose survival skills matched Suzanne's. Fruitful college years, marriage, and then a steady income gave the couple stability. They put a down payment on their first home. The house filled, one little one after the other, until there were four Fischers. It was, according to her, a life of benediction, and their sense of family dictated that no job was more important than mothering.

What makes Suzanne's story even more powerful is the couple's deliberate, almost ascetic, choices. "We stayed put while other couples, our neighbors, upscaled, moving into more expensive neighborhoods. We chose to spend our money on music lessons, summer camps, trips around the state. We took part in community programs, free music, and art shows. We laughed at how rich we felt and kept laughing, enormously glad at our unprosperous decision that I stay home with the children. Sure, we could have afforded more stuff if I had worked, but who needs another television, one more stereo?"

Reversing the cultural tendency to acquire, Suzanne and Jeff honored an age-old lifestyle that bred well-adjusted children. "The kids learned early on to make their own decisions, to share, to compromise, to find a life not without self-denial. It didn't hurt, even though it was austere at times," she said, a note of pride in her voice.

"We had to share, and often we were forced to arrange our schedules around a set of limitations. Some parents thought we were a little loony, but we determined that everything in our house belonged to everybody, not just to us, and, like the kids, we learned to share and to respect each individual's needs. If one of the girls needed a ride for a school meeting, and somebody else needed the car, we worked it out."

"It couldn't have always been smooth," I challenged. I could hardly imagine such a home.

"Believe me," she shook her head, "it wasn't easy, with four teenagers and one phone. Sometimes we plunged into crisis. But I don't think my kids were ever addicted to novelty. And I watched them flower in kindness. I've never been sorry that we *denied* ourselves."

After Suzanne's father died, her mother, Grandma Ellen, moved in with them. "Would anyone mind if Grandma came to live with us?" Jeff and I asked the kids at dinner one night. "We were ready, but were they? It was a unanimous yes! These teens had been schooled in the paths of self-sacrifice, so I'm proud to say they opened the front door wide."

But it was Grandma Ellen's bonding with the eldest grandchild that Suzanne relishes most. In her declining years, Grandma Ellen formed an unusual alliance with Peter. He asked no one's permission, but fell into the task of physically caring for his grandma. He'd come home after school, engrossed in the routine of feeding and assisting her to the very end. In that impressionable time, Peter received the most enduring gift of all: how to be with and honor a dying person.

"Pete's wisdom was born in Grandma's last moments. I don't think aging or dying will ever scare my son," Suzanne said.

After the last child left home, Suzanne and Jeff played newlyweds, weekends alone, music and dinner by candlelight, and sex without the "shhhh."

At some point, Peter, now grown with a wife and two daughters of his own, came knocking on the front door. Finances forced them to come to Suzanne's home to live, just temporarily, or at least that's what everyone hoped. Peter would obtain a music degree, get a teaching position, and then move his family into their own place. But each time a condition was met, Suzanne and Jeff sensed a subtle resistance, not only in Peter and Paula, but in themselves. They didn't want the young family to go. And there was evidence that intergenerational living could work. Paula's Cuban parents had fled Castro's government to negotiate a successful partnership of three families living under one roof. Paula was proof that it worked. And who could resist Paula's youngster, Paulette, toddling about chanting, "I don't want to leave Grandma!"

I'm completing my master's in social work, not for a career, but to better help others. My goal is not money, but the community.
—Suzanne F.

Eventually, the families finally admitted that nobody wanted anybody to move. In a three-bedroom, two-bath home, with a large yard and a street of friendly neighbors, Suzanne's family made intergenerational living work.

But what about money? "Who benefits most? I mean, financially?" I asked.

"Money isn't the foundation for our living together—love did that. But paychecks from Pete and Paula and our retirement surplus happily built the walls and roof," she smiled. Suzanne explained that their one set of original major appliances was required, one barbecue grill, one lawn mower, and, of course, one pool. They split expenses on food and consumables, utilities, and all household expenses. And, of course, both families saved an enormous amount on taxes.

"We're open. We both faithfully and carefully post our accounts in a monthly ledger," she said.

"Well, any drawbacks?" I could think of plenty, as Suzanne described anxiety separation from something very near and dear to her—her privacy.

"The primary drawback was privacy. I need my space, so we talked a lot! Finally, we found a plan. The house had been free and clear for years. Peter would buy it from us; we'd hold the mortgage, and he'd make monthly payments to us at a low interest rate. After that, we would renovate. A contractor friend helped us design a suitable master bedroom and library with a private entrance for Jeff and me. I wanted a walk-in closet, all the goodies of shelves and compartments, and an additional room off the bedroom for Jeff's office and library."

After that, the family looked at the most compelling room in the house, the kitchen. The new design stretched across the entire back of the house, with bright pine cabinets, a large island for eating, and a wall-to-wall window wide enough to see the pool and playground.

"My daughter-in-law can watch the kids while she stirs the soup," Suzanne said. "It was perfect except for one thing; I'd like a house big enough where all four kids could live with us!"

Suzanne's joy is infinite when she walks through the door and baby Paulette exclaims, "Grandma, you're home!" We clinked our champagne glasses one last time.

Lala: *A World Apart*

Lala's Iranian family fled the toppled Shah's government. For her own protection, they had sent her to Sacred Heart College in North Carolina. Now married and living in Paris, Lala has found happiness and stability. Her three children testify to that. But what's more joyful is her recent triumph over breast cancer. "My illness cast a new light on what makes me and my life real," she told me on the phone.

"What's it like coming back to visit America?" I asked, as we settled into a sofa in her hotel lobby.

"Do you want the truth?"

"Bad?" I raised my eyebrows.

Lala nodded. "I can't shake the feeling of what I saw while visiting Nick's friends. They were so changed, as if money has taken them over. They've settled into America, yes, but into the American culture also, and all their talk was about money." Count on Lala to speak hard truths, I thought, looking into her dark eyes. "They are living simply to make money."

I suggested that Nick's friends were, perhaps, the familiar story of immigrants falling in love with new money. She looked puzzled. "Is it the way here? Get rich, get a big house, drive a big car, and America will say that you are a 'success?'

"Take the dinner table, for example," she recounted. "Our friend Norman, his eyes kept shifting. He and his wife ate with us, but they weren't present, paying attention to the food or to us. Each time we sat together, they were elsewhere, ready to take off. They've turned their lives into making money," she said ruefully. "I pray Nick and I make money to *live*.

"Nick and I deliberately make dining a time of spiritual nourishment. We try never to rush, but to stay put after the dessert. We savor the wine, savor each other, savor the kids. Sure, Nick could leave, get back to making another client happy, but meal-time is our family time, to hear the stories of the day. Meal time is sacred; it's time for the spirit. We are given to it. It's the place where God feeds our soul.

"I don't mean to criticize," she hastened to clarify, "but I recognize that this 'rush' is very different from our life in France. I feel blessed that I don't like to live like this."

We surveyed the grandeur of the long hotel hall, and strolled outside. "Tell me about Paris. Expensive?" I asked.

"Sure. But we live in a small city apartment."

"Is Nick ambitious?" I asked.

"Oh," she laughed, "this is what I love about this man. He refuses to work overtime, even if it means more money. His priorities are with us."

Lala brought up Nick's friends again and how they give themselves everything and yet give themselves nothing. "They contracted for a colossal house," she sighed, "a palace, cathedral ceilings, marble entrances, the whole works. Yet, the way I see it, it was a misuse of time and money. Norman has to work all the time, including weekends, to find mortgage money. What's more, when I suggested that he and Sena come to visit us in Paris, do you know what he said? 'We haven't time for travel, Lala.'

"I felt such resistance in my heart. Not so much that they bought the house, but for what happened as a result. We had hoped to renew our friendship because we planned to accompany them to Canada. But they have fallen for something destructive, the American way, and by the time we were to leave, I felt so apart I didn't want to go with them. We were their visitors, but they remained at work until the last minute. Did they have to? It was Norman's own business; there was no boss watching the clock. So there we sat, their guests, missing their company!"

I invited Lala to the chapel where I had married my husband. Nick and the children joined us at the holy water fonts. I explained to them why we Catholics had water fonts, explained about making the sign of the cross as we entered the sanctuary.

After a full day, I waved the family good-bye. Lala is a down-to-earth woman who sees grass, weeds, sun, rain, and time as money, all part of God's theology. Her wisdom to let God's aliveness be present at her dinner table, to never let money compromise that time, changed the way Jim and I gather for our evening meal. Since then, our food has never tasted so delicious.

. . . . .

God, You smile broadly on these women, and they respond. What celebrities! Money is an adventure. Like the saints of old, they are models for me. They are Your saints, I say. Their eyes are open to see the sacred in all exchange. They live with nobility and gratitude. I love them for that. Please keep smiling on me too. Amen.

TIME
TALENT
TREASURE

Chapter Three

Working the Lode—Single Again

Money's dark cloud, though I pretended otherwise, continued to cast shadows on my new life. The nuns had been quick to recognize my discomfiture with money. I recall one evening before I had decided to leave when they had observed me grappling with money in a lighthearted moment. We were in the recreation room. To them, Monopoly was a game; to me it was something more. After a while, I was glowing with winner's pleasure, the rush of triumph in my eyes. I presided over my stockpile of play money and property cards, lovingly straightening each stack. I had the largest pile, and at the rate I was going, the other nuns' piles would be before me soon.

Sister Mary Ann struggled to keep the last of her properties, having been forced to sell the lucrative Park Place to me. She turned to me and smiled, but her words were serious: "Sister Adele, you've got precious money sense. We might need it some day. If we all leave the convent, you'll end up the richest." There had been a chorus of laughter.

I didn't smile back. She intended kindness, but at that time, I didn't connect possessing "good money sense" with a "gift," even if it were from God. I silently hoped that Sister's prophecy would go unrealized; I wanted only my share of God's world at that moment—or so I thought.

When I called my father and announced I was leaving the convent, I didn't know what to expect. What I got was his old anger. "Why do you want to leave now? You've given them the best sixteen years of your life."

I wondered the same thing when I exchanged my habit for street clothes and walked out of the wide convent doors for the last time. I clutched a small bag filled with modest worldly goods as I descended those familiar steps. I shielded my eyes, not just from the sun, but from the fear of heating up too quickly in a strange, new world. Standing on the bottom step, I prayed: *God, help me to aim well, to live simply.*

I drove my new beige Toyota up the Atlantic coast to Palm Coast, where, at the invitation of the pastor, my first "real" job awaited me. I whizzed past fields of undeveloped scrub and saw acres of mobile homes sprinkled along Florida's lands and parks. New towns had sprung up on either side of I-95. I was on my own in foreign territory. Pieces of prayers and fragments of hopes and fears sizzled indiscriminately in my head during that long drive from Miami. I felt naked, no longer shrouded by yards of black serge, no longer held close by ancient rules. The challenge of living simply, of not being seduced by a materialistic society, would require vigilance if I were to remain, as Sister Jane had dubbed me so long ago, "God's girl." And underlying all my queasiness wasn't fear of not making money but, as Sister had noted, of making lots of it.

Hadn't I already betrayed the rules of the community by secretly working with the Miami high school that last year while still a nun, sneaking off during the day to teach their girls chorus? I had covertly pocketed eight hundred dollars to help transport my mind and body back into the world. Not that the Mother House wasn't kind about my departure, sending me off with a one hundred dollar stipend. But I knew that sum would buy little more than my first bag of groceries. It was daring, this saving money business, and God knew I hated breaking rules. But I'd met too many nuns who had exited the convent without parental help, and had only managed their reentry into the world by sheer wit and will.

The savings paid off. When I waved good-bye to my sisters, the eight hundred dollars secretly earned secured a down payment on the Toyota and on my first apartment, an efficiency so tiny that washing dishes meant filling the bathtub with soapsuds after each meal. I would now be forced to make myriad tiny decisions without parameters set by a superior! Would I recognize God's guidance in department stores and gas stations, in supermarkets and mail-order catalogs?

Rejoining the outside world meant shopping for new clothes. No more black, loose-fitting garments that revealed little femininity. It was a time of high heels, miniskirts, and sassy shoulder bags. My mind whirled. When I bought a purse, how much money would I carry? How much did I need? How much was enough?

My Aching Back

I SHAKE MY HEAD TODAY, RECALLING THAT WILD LEAP. I ACCEPTED A position as music therapist at a local mental health center, and I also became director of religious education at the local parish. Then, one day a week, I drove down to St. Joseph's College and taught a music appreciation class, somehow determined to wring money out of every hour of the day. Overnight, my time for interior quiet vanished. The person I invented, this hyperproductive moneymaker, left no space for piety. I knew better, but I thought this was how one "did" a super-charged professional life. I enjoyed driving to the bank, depositing my earnings, checking statements, adding numbers, and driving away high, as if I owned the world. Occasionally, I did allow a few moments to glimpse God, sometimes to find a back pew and just sit a while.

Take time, perhaps in meditation, to know your money in all its giftedness.
—Jenny K.

Sunday was no day of rest for this frantic moneymaker. Not that I was alone; too many church workers, priests, choir directors, and religion teachers are caught up in the relentless serving of others, forgetting that the Sabbath requires them to give themselves some restorative time as well.

I had not yet learned that earning money is not about a separation or divorce from God, but about truly embracing the meaning of "Give us this day our daily bread." It would require a lifetime of curiosity about the very nature of money, asking questions that no one dared ask, putting hard questions to myself and to God, before I could absorb that undeniable truth: money and God do connect, quietly. Each time I consciously embrace a transaction, God is sacramentally present. But at this time, it was the hasty days and not enough hours to scoop up all the money I supposed I needed.

After an average day of nonstop activity, my head would hit the pillow like a lead ball. That was when I longed for the sound of the chapel's late-day Gregorian chants, as the nuns effortlessly intoned the simple, melodic lines. I missed the easy joys of community recreation, of the ditties and dances we learned from one another.

In my job as music therapist at the Day Treatment Center, I was eliciting sounds, no matter how thin, unsure, or feeble, from troubled men and women who stumbled into our program every day. They hovered sadly in their assigned places, sometimes staring at nothing, sometimes at me. I couldn't bear their eyes, and gazed at my piano keys as my fingers pounded on them. I knew somewhere deep in my heart that our jam sessions were as much for me as for my sorrowful friends. Like them, I was in transition, and life was all push and pull. One gray-whiskered man who refused to sing caught my eye above the sheet music. He wore the same wrinkled khaki pants and blue shirt day in and day out. I was drawn to him, his empty look, his thin frame. He occupied only the barest space at the sofa's end. Finally I walked to his side, admonishing him to participate. He rolled his eyes to the ceiling, as if calling on his Maker: "All I want is a little peace and quiet!" In his unique way, the bedraggled old man was God's evangelist pointing out my own spiritual hunger, reminding me of my long leap from regulated life. I was running in circles, undisciplined, without soul. And I refused to acknowledge it.

My efficiency apartment soon felt cramped and unwelcoming. My back ached from bending over the tub washing the dishes. I called a friend, another ex-nun. After leaving the convent, Maryanna taught inner-city kids in a Miami public high school, no easy task. Like Jews wandering the Sinai, we both suspected that we were moving aimlessly in our new lives. Sure, this life was our choice, but the results felt wacky. "God, this transition, as the kids say, sucks," she confessed. Trying to lighten our moods, I described my latest frugal purchase: wood crates for library shelves. Maryanna's parents, like mine, were children of the Great Depression—we had learned to make something do, stretch out its life, no matter how shabby. Why had I selected such a hole in the wall to live in? Are old habits that hard to shed? At least Maryanna had had sense enough to rent a two-bedroom apartment, I thought.

Later that night, I felt cheered. I sipped warm mint tea and I stacked books on my modest new shelves. I thought of the days when Sister Maryanna and I had taught grade school. She was there when I actually stalked a wealthy parishioner for an unpaid debt. I was the organist at chic weddings for brides who grew up in affluent neighborhoods. This particular mother-of-the-bride had neglected to pay for my organ services after her daughter's lengthy wedding. Feeling squeamish, and waiting until out of earshot of the other nuns, I had put in numerous useless phone calls to the woman. My patience blown, one Sunday I had waited while families filed out of church, pausing to dip their fingers into the holy water to bless themselves. The elegantly attired but embarrassed woman had tried to file past too, but I had stood firmly in her path. She had paled and furtively pulled two bills from her purse. "Sister, I was going to pay you," she had murmured, unable to meet my eyes.

I had smiled at her lie. I am both amused and chilled by this memory. (I wonder what that woman thinks of nuns today.) But I also think of myself, a grown, not-so-innocent nun aggressively using my uniform to pressure the woman.

The phone call to Maryanna had pulled me back from despair. Despite all the self-accusations circulating earlier in the evening, I felt God was close again. Perhaps I hadn't slipped that far from spirit after all. And money could still have a place in my life.

Buy 200 Shares

"When you play the big board, the game of money is like no other, honey," my Dad used to instruct me. Surely I wasn't supposed to be like him, calling my broker each morning. But something about the stock market attracted me. I couldn't resist. I had grown bored. Depositing Friday's paychecks into a savings account seemed silly and out of step with money's explosive possibilities. I walked out of the bank one morning thinking that I could do better. Long ago, I'd been introduced to that world of thinly disguised gambling and my appetite had been whetted; Dad had given me a hundred shares of Tucson stock, an up-and-coming utility in Arizona, and I was thrilled by it.

While on break in the Day Treatment Center's cafeteria, I picked up the daily newspaper, flipped to the financial section, and checked my stock. Tucson was up a point. Owning one hundred shares, I realized a paper profit of a hundred dollars, not bad for an overnight take.

Utilities were always safe, our family stockbroker, Bob, had advised. I smiled to myself. Images of me, rich and happy, flashed in my mind—money in the bank, a house paid for. I returned to my office musing the possibilities. Not that I would own a huge mansion or have fancy fish tanks in bay windows, but maybe I'd have enough money for that feeling of peace and well-being. I dialed the broker's number.

Bob's voice was cheerful. "Hello, Adele!" Suddenly I lost my voice. He waited while I managed a deep breath. "Bob, how about buying me another one hundred more shares of Tucson?" Then I hit a wall of doubt. *Oh, my God, can I really do this? All that money! Two years of vacation! Thirteen hundred dollars.* "Wait, Bob, check with Dad first." I hung up and lit the tiny vigil candle that I kept in a desk drawer. My heart beat furiously. What would God or my priest say about this risky and highly materialistic adventure? Nothing was clear.

That night, the moon was brilliant. Not a cloud drifted across it to signal that I'd made a mistake. I showered and then scooted between clean white sheets and dreamed, not of a rising stock market or of owning a Cadillac like Dad, but of special Sundays in Orlando when Dad closed the grocery store and drove us to the beach. Picnic times meant wonderfully seasoned shish kabobs made from the store's best meat. We played hard in the gentle Atlantic swells, jumping and dunking whoever was nearest and leaving the ocean's bounty only when hunger drove us out. We loved those picnics, the home-grilled feasts with a few traces of sand. Dad grinned like a kid as he dished out home fries cooked on our hibachi, with strict instructions to eat every one. My father looked content and happy, free as that ocean wind. I awoke and felt close to him. I had passed an unspoken hurdle. Bob called back the next day with a tease in his voice. "Your Dad said to buy two hundred shares!"

Buying those shares of stock was a defining moment in my new life after the convent. In the weeks that followed, I declared to my priest that while I felt comfortable about the gamble, I was strangely uncomfortable with the profits. Years later I came upon a beautiful passage in Marianne Williamson's *A Return to Love,* which expresses my truth precisely:

> Like everything else, money is either holy or unholy, depending on the purposes ascribed to it by the mind. We tend to do

with money what we do with sex: we desire it but we judge the desire. It is the judgment that then distorts the desire, turning it into an ugly expression. Because we are ashamed to admit that we want these things, we have insidious ways of pretending that we don't—such as condemning our desires even as we act them out. The loss of purity is in us, then, not in money or sex. They are both just canvasses onto which we project our guilt.

Of course, Dad was delighted by my leap into stock investments. After all, it was the stock market not the grocery market that had fueled his financial highs. Dad espoused the argument that God and money were mysteriously related, such that, for him, his risks in the market were part of his spiritual life. Words of an anonymous philosopher that I heard years after Dad's death reflect this philosophy: *The master instructs a young soul: "Come to the edge." The soul replies, "But I'm afraid." The master instructs again, "Come to the edge," and again, the soul resists. For a third time, he asks and this time, the soul walks to the very edge, and looks down, trembling. The master comes from behind and pushes the soul, and for the first time in its life, it flies.*

Dad had ventured near the edge many times, following the path that made the best sense to him. A full life was to be lived at the edge. He made that belief perfectly clear one night when the stock market had plummeted. His face was stricken; he wasn't used to loss. I sought to comfort him at dinner. "Dad, the market's got you depressed." I mirrored his frown and felt a surge to advise: "Why not quit, Dad? Play backgammon at the club, go fishing, forget the market!" Dad sat back abruptly. He looked out the window. Had I touched something deep in him? I was afraid I'd offended him, and I almost left the table. I'm so glad I didn't.

"You don't get it, honey," he said finally. "The grocery is sold now. We have enough." *We have enough? I knew that! Did he know that?* I was incredulous.

"But I can't just sit back and enjoy it. What fun would there be in that? I have to play in the *game.*" He smiled broadly.

Dad and I were talking adult to adult, and I actually felt like one. It was an afternoon never lost to me. Years later, each time I entered the gambling arena, I remembered his urgency to play the game, to take the chances that life presented to him. He wasn't afraid of life, and I loved that about him. There was always opportunity for one more try, one more margin of doubt to overcome. "Taking money risks makes me come alive," he insisted.

It was a great line, maybe not his own. But that evening, he led me to believe that gambling held the very essence of being alive, making bets on possibilities and never giving up, always playing. Stretching himself in the stock market in his so-called "retirement" kept my father vital. He took chances just to know that he was still wiggling, still in touch, still here. I leaned over and kissed his bald head, feeling we'd both won something great. For me, the biggest win of all was that I'd made a genuine connection to my father.

I felt a divine pull to stop my frenetic three-job nonsense as I peered in the mirror one morning and saw sorry-looking black circles under my eyes. I shook my head in disbelief. My olive coloring naturally breeds dark circles, but this? *The money isn't worth it, Adele! And feeling sorry for yourself, your face, and your health isn't going to get you anywhere either!*

I dialed work. "I'm off for a mental health day," I announced to my colleague. I kissed the receiver, then canceled every appointment and every rehearsal for the next few days. I wandered into the kitchen, brewed a cup of tea in my kitchen, all yellow and shiny. I felt tears. *You're rarely in this kitchen, you silly girl. You haven't cooked one hot meal here.* The tea warmed me. Sitting out on the back deck, I braced myself for some heavenly change.

It happened swiftly. A week later, when I was heading home on a familiar and lonely stretch of Florida back road, exhausted and spent after yet another late parish meeting, my faithful Toyota abruptly stopped. It gave no warning, no sputtering, no flashing light—just sudden death. And then quiet. I checked my watch. Midnight. *Oh, God.* Frantically, I turned the key over many times. The car had fallen into a trance. I looked out at a night totally black and sinister.

My heart pounded. I imagined the morning's headlines: "Woman Found Dead by Intercoastal Waterway." The hairs on my arms were stiff. I made the sign of the cross and tried the key again. I looked up, helpless. Through the windshield bright stars burned, but no moon illuminated the road. *How big You are, how great is Your name, how small my car, this problem, this moment.*

No auto passed and not a house or sign of commerce illuminated the night. There was no hint of life anywhere, just spooky motionless wee hours. My fingers played with the key that refused to ignite the motor. An avalanche of tears burst as if they had accumulated less from terror, but from my affliction of so much speed and, consequently, the sense that God was distant and had given up on me. I actually welcomed the tears, every tiny drop, and I sobbed uncontrollably. After a while, I rolled down the car windows and inhaled the grassy, clean, sharp smells that poured in like blessed assurances. Night sounds filled the car; an owl's hoots joined a chorus of crickets. I breathed deeply, trying not to be afraid. I lay my head back on the seat and realized that somehow this little nighttime crisis would end; God would get someone to me. I relaxed and surrendered to the steady rhythm of night sounds.

I wish I could explain what happened that rugged night; how, when the outer world grew so dark, utterly black, my inner world radiated with sparks of transformation, with divine light. Its brightness filled me with such full force, pulling me away from the mere fact of my car problem. Bigger questions sprang into my consciousness, some passing, some pressing me to follow them, to think about them, and to think hard. My mind whirled. *Money? Was it the drive for money that had delivered me to this spiritual dead end? Or was work the culprit? Work was ingrained in me. Endless chores in the grocery, chores in the convent: "An idle mind is the devil's workshop." One must keep busy to make it with God.* That night, alone on that deserted road, I was overpowered, forced to look at the mounting deceptions of my life.

Father P had even slipped me extra cash for added hours, once handing me a wad of dollars in a paper sack, whispering, "We won't let the parish secretary know about this." Now, in the quiet of this odd, Florida night, I was being properly admonished. My fingers wound tightly around the steering wheel as if squeezing out the nastiness of my past. I traced the outline of the moon on the windshield, yellow and full, playing atop the swaying pines. I bent my head, feeling the last tears. In my Toyota turned chapel, I begged God for strength. Soon after, I chuckled at the rush of solutions surfacing: quit the jobs, or quit one job. Buy a cow. Stay at home for a while. Bake something! I turned, pressing my nose against the window and actually laughed at the probable presence of dreaded snakes slithering about my tires. I couldn't resist the feelings of joy, of liberty. Suddenly, headlights shone on the road as a semitrailer roared toward me. *I'll get out only if you get out with me, God.* Trembling at the dangerous possibilities in store, I got out and waved the giant down. Brakes screeched. The driver, from the cab's height, surveyed me and my dead auto.

"Get in," he commanded.

"No," I had already prepared a truthful answer. "I'm too scared. Please call someone for me."

"Hell, lady, I'll treat you just like my wife. Get in."

I crossed my fingers. Treat me like his wife? What could that possibly mean?

I huddled close to the passenger door, my right hand tightly gripping the handle. We pulled up at a well-lit Holiday Inn. I got out, and he grinned: "You know, I get scared too, driving on dark roads at night. You could have attacked *me*."

God's Little Joke

WEEKS LATER, I WALKED INTO THE OFFICE OF AN ANGEL SENT BY GOD. A Protestant church employed therapist Ben Carroluci, whose work centered on Christ's law and love. He was not your "John the Baptist"–type Christian, calling a client to task for her sins. Ben was more like a familiar comfortable Thomas Merton with reading glasses, someone down to earth and easy to pray with. It wasn't so much what he said, but how he said it, and I was dazzled by the books on his shelf and his beliefs. I remember my first session, when he turned to ask: "What have you done for yourself this week?" I couldn't answer. The silence lingered. I retrieved a tissue. We were off. For starters, he and I addressed my workaholic issues.

"Find something lovely to smell, anything, that can remind you to slow down," he admonished me. In all my life, I'd never put a dime down for fresh flowers. Plants were okay, for I knew they'd grow branches. Plants were a long-term investment. But fresh flowers! Here now and gone tomorrow? I was astonished. But within days, pink and yellow roses or white daffodils, whatever color was available at the market, were cheering my kitchen table and slowing me down. Their fresh perfumes animated a new, slower world for me.

"Money is made for pleasure," Ben said in one of our sessions, pulling down a cream-colored, thin, dog-eared text titled *The Prophet*, by Kahlil Gibran. He began to read:

Speak to us of pleasure. And some of your elders remember pleasures with regret like wrongs committed in drunkenness. But regret is the beclouding of the mind and not its chastisement. They should remember their pleasure with gratitude, as they would the harvest of a summer.

He put the book down. "Pleasure," Ben said, "is as important in your life as work. Trust me on this!"

I stared out the window. I could hardly contain my shock. "The convent wasn't the best place to learn about pleasure," I stammered. "Even during our summers, after the kids went on vacation, we went on to higher learning and that included lots of studying and test taking."

Ben scribbled something on a piece of paper. "Adele, forget the convent right now. Ask yourself some new questions. For example, what's your salary for? Why is there money in the first place?" He paused. His thick eyebrows arched.

The silence stretched. I was shaken. Was I being led astray? I'm not sure why the questions stung so. Ben waited. Thoughts crowded my mind, but I couldn't speak.

Ben smiled. "I say that money is your friend!" Ben sounded strong, like a prophet standing in a pulpit. His tiny sermon pierced me like a bullet. Money a friend? Outside the window, a blackbird perched itself on the ledge, his beak directed down toward me, looking as if he knew exactly what was going on in that office.

"Well, I'll be damned," I finally managed.

Ben pulled out a wad of bills, including a fifty. He stuffed the wad in my hands. I looked down, fingering their corners, straightening them like Dad did when counting the grocery money. Suddenly, I held nothing more than green strips of paper. I felt like tearing them up and tossing them around the office like confetti. I'd show them who's boss!

Later, I laughed to think that I had paid a therapist to open my mind. Me, who had prayed as a religious for sixteen years, who had washed herself in the spirituality of saints and martyrs and countless other living heroes! I had to write a weekly check to a counselor, and one outside my religion at that! I had to *pay* to be led to another face of God, the minted God, established on every green transaction. Was *paying* for insights one of God's little jokes reserved just for me? Only later could I realize how sacramental the transaction.

After that session, car keys in hand, I ambled out to the parking lot a lighter, different person. I scrutinized my Toyota and for the first time, saw its worn and troubled dents.

"You gotta go! I'm moving up to an automatic." I laughed aloud.

"Meet me at the car dealer," I told Phil, a friend from my pastoral counseling group. Phil was a cautious type, not spending a dime if he could help it. My choice of a shiny black Buick, a luxurious first-rate car totally threw him. "Do you really want this fancy car?" He stared at it with alarm. He stepped back, scratched his head, and walked deliberately around the car, as if it were an exotic creature. Wide-eyed, Phil watched as I penned a check for fifteen thousand dollars and tossed it on the salesman's desk. It was the largest check I'd ever written; it was money from a profitable stock sale. Unknown to Phil, that check was proof that a very different sort of counseling had worked its magic. I was growing up, no longer embarrassed to spend money openly. Money had long sought to be my friend and was finally, rightfully, winning me over. I didn't try to explain, but Phil looked at my grinning face as if I were a madwoman.

My new Buick was positively decadent: electric windows and locks, all controls within an arm's reach, leather upholstery. It made a great story: abandoned on a dark road in a rusty Toyota, then hurled into a plush, velvet coach. As I steered my chariot about, I murmured, *How wonderful is Your wild bounty, O Lord.*

Money as Seduction

Once over that hurdle with money, I now faced another challenge: romantic love. To fall in love with a priest is a serious blunder; it promises, almost guarantees, nothing in return. Secrecy becomes the norm, hiding what the church denies. My case was even more unhealthy; by a mutual consent we had our financial transactions. This intimate episode of my life is included, not so much to report an affair, but to highlight what I've learned about how clearly money can seduce us when our emotions take over. It was that seduction that caught me in its grip.

From the first days I worked for Father P, I was in love with him. I was merely smitten at first, I suppose, and like other choir directors who fell for their pastors, it didn't take long to fully lose my heart. Never before had I felt this rush, this wonder! After working all day with him, I'd lay my head on my pillow, feeling at peace, certain that God approved. I had no idea how things would turn out, but as love blossomed, it felt good, right, even holy. Before I knew it, there was no going back.

No James Bond characters ever played such dual roles! It took enormous amounts of energy to foster the fiction, and I could write the rule book: don't answer the knock on your door when your friend is visiting; never, ever, answer the phone when you have company; travel in separate cars, even for simple trips to the movies, where you sit in the theater's dark recesses and pray that no parishioner recognizes you; buy vacation tickets for very faraway places, buy them separately, take separate planes, then pray that you will not get lost and will somehow meet in the appointed spot; live miles apart—my new condo was more than thirteen miles from the parish, designed to discourage the spontaneous visitor. The toll grew intolerable over years of late parish meetings, followed by exhausting trips back and forth to my condo and the inevitable weariness the next morning. Yet looking back, it was our private money exchange that robbed us of our integrity. Innocent at first, we simply continued to invest in two condos and an acre of Florida land. The property was contracted under my name to maintain the fiction of celibacy, and Father P always quietly paid me in cash from his own monthly salary. I convinced myself that we were building a future, that our comingled green bills held the promise that someday we'd be "Mr. and Mrs." But could anything bright and holy come of this? How could it? Secrecy of that kind erodes both body and spirit.

The deception bled us both, and, shortly, the lies exploded the charade. One day a former student, a young woman attorney and friend, visited my condo. Sandy examined the dinette set that Father P and I had purchased, running her fingers over the table top. I was on trial.

"Adele, you bought all this on a simple church salary?" I flushed. But how could I tell the truth? I could never convince Sandy, but I was practiced at trying. "I sure did!" I fibbed. I turned to the kitchen sink and ran the water for hot tea, hiding my flushed face.

God, take me back to that time when life was simple. When I could say what I meant. When I owned nothing. When I would never so much as think of breathing a lie.

I set a plate of brownies on the coffee table, grateful that she kept silent about her suspicions. Finally, I kissed her good-bye, slipped to the back deck, dragged over a chair, and fell into it, exhausted by my deceptions. Something had to change. I had to change.

The next day, I was back in Ben's office. He didn't judge me, but kindly said: "Change happens only in small chunks. As with the money, let's change just one thing at a time."

And so, slowly, I prepared myself to abandon my deceptive life. How quickly truth, like a bolt of lightning, shifts our perceptions. Never had I felt such grief. Ben turned his chair toward me and faced me directly. "Love for this priest isn't going anywhere except down," he said respectfully. The words were a knife in my heart. There was no going forward and absolutely no going back.

Again, something mysterious would change my direction. My father died. We had made our peace, and now, grieving the losses of both men, I drove to the vacant lot that had once held my hope for a home with Father P. I got out and walked the perimeter of the property, the smell of rain in the air. I sat on the wild grass, tossed blades in the wind, opened my journal, and wrote:

The rain is coming, but for this lingering moment, I am with the land. There is no deception here, no money lies, no fraud. Trees push their way upward as they are meant to. Scrub fills the empty places, and little surprises of red spring everywhere. Who am I to question things? A yellow wild vine, alive with a sprig of brilliant rose seduces with its poison. My lies have choked me.

I reread Thomas Merton's words printed on my journal's front cover: "You pray and suffer and hang on and then give things up and hope and sweat." A cloud of gnats ushered in the tiny drops sprinkling my face. Back in the car, I revved the motor and headed out. *Find me another place to live then, another hope, and while you're at it God, how about another God!*

The final push came from my brother. "Get the hell out of there! Church life is driving you crazy!" He gazed long into my eyes, disbelieving that I'd played myself so short. I quit all my jobs. Then I packed, piling my worldly possessions and my beloved cat, Company, into my Buick, and drove away without looking back.

With the uncertainty of no job waiting, I turned onto I-26 north for Charlotte, North Carolina, where Sarah, a former nun, was waiting with a shoulder to cry on. To my surprise, I didn't feel wiped out: I had my share of the property that we had sold, and the profits proved a soothing balm; they were a down payment on my new life. In God's mysterious ways, mercy and wealth followed me.

North Carolina in the 1980s bustled with new construction, and I found a half-finished apartment building. I was the first tenant. I rushed up the stairs, opened the door, and tried to forget, as I hauled in my suitcases, that I was back to the old world of rentals. Nothing would be permanent here.

Through sliding glass doors, unfamiliar trees shaded the grounds like sturdy sentinels. Oaks, dogwoods, and maples were in full summer dress, almost as if they were waiting for me. I tingled at the scene, the green beauty, and sat looking out the window for a very long time.

"Miss Adele," they called me. The choir's young voices of St. Gabriel's parish felt reassuring. I called home: "Gosh, Mama, it's so good to be needed once more." My new pastor, Father Tom, had had an opening for a religious director. "You're definitely a self-starter. I will count on you to create parent programs!" he said. I called home again: "But Mama, what's more important is that I feel that *I* can count on myself again."

Working with a children's choir was an absolute joy. I swung my arms in 4/4 rhythm, sweeping over the squirming young angels, prodding them to open their mouths round and discharge their pure music. The burden of work, like nothing else, soothed the unease in my heart.

At one of our last sessions, Ben had warned me that leaving would be hard, even unbearable at first. Little did he know. North Carolina's unfamiliar winters were no match for the cold swirling within my soul. After supper, with no one except my cat, I created a ritual in order to survive. Out came my pen, journal book, and rosary beads. I sat cross-legged before a blazing fire; only the ring of a phone could get me up, and there weren't many of those. Over the weeks, in some mystic way, I was rebirthing and I knew it, and I didn't have the strength to resist even if I had wanted to. While the church's confessional is powerful medicine, there is nothing like sitting before a burning log to fix what ails you. My pen helped, too. Words flew across the pages, pouring out the whole mess of my life. I recognized old sins, and they tasted sour. But I put it all down, the simple, ugly ways I had betrayed myself.

When my piano finally arrived, I played endlessly, loving the wrong notes as well as the ones that fit, carrying me beyond grief with the popular song titled, *The Rose,* crying with the bright hope it held out in its last line: *"In the spring, the seed becomes the rose."*

I suppose it was grace that drew me to those fires, which purged me, then left me exhausted but cleansed. What a strange way to rise—God's way—from the ashes of a broken heart. I look back in wonder at it all—the crying, writing in my journal, playing my piano, praying, and despairing. It required many tears, but I felt pure joy at last. I hardly pick up that worn journal anymore, but when I do, I'm happy for that frightening time. Today, it makes such sense.

After two winters, I'd passed through most of the darkness. Professional therapy, leading a choir of giggling elves, and numerous workouts at the gym directed me to tomorrow. I was ready and toned. And to my surprise, my bank account had not suffered for all that soul wrenching.

Single Again

MAMA FELL SERIOUSLY ILL, AND I NEEDED TO BE WITH HER. I POINTED my Buick toward Orlando, with Company curled up beside me on the front seat. I noted the passing roads, which had led me away from Florida, with gladness. I had taken a giant leap toward liberty when I first drove those roads. I'd been completely on my own for the first time—away from the convent, away from Father P, away even from the familiarity of Florida—though I was in my mid-forties now. I was only accountable to myself and God. The cold, lonely nights in front of the fire had been my crucible, and I felt pure at last.

Starting over would have been impossible without the gift of time. Lots of time. Try as anyone might, I know of no one able to rush their emotional healing after a breakup. It's foolish to try, and I'm convinced it is an irresponsible attempt that delays the lesson.

I had had to learn to cope financially after leaving the convent and again after ending my relationship with Father P. The women in the following interviews also had to adjust to the new status of being single. They found themselves swimming alone in a sea of bills, mortgages, insurance forms, tax documents, and other financial demands. They no longer had the security of their husbands' salaries. They were on their own and had to make all of their own financial decisions. Some women downsized, shedding houses for condos and doing with fewer appliances. Some started new businesses. Others leaned on relatives until they could manage on their own. But as one woman put it, "Staying in a marriage devoid of life is much more demeaning than living partnerless, even with less money in the pot."

New at being single, these stalwarts walked into a frightening financial world, but most of them discovered an unexpected adeptness. As they ran the money marathon—taking out loans, earning money, managing money—firm stepping-stones supported their surefooted inner selves. They laughed with their angels and cried with their demons, noted new insecurities and fears, and in the end, rejoiced in a newfound trust in God. In the crazy quilt called divorce, God pushed these newly single women to a heightened identity that they never would have achieved while married.

Michelle: *A Garden of Delight*

Trusting her intuition, Michelle Palmer divorced a hugely successful husband who had, in his compulsive acquisition of riches, filled her life with fairy-tale material goods—and little else. She's never been sorry! A Southern lady, Michelle is in her early fifties and, though used to the comfort and assurance of a high social position, a hollow ache within pushed her to abandon her privileged lifestyle and go it alone.

"I reclaimed my soul in the process," she told me. "Walking away from Bart's money gave me something far more important." Hearing Michelle's secure tone, I recognized her as the heroine of her story, one rich in self-identity. I liked being with her right away.

"When I fled that so-called Camelot marriage, I created shock waves among family and friends. No one could believe it." The dark-haired woman sitting across from me shook her head, as if she could not believe it herself.

As Michelle traced her finger along her chair's arm, she said, "I learned early in that marriage that money buys trouble!" Despite living in a gorgeous home complete with plush garden and accompanying lifestyle, Michelle had had to learn what was real and important to her. I wasn't surprised at how determined she had been to avoid an acrimonious divorce; she had asked for nothing, not a dime.

"Personal freedom means more to me than material security," Michelle said.

She was pleased to have made such a healthy financial start. I noted that many women would have taken their husbands to the cleaners. But Michelle wanted to earn her own money, to make money an adventure, not a weapon to right past wrongs.

"I'm not surprised that women fight for more. Fear prompts them to go to court, to get all they can! Women of my generation were not just ignorant about business and investments, we were abysmally deficient in information on how to provide for ourselves."

The first thing Michelle did was to buy a house, but not just any house, *her* house. "Friends thought I was crazy to take on this house. Of course, I was scared and swallowed hard when I signed the papers." The corners of her mouth turned up as she spoke. "Yet I considered my resources; Mom had left me enough inheritance to buy it from my ex-husband."

Michelle poured fresh papaya juice prepared from her own fruit trees. I sipped the sweet, delicious beverage and enjoyed the visual feast of her home. Surely, this woman has everything, I thought. How did she do it?

Rather than squeeze Bart and put herself through courtroom torture, Michelle developed a hidden self-reliance. She read and reread that tiny best-seller *Creative Divorce,* by Mel Krantzk, which led her to several business courses including how to manage commercial real estate. She quickly enrolled in a course on stock market strategies. Before long, Michelle was drawing profits on her own investment IQ. While she admits to making a few mistakes, her self-esteem—and her bank account—soared in no time.

Many women just like me have failed to see that controlling our financial lives has a good deal to do with controlling our lives in general.

—Sue K.

I listened, struck by the contrast between women who rise financially like Michelle and those who flounder. Granted, Michelle's initial resources helped. But stories abound of women from a range of means who pursue meaningful careers, open small businesses, turn artistic expression into income producers, or like Michelle, learn how to create a healthy nest egg. What is different about these women?

"Actually," Michelle broke into my thoughts, "if I had more money, it could be bothersome. Those who inherit money, have to deal with the horror of separation anxiety from those who have less money. Uneven economics can really separate friends."

Without a trace of rancor, Michelle described her former marriage. Her and her husband's radically different money attitudes quickened the marriage's disintegration. She described a brief history of living "poor," of feeling what that was like.

"We got off to a rocky start when Bart was working on his graduate degree. I hated the lack of money but more, I hated the lack of privacy in the dorm. Silly, giggly wives who thought I had something in common with them. At night, I'd get the baby to bed and settle in with the *New York Times* when, not even past the front page, one or more would routinely charge in, settling themselves in for a night of gossip while our husbands were crunching away in the library. I didn't know how to stand up for myself. The next day, I'd put the baby in a buggy and go off to the park but, again, they'd catch up with me. I'd have sold my birthright to get out of that dorm."

Michelle rubbed her eyes. "That's what I called the real poverty. My spirit was denied breathing room." In that time of scarcity, Michelle discovered that even a five dollar bill could nurture a person. She told me of a letter from her mother: "'Honey, here's some money for that last phone call home. You forgot to reverse the charges.' With that five dollars, I bought enough canned foods to last a week. Mom hadn't a clue how deeply that bill touched me."

I delighted in the oddity of hearing this story amidst such bounty and beauty: traditional polished mahogany chairs upholstered in pale brocades, Chinese rugs on a shiny wood floor, walls of bookshelves behind baskets of hanging lacy ferns. Over in the corner, building blocks and Lego toy sets had been shelved and neatly stacked, evidence of a grandchild.

Michelle refilled my glass, and handed it back to me. I wanted to know more.

"Your house is gorgeous, your garden is gorgeous, you are gorgeous. Do you ever get bored?"

She threw back her head and guffawed. "Dear me," she drawled, "I've never been bored. Right now, traveling is the one hobby I won't give up. Vacations teach me so much about myself. I travel with avid mountain climbers, who last year, insisted on Mt. Everest even after an avalanche scrubbed our first attempt! It wasn't my choice."

Michelle had traveled halfway around the world to see this natural wonder, but found herself hating it. The guide had given her a sidewise glance and reminded her, "Michelle, this mountain is neither good nor bad; it doesn't kill people. It's just neutral."

"I've had the same insight about money," she said. "Mountains or money. Both are neutral! They are both just there."

Later, I mused on Michelle's leap from a marriage that possessed all the trappings of the good life. No one can predict outcomes. But if, like Michelle, a woman ventures into singlehood again with her confidence intact, she might find it was worth the change.

Virginia: *To the Edge and Back*

When I left Michelle, my thoughts turned to another woman who had left a high-powered, monied man. I could hardly wait to interview Virginia Jeanoon, an Arab friend, who had nearly died of a heart attack at age forty-five, shortly after her divorce from a prominent insurance executive. I'd known Virginia since we were children. In all that time, we had never discussed money philosophies, fears, or dreams. One drizzly summer afternoon, she dropped by my house for a Middle Eastern lunch. I took her raincoat, her smart green silk suit offsetting her thick red hair. Virginia is one of the county's top education officials.

We sat on my screened back porch. To my delight, she was anxious to talk about the change in her money attitudes, and her words tumbled out. She leaned forward, elbows on her knees, chin in hand, looking girlish.

"Yep, when I nearly died, I finally relaxed, realized tomorrow takes care of tomorrow. I was going to live *now!* It shocked my children, but," she added with a twinkle, "I now get respect!"

"So you've rejected the old save-for-a-rainy-day philosophy?" I laughed.

Virginia nodded vigorously. "My entire philosophy has changed. I guess my red convertible is metaphor galore!"

Between bites, she told me of miraculous changes in her life. "Living in the present moment is now all-important to me. My children, suspecting this change, were scared when I began spending money. They were still in high school, and they called my new splurging behavior money madness. 'Mom, are you sure we can afford it?' they asked over and over. 'We can't afford not to,' I'd retort. 'Let's spend it while I'm alive!'"

Virginia's journey to the edge of life and back was dramatic. "Anything I can solve with money is not a real problem. I'll poke at that problem or this problem until it's resolved, usually with a dose of cash. But illness, that can't be fixed by money," she said.

I realized how far she had come from the terrible time in childhood when her father died while serving in World War II. Having no life insurance, Mimi, her mother, found that her tiny liquor store took on survival importance. Enduring exhausting nights in the bar with boozy night owls demanding drinks, Mimi scrambled to keep her children in food and clothes and school. By herself, she closed the bar each night, drove home for a few hours of sleep, then rose early to get Virginia and the other kids off to school. The grief-stricken young woman ultimately evolved into an independent, self-assured businesswoman.

I pushed a platter of humus, pita bread, and olives toward my friend. Virginia dabbed at the humus with her bread. "Being the oldest child, I took on Dad's role after he was killed. If Mom needed protection, I'd be the one. I'd save allowance money to buy her gifts. I really played the father. I've learned that money is a driving force in womens' lives. It sure played a major role in my growing up!"

> *When I was a kid, my first paycheck marched Mom and Dad and me to the bank to open a savings account.*
>
> *—Alice S.*

I let that point sit for a while. Virginia's money lessons were traceable to her mother's Middle Eastern roots. Virginia laughed, "She dickered with liquor salesmen, outsmarted car salesmen for our first car, a Buick, and then took on Mr. Cook, the contractor, when it came to remodeling our home. I watched her out-negotiate him as if she had a business degree. I learned it all at her knee."

Virginia frowned. "There's a downside to all that. On vacations, I can't help negotiating—it's in my blood—and I don't like myself when I do it. I always have to push for a better deal!"

I tossed an idea to my friend: "Hey, maybe Jesus haggled market prices. After all, he was a Middle Easterner!"

"Oh, yeah! 'Is that your best price for these sandals?'" We chuckled.

"But you're absolutely right, Virginia. How to settle on a fair price? I don't want to be a shyster, but I don't want to be a sucker either."

Virginia was a single parent at forty with two children to raise. She wondered whether, as we get older, we worry less about money.

"Virginia, for me, getting older and wiser about money is like evolving. Sure, I get past a particular sticky money issue and feel good about it. But soon, another problem hits me in the face, and I'm reminded that I still have more inner work. I'm growing and becoming looser; issues that used to disturb me deeply, don't get to me as much now, thank God," I said.

"I just feel so much freer now, free enough to give it away. I find that the more I give money away, the more it comes back," Virginia said. "My cleaning woman is another example. I'm providing her with a job; I'm sharing my paycheck to do so. I've even had her come more often than necessary. If I can brag a bit, my tax consultant commented, 'You give money away as if you had more.' Oh, did that feel good. It's true. If I inherited a lot of money, my lifestyle wouldn't change much. Maybe I'd remodel the house, have a maid every day."

Virginia has adopted the habit of paying handsomely for services. "When it comes to tipping a waiter, I go the extra mile with a lavish, 25 percent gift."

"Now, what about your divorce? What's different about how you handle money now compared to the way you handled it when you were married?"

Virginia looked pensive. "During that twenty-five year marriage, I lived in a survival mode. Joe brought in enough, but he spent enormous amounts on himself thinking I didn't know. Sometimes, we had only two dollars in our account. Talk about betrayal!"

The financial nightmares had escalated. Joe's drinking had too. Father O'Malley, Virginia's parish priest, was brutally honest. For years he listened to her stories of the man who could not handle responsibility or family life. Eventually, he said, "Do you like playing the martyr? Get rid of him!"

> ***Our highest use of money instills peace in our soul.***
>
> ***—Francesca D.***

"Freedom!" she said. She flung her hands in the air. Her mother's many gold bracelets jingled on her wrists. "Sure I'm different. I buy things. I live for today," as her red convertible and frequent trips to the old country aptly attested.

"The miracle for me is that after the divorce, I worry less and less about money." She reached into her purse and pulled out a small, dog-eared prayer book, saying, "I depend on God more and more." This gesture seemed unlike the Virginia I thought I knew. "Consider the lilies of the field, your heavenly Father knows them and provides for them." She snapped the book shut and sighed with satisfaction.

I walked her out to her car. I thanked her, then waved as she headed the flamboyant convertible out of my driveway. I realized that Virginia speaks for the feelings of many of us when she declares that money is the driving force that fuels womens' lives. It is, of course, a driving force. But for what? So we can buy a new house, a car, another outfit? I was reminded of my mother's blunt remark from her sick bed, as death lurked nearby. "Honey, why would I want to linger any longer? To meet another friend for lunch?" It was hard to hear then, but now I finally got it. All the experiences money could buy, including intimate meals, no longer mattered to her. Mama had experienced enough.

Outside the rain let up, leaving patches of sparkling sun on the yard, renewing my parched lawn. Virginia was completely renewed in her money attitudes since her close encounter with death. She reminded me of Mama's oft-quoted dictum, which we almost inscribed on her memorial card: "Live for Today; the Hell with Tomorrow."

Mona: *A World of Possibility*

"I'm here. Come on up!" Mona Greenberg's voice bounced down mahogany stairs and into the entrance hall where I stood. Mona was the opposite of Virginia in many ways, and I wondered what I would learn from her. I made the steep climb to her graphic design studio, feeling out of breath.

"Make yourself comfortable," said Mona, a soft-spoken woman, shapely and attractive, with her hair pulled back in a silky ponytail. Her pale eyes lit up as I handed her a clay pot of velvety purple violets. "They're beautiful," she said. She leaned in to smell them, not knowing that violets don't share their smells. "Let me put them in the window."

I surveyed the simplicity of her space. Mona's design studio had a new computer and not much else. Dramatically spare! Monks would feel right at home. A plain stuffed chair sat beside a tidy small desk. On it stood a framed picture of a praying child. Contrasting images of Virginia's and Michelle's designer wardrobes and expensive jewelry flooded my mind.

We settled down on a black futon. For whatever reason, our awkwardness was palatable. Mona cleared her throat nervously. "Wow," she exclaimed and covered her mouth with her hand. "I had no idea talking about my financial situation after divorce would be so, well, nerve-racking."

"When Hershel and I separated," she began, "I was the one who wanted to move out. As usual, we fought, and this time it was about my condo choice. I'd located one in a modest neighborhood at a great price. Hershel, on the other hand, insisted that I locate in an upscale neighborhood. We were at it again, fighting over money."

I could hardly contain my surprise. Here reads a strange divorce text. A wife resisting a husband's wish to give his exiting wife an extravagant settlement? I said nothing.

Mona looked at me earnestly: "I've always resented Hershel's values. I couldn't feel comfortable in an expensive condo. He always wanted to give me what I didn't want. Hershel should pay about half of what he wanted to. That's my style."

Women are locked into old money patterns for reasons all their own, patterns that they believe protect them from chaos and whim.
—Martina L.

Did she have a fix on the ethics of prices? I felt a growing restlessness, and it was difficult for me to detach from Mona's words. There were too many undertones here. I couldn't comment. "Should" is such a charged word, and Mona's rigid attitude about money was uncommonly close. In all my interviews I worked hard not to judge any woman's conflicts regarding money. Here was one of my hardest interviews to apply the working model to. Maybe some of Mona's rigidity was actually my own.

Mona smoothed her skirt over her knees. In her gauzy, batik-dyed lavender dress that emphasized her youthful appearance, she appeared to be a sophisticated hippie, but without the innocent joie de vivre, and carefreeness of the flower children. Dimples played on her face, but I saw no gaiety there. For Mona, talking about money was talking about a black-and-white subject with no middle ground. Her mouth pulled tight, punctuating it all.

"During the marriage, Hershel and I couldn't talk about money. For years, we danced around it as if it were a fire burning in our living room. I paid the bills, but I resented that he didn't notice or care what each bill totaled or how much we owed. If he occasionally leaned over my shoulder to see my figures, I resented that too, as if he didn't trust my accounting.

"I resented his spending. I knew what was valuable, how much money should be spent, and on what," she explained. I was saddened by the edge in her voice. Her story seemed to center on her former spouse's faults.

"Hershel would send money flying out of our lives. Stereos, cars, furniture! It made me so mad. I could hardly keep my mouth shut."

This union was evidently a classic case of spender versus saver. One hoards while the other disburses money casually. Most counselors suggest that money is not the real root of this conflict, but it is an obvious symbol of the deep woundedness in each partner. Plainly, love had been on hold between Mona and her ex-spouse.

"Know what my biggest fear is? It sounds funny, but I'm scared that I might become a bag lady." My heart lurched hearing this, and I reached out instinctively to touch her hand. We didn't say anything. I found myself slipping back to the time when Ben, my counselor, had said, "No accountant, or financial advisor, or even God himself could convince you that spending money will not deplete your resources if you feed yourself this toxic insecurity."

I picked up Mona's hand and gently asked, "The thought of becoming a bag lady, what's behind that feeling?"

"I'm not sure. I can't help it." She took her hand away, to tightly enjoin the other. She returned to the relative safety of discussing her husband's problems.

"I'm not sure that it has anything to do with Hershel, but when he bought another set of speakers, I remember lashing out: 'Why another set? We already have four!'" Her eyes blinked furiously, to avoid tears. Was her husband as compulsive about spending as she apparently was about saving?

> ***No woman need play victim to childhood poverty.***
>
> ***—Patty L.***

"Mona, let's forget Hershel for a moment. What has it been like for you as a divorcée?"

Suddenly Mona smiled, revealing that being single again *had* loosened her up a bit. "I buy more than I ever did, just for pleasure," she said softly.

"But soon I'll have all I need."

Despite my inner *Oh, no!* I waited, sensing that she was beginning to trust me. "Tell me about your parents," I urged. She bit her lip and her eyes saddened.

"Money was like a rubber band, tight and totally controlled by my father. He didn't believe in credit, so necessities were put on hold until cash arrived. He paid cash for a house. For a car," she said softly. "We did without a lot."

Bull's-eye! Packed away in a memory disk were fears that pushed Mona to behave like a squirrel collecting nuts for the winter.

"Dad gambled. Mom fought him. Once she threw a cup of coffee across the room at him." Bull's-eye again. Mona's silence was eloquent as she ran her fingers along the table's edge, tracing the wood back and forth. "No doubt, my sense of self-worth has been wrapped around this money stuff for years."

Mona brightened: "But I have grown aware that *people are willing to pay for what I do.*"

"Imagine that!" I kidded her.

She drew both hands together under her chin, as if about to pray. "It's a new pleasure," she said. "For the first time, and totally unlike my mother, I'm gaining financial confidence. I balance my checkbook to the penny."

The phone rang, and Mona excused herself. I looked at her strict, controlled environment and at the one small red pillow, a striking first note of whimsy too long denied.

Joan: ***A Love Affair with Money***

Unlike Mona, Joan, a vivacious blonde whose real estate savvy has put her on top, is one of a rare breed who openly admits that she loves money! She isn't afraid to let you know it, either. Joan fascinated me because she seemed to have grasped a basic spiritual truth about giving and receiving. She has long practiced tithing to charities of her choice, and she luxuriates in a green river of wealth overflowing onto her shores. Divorced several years ago, Joan was left to her own devices to make her way in the world.

> ***Only fools judge anyone else's money habits.***
> ***—Nara L.***

"If I'm blessed, I've got to give it back." After a bitter divorce, Joan prospered like never before. Was tithing her only secret? "I love to talk money," she volunteered when I first contacted her.

We met at her posh office on a brick street in Winter Park, where gardenias grow by the door and clients are greeted with coffee on a silver tea service. Joan is classic looking and the picture of the power woman.

"Sit down, sit down," she said, gesturing toward a Queen Anne chair in front of her desk. She sat across from me, hands crossed loosely, a simple topaz ring on one finger. While we chatted, she fingered a Baccarat crystal vase cradling a yellow rose on her desk. We talked a bit about the real estate market, and she showed me, with great relish, photos of several houses, some of them practically mansions, that she is selling.

She smiled a knowing smile, and started, "I think I've always had a strong work ethic. But it's more than that. My mother and I worked together in our house when I was about sixteen. When my girlfriends drove by in their own cars, they enticed me, 'Come on, Joan, let's go to the movies.' I'd tell them I had to work!"

"I've earned everything that I own," she said proudly. And she owns many lovely things, including a rambling, beautiful lakefront home. Suddenly, she surprised me with an unusual belief: "I think that my work is one of the reasons I don't play the lottery."

I frowned. "I'm not sure what you mean."

"Well, don't you think lottery winnings should go to someone who can't earn money? Someone without income? I don't need money from the state, and if I took it, it would feel as if I were on welfare," she said.

That sort of thinking, understanding that money is spiritual energy, underlies all of Joan's financial decisions. Before she writes out checks for monthly bills, she writes checks to her charities. Ten percent, not a dime more or less. And because her monthly income varies, the amount of the donations do too; they are always 10 percent.

"Actually, it [writing checks] is one of my favorite things to do," she said beaming.

This woman defies the myth that divorced women can't handle money, that their creative role in life is to find another husband or rush off to more luncheons. She dropped a large chunk of money into what became a successful real estate brokerage; phones rang nonstop and secretaries knocked at her door constantly. She laughed at the chaos as something that fueled her excitement.

"In real estate, patience is a priority. Money doesn't come in regularly. You have to plan far down the road. Selling real estate means not holding your breath before the check is in your hand." Hmm, I think to myself, good advice for all women.

"So how would you relate that to other recently divorced women?" I asked.

"I'd tell them first of all not to panic! Sit at a desk and list your assets. Most likely, you'll discover a well of prosperity." She waved a pen to make her point.

Joan made her own list at a time when she found her bank account dwindling to a couple hundred dollars. She had just acquired a home that had escalated her mortgage payments from five hundred to twenty-four hundred dollars monthly. She thought the increased payments wouldn't be a problem as she anticipated a contract on another deal to quickly sweeten her money supply. The deal fell through. The bank denied her more money.

"What did you do?"

"First, I told myself to forget discouragement. I'd survive. Then I went back to my original mortgage company, where I had an open-end mortgage. I explained that I wanted another loan. The executive gave me some lame excuse about lowering the value of the house."

Joan was not the kind of person you say no to, I thought.

"I found a woman to help me," she said, shaking her head. "Sometimes women have to seek other women who really understand. This gal asked me to list every single thing I owned. The woman surveyed my list, which included everything from art and jewelry to furniture and real estate, and said, 'I know that your credit is good. I think we can get you more money.' "Words from God! When we tabulated it all, I was stunned to find that I actually had over one million dollars in assets!"

Joan's secretary knocked again and stuck her head in the door, announcing that a client was waiting. "Be right there," Joan said, checking her watch.

"You seem happy, despite the divorce," I offered. "I'm glad for you."

"Money didn't create my happiness," she said. Her blue eyes danced. "Rather, the opposite is true. My happiness created the money. When I'm up, I attract people. They want to do business with me. It's that simple!"

Driving home, I thought about Joan's confidence and her willingness to go toe-to-toe with men in a man's world. So many women shoved into sudden independence are desperate to stabilize their new lives financially. They read the latest how-to books. Some try get-rich-quick workshops. They may repeat prosperity affirmations until they're blue in the face. For Joan, her tithing habit, launched when she barely had enough for herself, stood at the door of her prosperity.

I read somewhere that—rich or poor, single or married—we must make peace with money to avoid inner turmoil. Call it the zen of money, a consciousness that allows us to appreciate and divinely trust money.

Marilyn: *Money Mixed with Sex?*

The afternoon sun slanted low as I bumped up the road to Marilyn's Malibu beach house. Marilyn stood on the balcony, waving to me.

As I stepped out of the car, exhilaration filled me. The ocean was glorious! I scanned the endless green, the foaming, crashing waves, the grand Pacific. Its deafening roar deposited me at the feet of God.

Early the next morning, streaks of pink and purple slashed across the predawn horizon. Marilyn and I converged on the main deck, cupping mugs of steaming coffee. The mantra of the ocean waves mesmerized us. We slipped off our shoes and headed for the dunes. We hiked a mile amid crying gulls, the sun warming our skin. Where Marilyn lived, the beach was often deserted. I bent down to pick up a pink shell and a lavender one, slipping them into my pocket like I had in my childhood days at the Atlantic.

Back at the house, Marilyn grew solemn, ready to broach my subject of inquiry. "Money ain't it, is it? I don't know what 'it' is, but it ain't money!" Recovering from a painful divorce, Marilyn had not found her footing yet. She had fled a fourteen-year marriage, and her words and thoughts were tainted with sadness and resentment.

Financially, Marilyn was a winner. She owned a Spanish villa on a lake in north Georgia, a mountain home in Tennessee, this Pacific beach home, a cache of fabulous jewelry, elegant furniture, and a bulging bank account. Other new divorcées would see green at her fortune. But when I suggested this to her, Marilyn shook her head, her blond locks swinging. She took off her sunglasses and cleaned them, looking at me thoughtfully. Her green-flecked eyes were wide and sad.

Mustering her courage, Marilyn revealed the roots of her money pain, one unimaginable to most women. I sat tensely in my chair. Her voice was subdued. "An old man molested me when I was three. That trauma has had, in every way, the greatest influence on my disastrous male relationships. He was my first encounter with money. He gave me coins to allow him to do things to me. Consequently, I've always connected money with sexual abuse.

"For me," she continued, "this divorce meant the beginning of security, of safety, of control over my own life. You see, Adele, it may appear strange to you, probably strange to everyone, but I need to have control over the one who gets to use my body."

Marilyn picked up a leaf from the deck and as she talked, her face aflame, her manicured hands played with it nervously. She looked out at the Pacific, as if searching for more than an ocean. "It has taken a lot of therapy! But in some out-of-control way, even though it happened so long ago, I continue to associate money with the power to control my body. It ruined my marriage. I have this compulsive need to control both my body and my money!"

We sat quietly, the import of Marilyn's relevation heavy in my heart, almost too much to take in completely. I remembered something I'd read and recorded in my journal: *The secret of life is in the shadows and not in the open sun; to see anything at all, you must look deeply into the shadow of a living thing.* This childhood shadow had affected Marilyn's attitudes and actions all her life. God, I thought, how clear it is that no one can judge another. We don't know the heartaches that lie within someone else.

Marilyn continued. "I had seen myself as an independent, goal-oriented, hard-driving woman. Finding a therapist saved my life. Forty-five years had to pass before I faced this abuse thing. It was my deep, dark secret. Money made sex dirty."

Words were spilling out rapidly now, with unexpected force and anger. "You can understand how, for me, money was, and still is, God-awful confusing! I had to go back to school for a career of my own. No matter that my husband made piles of money. I felt he was in control of everything. I simply had to take charge."

Marilyn's shoulders slumped as she continued. "Thank God that I live comfortably and that my children will be educated. Thank God that I can travel and enjoy life fully. These are things I never knew as a child."

She spread her hands in a helpless gesture and related how she and her brothers and sisters had hungered for affection and emotional

Is there a possibility that I may have more than enough at every given moment?
—Emily C.

warmth. And even though a beauty, she had never felt attractive. When someone complimented her, her mother had squelched it with, "Don't tell her that!"

"I wasn't allowed to feel the power of attractiveness. And in fairness to my former husband," she continued, "I've reached a place where I begin to understand something about him. He was feeling his own father's displeasure that he didn't make enough money—that he couldn't, no matter how hard he tried—even though he raked it in. And that ruined *his* sex life. Feeling unsuccessful pulled him down. Everything stopped working. God, is there no end to how money can ruin a person's sex life?"

How curious that Marilyn chose a husband who, like her, would equate money and sex. They both acted out of fear, each wrangling for control, each feeling desperately inadequate, and each hoping that acquiring money would somehow make them whole.

Marilyn stood, slipped her hands in her pockets, and stared out to sea. She looked drained. We collected our coffee mugs and straightened our chairs. The wind knocked over a flowering plant, and she bent to stand it up.

. . . . .

You know, God, this was hard for me. The stories of these broken lives bring up memories of my own dark days—that cruel separation, being ejected, the dull uncertainty, and being so alone. How incredible that each of us managed through such difficult times! And here we are! Who could account for our coming alive again? It had to be You. Besides, Who else would be so welcoming when we found our way?

Chapter Four

Gathering the Manna—Women in Their Prime

I had been spilling my money woes to several therapists, hoping to untangle the conflicts long rooted in me: disapproval of my father's singular pursuit of money, followed by a regimen of officially sanctioned poverty, then working nonstop pursuing the very thing for which I'd blamed Dad. I even confessed to the underhanded practice of accepting undeclared cash for extra work in a previous job. I was working toward an emotional acceptance of God's abundance in my life. But it took a sudden windfall to blow away the sticky traces of what was still ailing me.

Mom didn't linger after I came home. In November, on All Souls Day, she gave us her final good-bye, in the process bestowing on me a whole new set of money conflicts.

After taxes, estate debts, and lawyers' fees, her will left a lump sum of nearly half a million dollars to each of us. I'd never seen so many zeros on one check. They floated as if surreal, popping off the paper to mark the stepping-stones of a new path. The details of the day I accepted that inheritance check are etched in my memory.

The February sun was high, the air was cool, and the garden glistened from a recent bath. My brother's car pulled in the driveway, and I ran out to greet him. Roland waved his check up and down, a big smile plastered across his face. "Thank God, *that's* over," he declared, as if having left a courtroom battle. As executor of the will, he had taken my mother's death the hardest. There were dark rings under his eyes. He rolled his eyes heavenward. "Did you have a clue, Mama, what a mess you were laying on me?"

At my kitchen window, clutching my check, I stared at a long line of wildflowers dancing in the distance. Huge clouds rolled by in the spacious Florida sky. A flash of tenderness swept me away and tears misted my eyes. *Is that you, Mama, Dad, floating over me? Are you grinning as you see me now? In your fondest moments of generosity, Dad, did you ever dream that you would leave such a bundle of money? All those backaches, the sweat, the contracts that kept you up at night. And Mama's blue varicose veins earned from so many hours behind that grocery counter.* Roland had followed me to the kitchen. I could tell he had no stomach for hearing another word about the matter. Unlike me, he took his inheritance in stride and completely welcomed it.

"Go with me to the bank, please. Look, my hands are shaking!" I held them out. "I mean, how do I deposit a gold mine?" He rolled his eyes, but we set out in the car. The bank lobby was bustling; people were lined up to negotiate various transactions with the tellers. I joined the line. As I approached one teller, I spotted her stick pen; *Jesus is Lord!* was emblazoned on the side. So Jesus was in this bank? I searched her thin young face, tightly coiffed hair, and pursed lips as I listened to her cool voice checking my numbers. But this was my mother's bank. Hadn't it always been a friendly place?

I remembered Mama being treated like a queen at this branch. "Yes, Mrs. Azar, a glass of juice?" they had offered as she swept through the doors. How easily she chatted with everyone, tellers and managers, strangers and old acquaintances. They called her by name. "They like me here," she had whispered once as we sipped their orange juice. *Why not, Mama? Your bank account of over three hundred thousand dollars should have bought a smile or two.* But now, I was unceremoniously ignored. No smile, no reaction of any kind. Her cool disinterest angered me. *Are you a robot? Do you see half a million dollars deposited every day?* I lowered my head to hide the heat of my feelings. Clearly, I was already slipping. *Watch out; the money's changing you already!*

Seek ye first the kingdom of God and all these things shall be added. The familiar words bounced around my mind, feeling foreign. The inheritance bewildered me. When the grand check arrived, I had enough money to throw my attitude toward life, toward friends, and toward God into orbit. And that's exactly what happened. As the days passed, my confusion mounted. My life felt upside down, even haunted, as if I'd done something wrong. From my desk every morning, that unbelievable bank statement glared up at me. I wouldn't put it away. *You won't let me lose it, will you God, the inheritance I mean? Lots of people do, you know.* Prayer was my foundation. It had always been. It took months, but the new fortune eventually taught me to recognize God's outstretched hand.

"You mean that this windfall is causing you problems?" My close friend Mary stared at me. Then she stared at the bank statement disbelievingly. "You've got a problem with this? I wouldn't let that be known, dear friend!" Mary could be trusted, but I couldn't trust myself. Not only did I hide the fact that I was having problems accepting my inheritance, but I tried, as best I could, to hide the inheritance entirely. I brooded over foolish images of the wealthy, full of snobbery and spiritual emptiness. My thoughts were agitated: *Nobody feels comfortable around rich people. Most of them lead isolated lives. The Bible clearly states that a camel pushing his bulk through the slender eye of a needle will get stuck; so, too, will a rich man struggling to get into heaven.*

I tried to grasp a larger view. What exactly did inheritance *mean?* Normally, I'd take the question to my most-trusted therapist, but Ben wasn't available. How I missed him. I read stories of families accepting or not accepting provisions imposed by a will. Some were able to glide through the process, but often, there were those who experienced untold stumbling before the will was settled. I reverted to an old trick of gathering friends to probe different viewpoints. I invited several friends over for tea and talk hoping their input would be enlightening. After sweets and small talk, I threw out my big question. What is an inheritance? I asked. Silence and a few raised eyebrows followed for a moment, and then they warmed to the subject.

"It's a bonanza from a dead relative, what else?" said one person.

Another piped up, "You get the money and sometimes the property!" She rolled her eyes. "And that's when the trouble begins." Everyone laughed, yet it was a hollow sound. Families don't always behave well after a death.

Tina furrowed her brow. "My husband's inheritance certainly gave us an occasion to take pokes at each other." That opened everyone up. Stories bubbled around the room that reflected infighting and quarrels fueled by the wills. Boundless issues swirled around the subject, but I wondered if any of them had struggled with guilt over the money, like I did.

"Is it just about the money, then?" a lawyer friend asked. I always liked her spiritual take on things.

"Well, the way I see it," Tina answered, "an inheritance is a sensitive mix of grief and joy. You mourn for the beloved; you ride high on his prosperity!"

At the end of the afternoon, we all agreed that dealing with an inheritance is a risky adventure, an emotional roller-coaster ride. We discovered that God often appears to play favorites. Some folks inherited money early in life, some later, and some never at all, and the latter didn't seem fair. Tina, who had never inherited a dime, was honest: "I want someone's estate, too."

Everyone would like to jump on the inheritance ride. But for all our talk, I was the only one actually boarding that day, and the terror and the thrills were mine alone to experience. But the visit and conversation validated my feelings: yes, an inheritance *was* a big deal. And yes, those loops and spirals ahead could take anyone's breath away. I bid my friends good-bye and when I shut the door, I sighed loudly, *Oh God, stay close!*

Years later, married and finally able to rejoice in a shared bank account, I asked my husband what the word *inheritance* meant to him. I sat by our pool, watching him rest at the edge after swimming several laps, water dripping from his eyelashes. It seemed to me that he, a poet who dismissed discussions of money, granted me the finest definition so far.

He took his time, then said, "Inheritance is about planting. I think it's a kind of invitation to accept a new seed," he continued, "one pregnant with promise. Maybe I read it somewhere, but inheritance is not about something that you get, but about something you grow."

I seized a pen and stored his words. He splashed away, laughing like a kid. "See how your inheritance has grown me?"

Jim's imagery fit my desire to sanctify our good fortune. In my writing I sought to untangle the knots of various myths and biases handed down to me from a long line of Arab forebears. I was also drawn to update what I considered antiquated teachings by my church on the subject. Truly, the inheritance had been a seed freely sown. The heavens had nurtured me, and then Jim, as I grew from having such money. I felt God's presence that day. *Will you accept what I pass on to you, love it, work with it?* A sweetness filled me. I walked away from the pool feeling newly animated.

I had once confided my confusion over my fortune to a priest, and he had answered, "An inheritance has the makings of grace, extraordinary grace." Having ministered to the wealthy for years at an upscale Coral Gables parish, he knew greed and he knew grace. My challenge was to recognize the difference. I read numerous religious texts to bolster my confidence about being a wealthy woman. I found Buddha's words comforting: "Do not treat lightly the things that enter into a person's life, receive them for what they are and then try to make them fit tools for Enlightenment." I didn't precisely recognize what Buddha was getting at, but his message soothed my resistance to my inheritance, and enlightenment was definitely on the way.

The disbursement of my parents' household treasures was a decidedly less upbeat event than the cash distribution. From out of nowhere, pain and greed surfaced among us kids. One chosen night, we gathered to parcel out their things. Mama, the center of our family life, was gone, and without her we were suddenly a family at war: adrift, separated, mistrusting. The lifetime of familiar material goods stacked around us was transformed into ugly weapons that, emotionally and spiritually, wounded and divided us. It was almost too much to bear. Who could stand to let go of any one item? Each of us had a deep, cellular attachment to every precious memento. Before our eyes, the crocheted dining room tablecloth, the blue crystal vase, and the ceramic camels that had lived on the mantelpiece for so long took on supernatural meaning. We grabbed at them like the orphans we suddenly were. The words and tears that escaped us seared my heart for a long time to come; that night burns shamefully in my memory.

I was so muddled after that night that I couldn't think straight. Was I really fighting for *things?* Had sixteen years of convent detachment vanished overnight? A friend had advised me to turn over Mama's precious crocheted tablecloth to the sibling who'd cried over it. *It's the Christian thing to do!* Maybe so. And maybe that kind of gratuitous help from a friend standing outside the mess was simply too easy to spout. Mama had crocheted that lace cloth nightly as her tears had often spilled onto it. I confess I still want it.

Our family can barely mention that night. What *was* it all about? That may be the first question on my list when I meet God face to face.

During that disturbing period, reading led me to a divine voice. In her book, *Wasted,* Marya Hornbacher writes of her terrifying experience with bulimia and anorexia, speaking of the deep-seated questions these diseases raise. She writes that an eating disorder is "a response, albeit, a rather twisted one, to a culture, a family, a self. It is a bundle of deadly contradictions, a desire for power that strips you of all power, a wish to prove that you need nothing, that you have no human hungers." Had I become monetarily anorexic?

No one, including myself, could fully understand why I irrationally denied a normal hunger for money. I was aware of an old voice in the wings: *Give it away! It's the holy thing to do!* Give it away? The way my friend advised me to give up the beloved tablecloth? Is possession such an evil thing? I kept hearing the same "Christian" message. This time, I prayed not to fall for it.

I thought a lot about St. Francis during those days. He left his father's wealth to roam the countryside penniless, depending on others for his survival. And the Church elevated him and countless others, men and women who'd abandoned material goods to follow God. Yet, for whatever reason, something in me wouldn't go there. I'm glad I followed the suggestion of one even-minded friend; she put her hands on my shoulders, looked deeply into my eyes, and with a heartening smile said, "Honey, the inheritance has made you crazy. Why not relax and enjoy it? Can't you accept a gift coming directly from You Know Who?"

Generative Generosity

THERE WAS NOTHING TO DO BUT FORGE AHEAD AND CREATE A NEW identity for myself. My journal went everywhere with me. Dad's familiar *Nuschur Allah* was scrawled up and down the margins. So was Father Caulfield's admonition, "Take what God offers you." Slowly but steadily, I made peace with my inheritance.

My first leap of faith was to relinquish my career, though that felt like letting go of a life raft. I'd be adrift without a job! Not showing up as part of the labor force was like not showing up for dinner. Or not showing up for myself. A friend rocked me with her comment, "Much as you might not like to think so, Adele, you no longer *do* belong to the working class. Face it!"

And so I endured the awkward transition period, to being "independently wealthy," including bearing the inevitable discomfort when a stranger asked, "What do you *do,* Adele?" That question irritated me. Why do I have to *do* something? I thought of my days in the convent. No one ever asked what I did then. My habit said it all. The larger question might be why do we judge one another by what we do? Having money was exposing another cultural illness: job labeling, a cruel and unfair burden, a total invasion and a ridiculous notion that we could ever know anything real about another human being from their job description. Does suddenly not being on a payroll make you worthless? I resolved never to ask that question of anyone again. And I never have.

But that was only one lesson. How often and how much should I donate? I began some serious check writing. In fact, the early days of my wealth saw me tossing checks to just about any person or nonprofit who asked for a contribution. It seemed the right thing to do. After watching a prolonged round of this behavior, a mentor finally put it to me: "Wait a minute. Don't be so hasty. Take your time. You don't *have* to give it all away."

As I got nearer to feeling the truth of that advice, my supportive stockbroker, Bob, who was Jewish, introduced me to a peacemaking group that would change my life. The Foundation for Mideast Peace sought to reconcile Arabs and Jews. Here was a cause that went straight to my Arab heart—making peace with our ancient cousins seemed like a sacred duty. I plunged into the work, a cooperative undertaking that reminded me of the best aspects of the convent. I met many passionate Jewish and Arab people who wished to explode the old myths about the two worlds. Once engaged, my money woes took a backseat, and along the way, I got straight on what money I wanted to give to good causes.

One Irish fireball and nun friend, Sister Toby, a gracious recipient of much of my generosity, described the beneficence that I enjoyed as "generative generosity." I soared on her words. "Hey," she said, "it's like saying to someone: 'Here, take this money! Go and help yourself!' But really you're giving to yourself because long after your gift is forgotten, even by you, your soul is still unconsciously reaping the rewards." How right she was. Once, when I responded to a call for help from a Palestinian-born student, I thought of Dad and his hard-earned payback that I now held. Both of us, Dad and me, helped put that young student through Ohio State University, and it thrilled me when he graduated with honors.

But there is a flip side to generative giving. Sometimes I was confused when I didn't get the kind of thanks I felt I deserved. I'd harbor sour feelings toward the beneficiary and blame myself for my feelings. But I was not the first to feel this way. Jesus Himself, it is written, miffed after curing the ten lepers, took them to task for not saying thanks.

We give praise by a quiet blessing on the check, or cash, or plastic that we hand over to another. Our awareness of this act as a spiritual exchange heightens the meaning and purpose of our monetary engagements.
—Jenny R.

Help came from May Sarton's *Journal of a Solitude*, where she quoted the writer, Melanie Klein: "Even the fact that generosity is often insufficiently appreciated does not necessarily undermine the ability to give. By contrast, with people in whom this feeling of inner wealth and strength is not sufficiently established, bouts of generosity are often followed by an exaggerated need for appreciation and gratitude, and consequently by persecution anxieties of having been impoverished and robbed." Mercifully, my less-than-noble feelings rarely stopped my donations.

Not long after my mother's death, I took to visiting her condo for comfort. Under a bright moon and bowlful of stars, I felt close to her there. I thought back to the time, after Dad's death, that she soared like a bird let out of a cage. Memories flooded back, and I wrote to my mother. I've read over this letter many, many times.

Dear Mama,

Gosh, how you managed to soak up all that legal tender. And so casually. You instinctively adopted a graceful money style. I was in open-mouthed awe.

Surely Dad would have dropped dead at the price tags of your purchases. You replaced years-old furniture with an art deco mahogany bedroom set. You turned the kitchen inside out and made it beautiful, refurbished countertops, and added an eat-in center. You spent thousands. You were having a ball, while curiously, I found myself taking Dad's role, sitting back, asking, like Judas: "Couldn't this money have been given to the poor?" You went all the way, got that top-of-the-line four-door gray Cadillac complete with every bell and whistle. No one could tether you again. "People look up to me, honey," you told me. "They think I'm somebody." You were somebody all right, somebody fresh, a new woman on the block.

You did toss some morsels of that good fortune where it was needed. Your sewing partner, Renee, later told me about your Tupperware parties for cash-strapped friends. You'd pledge and buy more than anyone needed simply to help them out. Some of that Tupperware is stacked today in my own kitchen cabinets. Then there was three thousand dollars worth of Festive china you donated to the Syrian American Club. How they cheered the new dinnerware. And, of course, I'll never forget the day the doorbell rang, and a weepy Amica stood there. You knew why she was there, but you let her say it anyway. Her grocery had burned down. "The bank refuses to finance us!" she cried. I witnessed you, ever the kindly banker, walk to your desk and write a thirty thousand dollar check without blinking. A sacred moment. "Amica, write a promissory note with the going interest, and start paying it back when you can," you instructed her. Mama, no doubt about it, you're my greatest money mentor.

And then there was Tony's Bakery. Today, your picture hangs like a relic behind the counter, and Tony, when asked, sanctifies you: "She's the angel that loaned me the money for this start-up business."

Still, I confess at times I found your high-flying ways frightening.

"Mama, you're not the only monied woman in your crowd," I objected. "Others can foot the tab sometimes. Why not let them?"

You laughed me down: "If I go overboard, honey, so what? It's the first time in my life that I can throw money at friends. I come and go, and I don't take orders anymore. I'm free of a grocery counter. What did I know then of clothes, perfume, and jewelry? They were alien luxuries." Yes, Mama, your worry lines softened. The facials and manicures and coiffed hair, all from dollars well spent, had birthed a new, radiant woman.

Remember that gambling ship that cruised from Cape Canaveral, and you let the one-armed bandits claim two thousand dollars of yours? I felt sick when you told me. You did too. But I've had new insights on that loss. Pouring those coins into a slot machine may have helped you stand tall. You joined Dad's leap into risk taking, the very thing you blamed him for, while abandoning your role in scheming, scratching, and saving every penny. You lost that money freely, but not your dignity. I love your oft-quoted quip during our last holiday together, when you took us to Greece and spent thousands: "Live for today, honey. The hell with tomorrow!"

I closed my journal. I wished I'd written that letter while Mama's eyes were open.

I had much to learn in those turbulent post-inheritance years. The biblical word "steward" kept popping up, an expression heard in Sunday sermons. Good stewardship seemed to mean using God's gifts appropriately. But good stewardship, I figured out, must also mean that I mattered too, that I shouldn't sell myself short. I must be a good steward of myself. It was wrenching, but I decided to avoid the sales racks and tables. My new contract with myself and God read like this: *I will be a good steward even in the seductive world of high fashion. I pray not to sell myself short even as I pray not to go overboard. But You will be with me. Give me eyes to know when enough is enough.*

Shopping became a discipline. I created a ritual, pulling God into the store with me. In a dressing room, for example, with a garment on, I'd check myself in the mirror. *What do you think? Yes or no?* No matter what I thought or bought, no matter which department I shopped—dresses, cars, or refrigerators—I felt God beside me. No purchase was excluded from prayer. When I left a store, I soared, my high heels in perfect rhythm with the fashion world, but more important, in rhythm with my new-found stewardship.

Actually, that ritual wasn't entirely new. Bringing God into the buying process recalls a bit of old Church ritual, a medieval practice when the village priest blessed a new roof or the birth of a horse or cow. The idea was to recognize that things merely pass through us, they do not belong to us. One of my Italian classmates in grade school did it her way: "If I get a new dress or blouse, I have to wear it to Mass first, like I'm giving it back to God." Such creative rituals are open to everyone of us. There are immeasurable connections to God waiting to be discovered in the sacrament of money.

I was tested and retested in my new life as a woman of means. But nothing jarred me as much as a shiny, new, four-door Cadillac Seville. Prior to that, I could hide behind private shopping sprees, anonymous donations to the peace foundation, or hidden accounts. Now, taking on a Cadillac, really against my better judgment, raised the curtain and shone a spotlight onto my circumstances for all to see. I'd asked my brother, Roland, to choose a car for me from an auto auction. I never dreamed he would select a Cadillac, of all cars!

"Can't you enjoy this car like Mama enjoyed hers?" He shook his head sadly. Dropping off that luxury car at my home was like setting up a loudspeaker, broadcasting to the world that I was in the money. I blew up at Roland, at the car, and at my foolishness for not going with him in the first place. But I kept thinking, *Wake up. Your conflict isn't about this car.* I noticed a little yellow hibiscus I had planted by my door, clearly part of God's plan. Could God's will be that I own this beautiful car? Am I being silly? Most people think of God's will in terms of accepting the bad things that happen to good people. I grasped an old truth in a new way: God's will includes accepting everything, even the bounty.

Eventually, I came to accept what a priest friend had written about my inheritance: *Whether you take a vow of poverty or take ownership of a Cadillac, it's all about accepting the gifts God puts before you. All is gift.* So I drove that car. I drove it up and down lonely roads at first so no one could see me. But, secretly, I began to love the outrageous vehicle. Yet, while still working in the church, I refused to park in the parish parking lot. I hid it among the towering oaks across the street and walked the distance to the volunteer office. The same held for meeting friends for lunch; I stationed the car a decent distance away and walked the extra blocks. At the supermarket, when a bag boy asked, "Where's your car, ma'am?" I'd mutter under my breath, "That one over there." The truth was that my lips refused to shape the word Cadillac.

How jealous I felt when a young woman drove out of a grocery parking lot one day in her white Mercedes convertible, with the top down. Talk about liberty! She smiled at me, and my gaze followed her as I got behind the wheel of my car. Then a familiar face addressed me from my rearview mirror: *Adele, could it conceivably matter to God what brand car you drive—Toyota, Buick, or Fiat? You have a Cadillac. Drive the damn car and be happy!* I started the car and enjoyed the smoothest ride imaginable. With God's ever-present grace, I was winning this war.

I took comfort in author Marianne Williamson's words in *A Woman's Worth*: "It is God's will that each of us, every woman, man and child, be happy, whole and successful. It is impossible to overestimate the psychic damage done by the delusions, pseudo religious and other notions that God is happier or we are somehow purer if we are suffering just a bit. The truth is not that God is happier or that we are better, but that the institutions that told us so are happier, because suffering keeps us in our place, where we are easier to control."

I clutched my old religion longer than I wanted to, all through the struggle with my inheritance, believing that I was much closer to God when nailed to a cross, any cross. To believe that happiness is our right is not easy for me, and at times, I simply take it on faith.

Anna Dickinson, whose story appears in Chapter Six, dreamed of diamond earrings, and discovered that she wasn't meant to wear them. She lost one, found it again, had the clips tightened, then stopped wearing them because they now hurt too much. "What my money buys me sometimes only frames a letdown," she said beautifully. That's what happened to one of my biggest dreams.

My True Language

CURIOUSLY IT WAS MY NEW FRIEND, RABBI ZALMAN SCHACHTER-Shalomi who, in the course of an ecumenical workshop, urged me to connect with my Arabic roots. Not long after, I enrolled in an accelerated, nine-week course of total immersion in Arabic at Middlebury College in Vermont, a small Ivy-league college that was widely known for its summer language programs. My ambitious fascination had all the makings of an academic disaster: a strange alphabet, unique calligraphy, and guttural phonics, not to mention the fact that I was the oldest student enrolled. But I figured I could do it. As a child, hadn't I translated from English into colloquial Arabic for my grandmother? So I signed a contract that forbade speaking English for nine long weeks. And to prove my resolve, I forked over several thousand dollars to do so.

Initially, I loved the program. *So I am the oldest student, so what?* I'd always cherished younger friends, and friendships here should prove no different. After registration, I sat under a large maple tree that looked over the commons. I visualized my return home, how I'd dazzle everyone, Arab and Jewish friends alike and my siblings! I smiled to myself.

But once in class, the language proved elusive. I couldn't keep up. I stuttered; my mind froze. I stopped raising my hand and avoided my teacher's glances. For the first time in all the classrooms that I had sat in, I faced a full-blown academic disaster. I could only stare out of the classroom window, seeking solace in the magnificent maples and sycamores and the luscious blue skies. I began to panic. I should be getting this stuff, but I wasn't! It was a nightmare of the highest magnitude, especially with all that money riding on it.

Classrooms had been my home. I was comfortable with the student-teacher dynamic, especially in my role as teacher. Now, with the absence of language, I spiraled horribly into a vortex of lost identity, clinging to the dwindling reassurances that unlike the others, I had, at least, a native sense of Arabic. But rather than study after class—studying only evoked a deeper feeling of rage—all I could do was head for the cafeteria and fill my confused self with candy from the vending machine. I couldn't go home. I couldn't go on. In late afternoons, I biked up and down the nearby country roads, tears flowing, wind whipping my hair. One day, I parked under a giant tree and looked up, *What did I ever do to You that You should treat me this way?* I let all the pain flow into my journal. Despite the cool breezes, the grassy knolls stretching before me, the farms that lay in the valley below, I was in no mood to thank anyone. *Where the hell are You, damn it? You've slammed me down. I'm nobody anymore!*

By the next Monday morning, Arabic sounds repulsed me. I had to get away or I'd end up in a loony bin. Back on my bicycle, I tore down the grassy hill, across the cobbled Middlebury streets, and found the small town bridge nearby. I leaned against the railing, breathless, unable to go forward or back. In that moment, the joyride of all that money I'd inherited, and its accompanying feeling of power, crashed. Nothing seemed important now. I stared down at the river pounding the rocks. *Money can never make wrong things right! I'm never going back to that classroom.* I turned toward town, a block away, and found a snug corner restaurant. The waitress spoke kindly to me. Something snapped. *English! My language.* She spoke words that I understood for the first time in weeks. I answered without thinking, savoring the sweet words with my tongue. *To speak and be understood!* I kept looking at her with relief. I ordered several cups of coffee just to keep our conversation going.

The next morning, I was a woman with purpose. I jumped on my bike and sped to the college library. I parked, gathered my notebooks, and pushed the giant wooden doors open to a breathtaking supermarket of unlimited reading delights, all in English. That summer I fell in love with and simply couldn't fill up enough with my *true* native language. Journals by May Sarton, novels by Steinbeck, and memoirs by southern women writers. All in the language that my parents, in their eagerness to Americanize their kids, had mandated to replace old-world Arabic in our home. I rejoiced in the truth that I thought and prayed in English, the language God uses in my mind when calling me to Him.

Returning to Orlando, however, I felt lingering shame, and for weeks, I couldn't face friends who had seen me off to learn Arabic. Instead I sat, ate, and read alone, a happy hermit hidden in a cave made of the English language. The practice of silence, learned during days of not speaking at all, had also come home with me. It felt very natural and still does. Most of my talking was internal.

The loss of face was tough, but it cut through my false concept of "success." I had paid, and lost, a bundle of money to find something far more spiritually significant than a new language. I've learned to look at loss in this way. That lesson has proved more valuable than the gift of reawakened English; that out of every loss something new is discovered, something more precious, something perhaps even destined. Would it be too much to suggest that the greater the loss, the richer the discovery?

Recently, I opened Belden Lane's treatise, *The Solace of Fierce Landscapes,* concerning mountaintop spirituality. "When everything is irretrievably lost, life does not end, but is at a point of new beginnings. 'Except a grain of wheat falls into the ground and dies, it remains alone; but if it dies, it bears much fruit' (John 12:24). When language utterly fails, the dumb but patient tongue will someday speak again, with golden, winged words, carved in silence."

The inheritance had done its work after all.

Women in Their Prime

I WASN'T A YOUNG WOMAN WHEN I RECEIVED MY INHERITANCE. My hair wanted to be gray, a few wrinkles wanted to divulge themselves, and no one had ever thought to "card" me. But at this age, my maturity cast a different light on things. I was becoming truly aware of the gifts that surrounded me. Whereas before, trees were trees and grass was grass, now I would gaze long at an oak, imagine what it would be like to be one of its branches, touch them, and lose myself in the varied colors of its leaves. When I beheld a flock of birds flying over a stand of laurels or heard the sweetness of children playing in a distant sandbox, my body stilled. Did I ever really see these things before? Early walks in the garden grabbed my heart as dew sparkled on leaves and petals. Everything is part of God's cosmic dance. Clearly I was in a new place, and I'm convinced that this place of aging is a place of awakening. There are unique compensations for gray hair and wrinkles. As we enter middle age, we enter our prime. And it is a time, usually free of demanding young children, that we have the opportunity to be our greatest selves. "Ah," one interviewee added to my observation, "in that, my dear, lies precisely the beauty of aging."

Enormous possibilities unfold in middle and later years, a fact I am just fully grasping. A dear Jewish friend, a Holocaust survivor, celebrated her eightieth birthday with a toast to life: "I had a miserable youth, but by God, I'm having a happy old age!"

My husband recently celebrated entering his sixth decade. It was a good birthday; the festivities clearly marked Jim coming into his own. To solemnize the event, we climbed a small, rugged mountain in Provence on a clear spring day. Up we crawled, several thousand feet. I stopped, winded, and waited while he struggled ahead to the top on his own. Once there, he stood tall, arms outstretched like a giant Christ.

He exploded with laughter that echoed throughout the valley. At dinner that night, energized, Jim grasped a bottle of Cambrio and toasted himself, then everyone else advancing in age. "Aging is like this bottle of wine marked by time," he beamed. "It only mellows."

Psychologist Jean Houston's essay in Rabbi Zalman Schachter-Shalomi's best-selling book *From Age-ing to Sage-ing* says: "No longer needing to compete and be acceptable, likable, and all those other things considered respectable in society, people are finally uncaged in their elder years, free to release energies and capacities that the culture restrained in them when they were younger."

Aging awakens many latent virtues. Good financial habits developed in our youth, such as detachment and generosity, have room to flourish. Beloved American writer May Sarton knew this well. In her final journal, *Endgame,* she records a sobering account of her seventy-ninth year, replete with bodily discomforts, a creeping weakness, and a rising anger at her diminished strength. Yet she maintained an old habit that shed bright light on her character: "I manage to pay bills, and I love giving money away. So when I get up to the study with the idea that I am going to write a letter, it very often ends simply in my sending a check to one of the many things I love supporting and want to support."

Like other women, Sarton recognized her need to heal a spiritually flagging world before she left it. Her checks flew out the door on the wings of angels. She, like my mother, believed that we ought to make money flow. These women knew that money is sacramental, a nourishing river of energy. Some older women also give away their possessions. Eager to simplify and shift the "stuff" out of their house, many bid good-bye to material memories without raising an eyebrow. And if they can't give the stuff to family and friends, they pass it on to Goodwill.

One older friend, whom I shall call Betty, fell prey to her attachments, and they are strangling her. She sucked up a lifetime of "things" off sale tables—jewelry, cosmetics, toasters, and trinkets—then lugged her purchases home to be displayed on crowded shelves. Betty's home is so packed, so tightly stuffed that one gets a choking sensation when visiting her. There is barely room to walk.

There's a bit of Betty in all of us. Author Kathleen Norris speaks to this issue in her spiritual classic, *The Cloister Walk.* "What is enough? Are there enough trees here? As always, it seems that the more I can distinguish between my true needs and my wants, the more I am shocked by how little is enough."

The following women have spent money on their grandchildren, on beautiful art for their homes, and on a good pair of shoes. Some have collected unemployment, lived on welfare, and battled the squeeze of limited income. Whether these women have a lot of money or only a little, they are all savvy about its worth in their lives.

Ami: *The Cash-Only Lady*

If there's someone I wish to emulate when I reach my eighth decade, it's Ami Cohen, who lives as well as a Rockefeller. Not that she has millions, quite the contrary. But what this twice-widowed lady possesses is a magnificent sense of style and exquisite money management skills, handling her two pension funds on a par with the world's best financial planners.

Her small apartment resembles a two-page spread in *Home and Garden*—tasteful artifacts in all the right places, framed paintings, large green palms setting off Florida bay windows, and crisp white and black leather furniture placed invitingly. Surrounded by such striking beauty, Ami loves to tell how she lives on a modest retirement income. She was a decades-long friend and neighbor of my parents, whose next-door neighborliness blossomed into deep friendship. Dad the Arab and Ami the Jew managed to connect on vital Mideast matters—like how to bake flatbread, stuff grape leaves, or mix tabouli to perfection. Food talk, and of course money talk, proved an animated, endless exchange between the two.

This day, Ami sat on her porch, a steaming cup of spearmint tea beside her, and described her colorful past. Every silver hair was in place, and her freshly manicured nails glistened. "I've lived many diverse lives, good and terrible, better and in-between," she said, warming to the subject. "Each life taught me more about who I am. And how I want to spend my dollars. One cannot get this old and not leap into some kind of wisdom."

Ami recounted her escape to England from the Nazis, a story she had never mentioned to me before. Penniless, she had managed to sustain herself while sequestered in a tiny rented room, a lone boarder. "People used to send refugees Reply Postage Stamps, and I banked them. I must have been the joke of that little English town when I deposited the stamps. In a while, though, I had a few shillings and then a pound here and there. Finally, I was able to escape that little room." Ami's eyes narrowed, and I knew something important was coming. "But let me make it clear; it was never about money. Money has always served me instead of the other way around."

Money has always served me instead of the other way around. No other woman had said it so succinctly. In that simple statement, I realized how women can neutralize years of poverty. Trained early in her life by frugal parents, Ami lives by one rule: Save until you have enough to buy what you want. She seemed to read my thoughts.

"I'm proud to say I've always paid cash for everything. And if I see something I want, I save my money to get it. Even if it takes months. Or I do without. In this way I've consistently managed to live below my means." Ami manages to match stark discipline with a lavish lifestyle.

I glanced around the room. I told her, "No one would ever guess. Is there something you're not telling?" She described savings habits that were a carbon copy of my father's. "You must save," he admonished all of us, "no matter how little. If you make ten dollars a week, pretend you make eight. Put away two dollars and pretend they don't exist."

Ami's monetary style gave her confidence; she was a vital woman whose high standards never flagged. "I can assure you, I'll go without, rather than not go first class!" And first class is definitely how Ami carries herself in the world. When she first migrated to the U.S., she told me, her only brother opened his arms, his house, and a bank account for her use. She reluctantly piled her few belongings and her eight-year-old daughter into his second-story apartment. But as for accepting money from his bank account, she balked. "Absolutely not!" she said to him, despite having no idea how she would survive. After bouts of tears and depression, one blessed morning, she came up with a plan.

I keep to the speed limit, not because I am supposed to, but who wants to pay traffic tickets?
—Beth V.

"I opened the closet door to the few clothes my brother had generously put there. I laid them out, coordinated, mixed, and matched them until they worked together. I skipped eating and caught a bus to Chicago's largest department store. I took the elevator up to personnel. Hiding all my jitters, I put on a proud smile, extended my hand, and greeted the managers. They gave me a look over. My dear, they hired me on the spot! I had an office the next day with the letters on my door reading Bridal Consultant. I didn't know a damn thing about bridal gowns, weddings, or receptions. Pure determination got me that job! I did it for the money that would serve me. From then on, nothing stopped this refugee!"

Even with a regular paycheck, Ami refused to slip into consumerism. Self-imposed boundaries allowed only a few luxuries, such as a small glass of Beaujolais before dinner and always, fresh-cut flowers. "I have to have live flowers. Most weeks, I spent only five dollars on a fresh bouquet. And some clothes for my child!" But that was in her early days of prosperity.

"So, still no debt, Ami?"

"I never, ever, paid a carrying charge on anything. And I never will. I bought my first house in America when I was widowed; my brother's loan was the only one that I ever allowed myself. My first car was fifteen hundred dollars, and I found a way to scrape up the exact cash."

Ami's appearance, slim and chic, is like that of a much younger person. She told me about her single recent indulgence, a Visa card, which records every purchase she makes, right down to the smallest book of stamps. Why would a widow note every nickel, dime, and even penny she spends?

"Every dollar is a plane mile," she grinned. "I buy everything with Visa: gas, theater tickets, Blockbuster videos, postage stamps. If Visa forgets to record a purchase, I scream a little on their 800 number. In return for my bookkeeping, I get to go to London again this spring—totally free." I should have known.

I felt my father's spirit in that room. Surely he was smiling. No wonder Ami and Dad had stood together on so many issues. Both were savers, money-conscious, bargain hunters. It was their very life force.

What are Ami's plans? She told me she discovered an expensive retirement home that was "genteel, a deluxe way to retire." I was not surprised, when, a few years later, I got a note from Ami from her new "deluxe" address.

Carla: *On Being Poor*

Ami Cohen and Carla Amelio both experienced acute poverty in their youth, but that is the only common thread between how these two ladies have lived with—or without—money during their adult years.

Carla's social security pays her rent on a tiny plot of land in a mobile home park; she scrambles from one check to the next, barely stretching her pennies through the month. Her adult children help out with prescription drugs, trips to the grocery, and unexpected expenses.

But Carla's situation is not to be pitied. She burns with a passion for life; Carla, in her mobile home, is undeniably wealthy. She told me, right up front when she agreed to talk to me, "I won't let low income absorb my thoughts. I turn my mind to the riches around me: my gardenia bush, my square-foot vegetable garden of tomatoes, squash, and green and red peppers. I sing the arias of my beloved operas to my heart's content. I follow the stories of many heroes in my library books. I host my friends, and I prepare the finest Arabic cuisine my tiny kitchen is capable of. I don't have to prove to anyone else just how rich I really am."

Carla had agreed to meet me at a small restaurant near her trailer park. We settled in a booth and ordered soup and salad. Carla chuckled when I put down the menu and got right down to business. "How do you do it, Carla?"

"Mainly, I guess, I've got faith in myself," she said slowly. "I keep my rosary beads busy, always handy by my bedside and another in my apron pocket. And I've got so many friends!" I recall Carla and my mother laughing over their sewing, needles always flying, knitting a special closeness as they figured out difficult crochet patterns. Today, it's country quilts that contribute to Carla's spiritual wealth. Her lovely quilts could easily take top prizes.

Carla never stops; she's one of the busiest women I know. "Such creative achievements! Tell me about your quiet moments."

"Well, there aren't many," she smiled. "Sometimes after making a quilt I feel alive, reborn. I'll make myself a cup of tea and enjoy a quiet home. No television, no arias, no anything for an hour. I breathe away stresses right there at the kitchen table. And maybe if I've still the energy, I'll water all the African violets."

Carla sipped her tea. She is a woman who is attentive to life, who doesn't overlook little things, a seeker who turns to good books, good conversations, and even silence for meaning. Carla might welcome more cash, but it's absolutely unessential to her inner being. In a throwaway world, she makes the very act of unwrapping a tea bag holy. "Did I forget to thank you for this soothing tea?" she asks God. Undoubtedly, this is a rich woman.

Carla had always battled poverty. Her childhood resembled *Les Miserables*: no bread, no electricity, no hot baths. It was the early 1920s. Welfare didn't exist, even in the minds of politicians. Families either prospered or suffered on their own. "My father died when I was twelve. I cared for my brothers while Mother worked. I'd stand for hours in the city's charity lines for handouts: flour, milk, or cheese." Carla's eyes took in the butter she had spread on her roll.

Brilliant in school, stellar report cards, and teachers' praising notes followed her home. But she hated school. Even after being applauded for singing the *Star Spangled Banner* before Friday assembly, she burned in shame, thinking instead of the noise the loose, flapping soles of her shoes made as she approached the stage. Carla finally dropped out of school.

I asked whether she and her husband traveled, and she looked a bit wistful. "Nicholas and I can't journey out like our friends, but my library card is worth more than a travel visa. Library books come delivered to my mailbox! All free! Novels, cookbooks, travel logs. I forget my aches and pains because reading is my soul's medicine. And my trips are a lot quieter than those roaring planes and noisy airports!"

Carla took a spoonful of soup. "Meat! Now, that's another story! Mother would reach over at the table, dig into my piece, and pass it to my brothers as if that was normal. She never apologized. 'Meat is for boys only,' she'd say. Mother's preference for boys, an Arabic tradition, was everywhere." She leaned forward and smiled. "Now I enjoy meat at dinner, every dinner, no matter how small the portion."

What is it about money that makes us feel secure or insecure?

—Lorrie N.

I was reminded of a passage from Carol S. Person's book, *The Hero Within*: "We choose the world we live in, we see that each of our archetypes carries with it a way of seeing the world, and people who see themselves as victims get victimized." My friend obviously chose a world quite different from her mother's. One thing Carla was not, however, was a victim.

Carla and I split dessert, spooning the caramel flan slowly, stretching time, delighting in our cultural connections. She spoke of a friend, Louise, who had been diagnosed last year with cancer and had recently died. But in that last year, Louise had forged ahead on a planned Las

Vegas gambling trek. In one afternoon spent with a one-armed bandit, eighty thousand dollars had poured into seventy-year-old Louise's lap, tilting over her entire life. She came home a renewed woman. Like a princess, Louise bestowed scholarships on all her nieces and nephews, showered money where it was needed, and built a sunroom across the back of her house so she could "watch the sun disappear" every day that she had left.

"All it takes is one lottery ticket," said Carla, revealing a side of herself few ever see. The side that would love more money and buys a ticket every week. She looked at me evenly, saying, "Buying that one ticket keeps my fire stoked. A dollar for hope! It keeps me young." She and Nick rarely skip that dollar investment. Buying that ticket is like a practiced weekly prayer.

Carla loved the chance to talk about money. "I'm the richest woman on earth! I watch my children drive up to my trailer, bundles of groceries in their arms, smiling and laughing and healthy. There's nothing more I want."

I drove her home, where everything was neat and orderly, the corner rosebush beautifully tended. She got out, but she told me not to leave. She grabbed a pair of black scissors lying nearby and carefully snipped a magnificent red rose. "For you," she smiled.

Joyce: *Running with the Wolves*

If Carla is a pillar of stability and permanence, Joyce Andrews is a model of mobility and free spirit. They couldn't be more different, yet both of these mature women possess an enviable ability to live without much cash. One warm afternoon, sixty-four-year-old Joyce sat comfortably in my backyard gazebo, ready, she said, to handle my questions. Her answers were snappy as she described a free-wheeling lifestyle. She reminded me of a flighty young girl, and more than once, I wanted to lasso her in midflight and demand that she explain herself. Joyce's ramblings reminded me of Mahatma Gandhi, who once said that while he wanted to live in truth, what was true for him one day might not be true for him tomorrow.

Unorthodox, mysterious, and flirtatious even in her advanced years, Joyce's softly aging face and graying hair spoke of a seasoned beauty. There were few wrinkles anywhere. She was an amazing woman to watch. "God's a verb in my book, Adele. I'm *living* rather than *being lived.* I have to keep moving." Joyce's sister had warned me that Joyce was "mildly different." *Mildly* was putting it mildly.

Joyce had nomadism in her blood. Her family had lived in the Belgian Congo, where her father was a diplomat. There she had fit in easily with unfamiliar people, the distant geography, and a new language. Back in New York as a teen, she had also fit into the local Catholic schools, then college. After that, her blithe spirit was off to Italy, where she captured a masters in art history. By all accounts, Joyce could have been a prominent figure in the Renaissance arts, but she never settled down long enough to do that.

"Italy was an exciting time," Joyce said. "There were lovers, art was exhibited everywhere, but no money, always no money. How could there be?" she laughed. "I never stayed still. I took off again to Belgium, then France." Still the wanderer, Joyce loved to speak of her adventures. She's a natural traveler and was never meant to stay put—even at sixty-four. "I'm fated!" she said leaning close to me, her hazel eyes intense. "I must explore different campfires. What few clothes I own reside in suitcases, not in closets."

In New York a few decades ago, the city was getting to be too confining for Joyce. Armed with her father's inheritance and with her husband, Carl, she bought a Pennsylvania farm. The idea was to establish an artist's colony. Joyce's boundless imagination was a fertile field of ideas. The farm charged only what people wanted to pay, welcoming like-minded adventurers, some believing in neither God nor the devil nor even art. Needless to say, Joyce lost the farm. "Money and me don't get along!" She moaned in explanation.

Carl's sudden death didn't help Joyce settle down. Free of the farm and no longer compromising to her husband's wishes, Joyce took to the road again, refusing a friend's offer of a car. "I wanted to walk," she shrugged. When I stared at her, she responded with a somewhat strained laughter, which betrayed something less than total confidence at the idea of a mother of two teenaged sons, in her early fifties, hitchhiking to California in pursuit of another dream.

In California, she was penniless again. She seemed so naive, even now, a girl-woman well past childbearing, and so charming. "Well, that's the way it was," she drifted off, looking down. "Honestly, I don't know how to play the money game. Other people hold a number of jobs in their lifetimes, but how do they do it? Where do they get them?

Maybe I simply love the freedom of no house or garage or kitchen counters." Suddenly, my garden gazebo seemed important—stable, protective, an integral part of the garden. Joyce's words disturbed me. I admit that I'm a woman who loves protective, sheltering walls, including a bank account that keep those walls standing.

Perhaps to ease my increasing discomfort, I broke into the old Gene Autry classic: *"Oh give me land, lots of land, under starry skies above. Don't fence me in!"*

"Hey," Joyce laughed, "I love the freedom of my wilderness." Joyce's "no house/no walls" philosophy forced her, at one point, to live in a cramped RV. Nights found her searching for a well-lit mall or other parking lot that she could park in whatever town she ended up in.

I was astounded. "Weren't you afraid?"

She brushed a fly away. "No. Honestly, I wasn't." I believed her.

> ***Does the five thousand dollars that sits in my bank account define me?***
>
> ***—Anna D.***

Joyce told me about falling in and out of love, giving herself over to a man, an image, a piece of geography, then abandoning it as if it never existed. She confessed, "I'm really sad about a thirty thousand dollar loan I made to one of the guys on the farm. He never paid me back, always promising that he would, but there it is. Money slips away from me. I *do* have talent jumping from the tips of my fingers. But I can't plug into how to do the money thing." A warm breeze ruffled the flowers hanging in my gazebo. I sensed something like self-destructiveness gnawing away, unwittingly, at this wandering soul.

I left Joyce in the yard while I hustled up some scrambled eggs. Near the cream pitcher, I spotted Clarissa Pinkola Estes's bestseller, *Women Who Run with the Wolves.* While the coffee perked, I leafed through and found a familiar line: "When we break Convention's rules, then we leap into the forest or into the desert or into the snow and run hard, our eyes scanning the ground, our hearing sharply tuned, searching under, searching over, searching for a clue, a remnant, a sign that the wild woman still lives, and that we have not lost our chance." I nearly laughed aloud. Joyce, the wild woman, dancing as far as she could get from the ties that bind her. That's her!

I set the tray between us, poured coffee, and served the eggs and blueberry muffins from a silver platter. "I don't often get breakfast like this," she said smilingly. "Neither do I," I replied.

Joyce now lived in a single-wide mobile home on two acres in Nevada in the barren and gorgeous Mohave Desert. Out there alone, relying on her considerable resourcefulness, raising her own vegetables, fashioning an independent life. "I'm looking forward to going home and just sitting in the desert," she said wistfully. She had been in town only a few days and was ready to leave.

"Joyce," I said, "whatever happens to you, I want you to know that you are blissfully outrageous, and you continue to destroy my well-constructed ideas of the perfect sixty-year-old." She giggled, but I wasn't ready to let her off the hook: "But will you have enough income out there in the desert? I mean growing vegetables is okay, but what about money for fertilizer? Or for a water bill?" She finished the last of her muffin before she spoke. I was prepared for anything.

"Money? Income?" she repeated as if mouthing occult theories. Then a glint appeared in her eyes. "Actually, money does always come to me, though rarely in huge rushes. Look, when I needed a car, a Toyota appeared in the front yard, with a sign perched on top, Have Car, Will Travel, a surprise from my brother-in-law. Later, I bought the two acres in Nevada with money that popped up from a partial payback of a loan. Money isn't anything I can count on, and it doesn't last, but somehow, it always shows up when I need it."

Talk about a level of faith I don't possess! But was it because my own inner voices clamored against the idea of limited wealth? I applauded the way another interviewee had put it: "Possibilities of wealth always emerge from God's back door." *Spare me, God, my ever-present financial answers, my conviction that you can't move through the world without considerable fortune. This woman doesn't give a hoot, and like Elijah in the Old Testament, she is in the desert, content to eat from Your own hands, watching the stars. Who can put a price on that? What could be holier?* Still, I couldn't help but wonder whether Joyce didn't pay a heavy price for living out her nomadic dreams.

Marybell: *The Second Maturity*

Silver-haired Marybell Simmons, a wiry ninety-three-year-old widow, faithfully sweeps her driveway daily. In a systematic manner, she begins at the right-hand corner, sweeps halfway, then moves to the opposite corner and continues. Pushing in patient, soft sweeps, Marybell's wide broom shoves the litter into a black plastic bag that, when filled, dwarfs her small figure. It's a holy ritual, this public sweep, which contributes much to our neighborhood sense of rootedness, and we all marvel at our friend's success in keeping mind and body together.

Marybell is like a preacher; for her everything is black and white; she has no doubts about her opinions. Marybell is financially independent, able, if she wishes, to treat herself to household help, but she rarely does so. Marybell insists that an older woman, such as herself, should be frugal but always grateful. She insists on driving her '56 Chevy herself, scoffing at anyone who suggests different. Or, heaven forbid, at anyone who suggests a maid. "I'll do it myself, thank you. I got all the strength I need," she drawls in her soft Southern accent. Her house, like the driveway, is always spanking clean, a place of efficiency and order.

When she sees me, she calls, "Come visit for a while!" We settle into the white wooden rockers on the apron of her carport. Sometimes we rock a whole hour away. We say little, just note passing cars, hear the neighbors' dog barking, and comment on why this pooch or that cat needs a better home. One morning, though, I couldn't help asking her about money. How had money shaped her stalwart being? I mentioned the spotless blue Chevy that sat before us, which ran only to church, the hairdresser, and the market—the proverbial little old lady's car kept in mint condition. Marybell looked at me, cocking her head. "Why should I sell it? It runs as good today as the day I got it." I loved Marybell's feistiness, her sharpness. This was a resourceful woman who lived modestly, never allowing money to get the upper hand. "About all I require is two good meals a day and plane tickets to see my family in South Carolina. I buy what I need, that's that."

Growing up in rural South Carolina on what she called a farm but what, I realized as she talked, was more like a small plantation, Marybell never heard "we can't afford it." Her father was moderately successful, and they could indeed afford many things. But they chose to live simply, working the farm themselves. Drinking and smoking weren't allowed in her childhood home and debts weren't either. According to Marybell, money is supposed to be "comfort," and that's how she treated it. "My father had acres of farmland," she said. "Grew watermelons and cantaloupes and cotton, too. Shipped them all north by the trainload. We'd play horsey on the ginned bales of cotton. Cotton was our most excellent crop. The bales sat a long while 'cause Daddy was a good businessman. He'd wait for just the right cotton market." Marybell's white eyebrows were still thick and had an expressive slant. As she talked, they dropped, giving her face a fierceness that belied her serenity. This Southern steel magnolia had an assurance that ran as deep as her accent.

But she did get some help—from Herbert, the yard man. Often, I'd spot Herbert and Marybell huddled in her yard. It was an odd sight, the virile black man and frail old woman carrying on long discussions about a poinsettia bush or what azalea bush needed pruning. Driving by, I'd spot Herbert mowing the grass with her following, talking up a storm, a scene right out of *Driving Miss Daisy.* Herbert was keeping a promise to Marybell's late husband, who had originally employed him. "I'll watch over Mis Simmons," he had said. And for nineteen years, Herbert had kept his promise. This morning, Herbert wheeled into the driveway. "Mornin,' Mis Simmons!" "Mornin,' Herbert!"

Marybell's friend Lucy once admonished her, she said, for paying Herbert too much. "'Hell, no,' I told her. 'When I need a lightbulb screwed in, I get on the phone. If a limb falls off and lands in the front yard, do you think I can move it? I call Herbert.'" Marybell's tone, her nod his way midsentence signaled that this man was a treasured friend. Herbert would be there even if Marybell *stopped* paying him!

Marybell's tiny residence was immaculate and spartan to match the red brick and white shutters outside. Two bedrooms and a bath were appointed in Amish simplicity. The kitchen's white curtains, freshly pressed, blew at the window and the countertops gleamed, spotless. No wonder Marybell is wiry; doesn't she ever eat? She stood across from me near the glistening oven, pointing: "My sister wanted me to get a microwave. 'Sarah,' I told her, 'I don't want a microwave. I have a toaster oven and a floor oven. Who needs a microwave?'" I visualized my own kitchen and its multiple ovens—three at last count. Marybell's personal simplicity forces a mental inventory of one's so-called needs.

Scattered about the house, I glimpsed a half-century of mementos: an upholstered easy chair, a secretary's desk, a Victorian grandfather's clock. Atop the secretary, I spied a book of poetry, a tin of chocolates, and a large box of mauve linen stationery. Marybell's tour included them all. "My birthday presents," she said. She scowled at the stationery box. "Look at this! Lou (the next-door neighbor) knows I write a lot of letters, but this vanilla paper is much too costly. I'm asking him where I can take it back; I'm sure they've got a cheaper kind." I smiled to my-self. Such is the economy that Marybell chooses to live by, a private set of ethics.

We polished off glasses of fresh iced tea. I felt a deep respect for Marybell and her utterly counterculture idea of not needing much and nothing fancy. Who knows, Marybell might well be a millionaire. But this woman, so unlike my cluttered friend, Betty, was determined to reject anything that she doesn't need. She rocked. I sat still, silently taking in her peace and her truths. For some, the idea of spare is part of the aging process, passing on stuff no longer needed. No more stuff, period!

Walking home, I remembered I had left my pen and ran back to Marybell's house. At her door I gave her another hug. How fragile she felt in my arms, this "Mistress of No," this woman who lives so fully despite her frugality. There was something especially precious about that hug. I uttered a final prayer on my morning walk: *Thank you, God, for sending me back for that hug.* Marybell passed away not long after our visit.

Tabatha: *The Dignity of Asking*

Marybell was very much on my mind when I visited Tabatha, another aging woman who possessed the same composure. Once again, I found myself rocking in a worn wooden chair. This time, I rocked on the narrow porch of a clapboard cottage, situated just yards from a traffic-clogged four-lane highway, engulfed in sounds of racing motors.

Tabatha Tukes, an elderly African-American woman, invited me to spend an afternoon with her, in a space so slim that it allowed for only two rockers, a space where I would learn about money as hope. Tabatha revealed her history to me slowly, in her Southern black dialect. Her story was a testimony from one of God's poor.

"I came up rough. I was eleven years old picking cotton in the Georgia fields. I used to work the fields by myself all summer. Couldn't go to school except in the winter. I got paid fifty cents to pick one hundred pounds of cotton a day." Tabatha shook her head at the memory. Her story sent me back to Marybell, whose father employed young black women to work their farm. Both women were a part of black history; one as owner, the other as being owned.

I asked what the hardest part was. She replied, "Shoes!" She tightened the lace of a worn sneaker for emphasis. "I had just one pair for picking cotton and for going to church. I sure could have used another!" I asked about her parents. "My father could read and write, but stopped school in the tenth grade 'cause he was out in the fields every day 'cept Saturday and Sunday, and sometimes he worked Saturdays. I accepted the Lord's will that we would never have money."

Tabatha and I had reconnected when she found my name through a mutual friend, then called and asked, "Sister Adele, remember me?" I had noted anxiety in her voice. We hadn't talked in over thirty years. "No," I replied honestly. "It was back in the sixties that I cooked for the Sisters at Bishop Moore."

Slowly, memories of a younger Tabatha surfaced, a black woman with the widest eyes I'd ever seen, a plump body, and sandals, always wearing sandals in the convent kitchen. Her innocence and modesty were palpable, yet when it came to Southern fried chicken, she knew she was tops. The nuns swore that no one equaled her culinary skills. Most of us gained a few unwanted pounds our first year there.

I also remembered Tabatha's generosity. She'd come to work early and prepare sandwiches for weary nuns wanting a classroom break. There was always something good to eat to quell the constant stress of students, schedules, and assembly preparations. I had tried the missionary thing, doing all I could to convert her. She shut me up fast. "Sister, it was bad enough to be black in Georgia. I didn't need any more problems as a Catholic."

"I sure could use some help," she said softly on the phone. Immediately, I was sure I knew what help she required—money! I didn't warm to the idea. Yes, Tabatha and I shared history. But did that require me to pay her gas bill? Was it that simple? I had money; she needed it. Why did I balk?

"I'll help you this time, Tabatha, but don't make it a habit." I had only acquired my inheritance recently and was anxious about doling it out, afraid that I'd become everyone's easy target. Blessed Tabatha wasn't a bit cowed by my firmness. And now on her porch, I heard why.

"Mammy always told me, 'Tabatha, if you need something, ask for it. If they can't give it to you, it isn't worth having.'" According to

Tabatha, her mother left her two heartfelt teachings: "Don't steal or lie. But do ask!"

In a voice cold as ice then, and for which I'm terribly ashamed, I tossed Tabatha a frigid "yes" and mailed her a check. One month later, she called again: "Sister Adele"— she couldn't stop calling me Sister Adele, and truth be told, I liked hearing it. "Could you help me again?" While I never denied her, I admit that each time I scribbled those checks it was with a reluctant heart. But as the years went by, I came to understand that this dear woman was what the Hebrew scripture calls *anawim,* God's poor, the poor always-with-us, as Jesus called them. At some point, I accepted my role as Tabatha's monthly donor.

Whizzing trucks and the sounds of horns battling for access onto the highway in front of us didn't deter our chat, although I covered my ears once. Tabatha looked serene despite the chaos. What possible peace can come from a front porch assaulted by traffic noise? But Tabatha continues to teach me lessons; today's was that inner peace doesn't depend on what does—or doesn't—go on outside.

If my friend had invited me in, I don't think I could have accepted. Something about the darkness, the broken furniture, and the sagging wooden floor peeking through the screen tore too painfully at my heart. Tabatha lived on Winter Park's West Side. Tenants, all poor blacks, occupied the entire block.

Tabatha rested her head on the rocker's back, and like a polished storyteller, she unfolded a hard life story. "How grateful I was when Sister Mary Thomas hired me. You sisters were patient. And you paid me good. But I worked for you three years before I realized that I had no social security building up." Tabatha described approaching the head nun to request that they begin to take a sum from her weekly paycheck.

"Tabatha, did it ever bother you to see the nuns eating good food, living pretty high class in that spacious convent on the lake?"

She appraised me with her dark eyes. "Really, Sister, it never did." No angry backward glances here. Had oppression worked its way so deeply into her spirit that it numbed her? Could this woman be so content with her lot? We rocked in silence for a while.

> ***Money's use portrays the who inside us.***
> ***—Natalie D.***

"Every day, Sister, I thank God for that Social Security check." She grinned widely. That wise money choice she made long ago still pleased her.

I silently thanked God for Tabatha, my living Sunday collection basket. The gift of being able to help someone like her was spiritual food for me. We chatted until the sun faded. I hoped that she had enough to eat. I hoped that she would ask if she didn't. We bid our farewells, and Tabatha walked me to my car.

As I joined the din of traffic, I happily reflected that Tabatha, to her enormous credit, had not diminished herself in the least by asking for help. Nor had her asking me for money in any way lessened my respect for her. That early phone call was actually a call to community, even though I had to grow into that awareness. She bonded me to her, to the chronically poor, and reminded me once again that no woman is an island.

Kirstin: *Money and Inner Peace*

Tabatha's serenity is matched by that of Kirstin Anderson, another unusual, older woman who has made peace with money. Kirstin is an angel whose feet barely touch this earth. Spiritually attuned, despite years of overwhelming losses, Kirstin's security, like Tabatha's, lies within herself. She keeps in touch with a deep sense of personal worth. Yet unlike Tabatha, her sense of beauty is the wellspring of a vigorous life support system. While Tabatha seems oblivious to her surroundings and has managed to overlook aesthetics, Kirstin thrives on her environment. When with her, one is caught between rejoicing in the glory of her spirit and feeling the pain of her skimpy resources. Kirstin exemplifies the first of Anthony De Mello's two ways to be with money as described in his book, *The Way to Love:* "One person feels quite secure with practically no money in the bank, [while] another feels insecure even though he has millions."

One warm Florida afternoon I drove to Kirstin's home in the country outside Orlando. Flinging open the front door, she stood tall and greeted me as if I were someone she couldn't wait to see. I told her she reminded me of Flip Wilson because what you see is what you get. She grinned widely, offering "Welcome!" My glance darted to the furnishings. Despite constraints enough to hobble a lesser being, Kirsten had turned her home into a miniature showplace. I was reminded of Ami, who always went first class. Polished antiques, porcelain vases, and art filled each space. A tiny blonde European piano graced one side of the room, a woven tapestry made a striking accent on the opposite wall. She proudly confessed that she uses her best china and crystal for all of her solitary meals. It appeared that Kirstin's surroundings existed to honor her. To say nothing of what they did for me, her guest, who felt welcomed and warmed.

Kirstin mentioned that her finances were perpetually tight. It was all she could do to afford the modern house she was renting. I suggested what I thought was an obvious solution—a roommate. In a snap, Kirstin set me straight. "Serenity and solitude are far more important to me than having funds required for the moment," she declared. Kirstin was right to resist. Throughout her ongoing money trials, she had never lost the house or felt a hunger pang. More important, she had held on to her treasured privacy.

As was her habit, she served us on a silver tray—freshly baked orange bread, coffee, and slices of cheese. "This money discussion must be where I need to go," she confessed. She straightened, pushing her fading blonde hair into a bun. "I *don't* want to look at it. I really don't!" I laughed, totally surprised at her. It seemed uncharacteristic for Kirstin to avoid any conversation, especially about the topic she'd just set me straight on. Money must be one major sore spot.

Outside, a summer shower drummed at the windows, increasing our sense of intimacy. Kirstin sat close on the sofa, and, in her refined, deliberate way she began, quietly.

"My childhood was steeped in deep poverty. Feelings of powerlessness followed me as no money was ever saved for electricity, or warmth, or food. My fear of money is natural. It's in my blood." Her worst experience with money happened in 1989, when Stuart, her beloved husband, died suddenly. He'd been a holistic physician who supervised a large clinic on Norway's south coast. Kirstin had worked with him for many years, learning from him. She had also sung in his choir; he was an accomplished musician as well. A huge influx of clients had enjoyed mental and spiritual healing at Stuart and Kirstin's clinic, and their reputation spread throughout Scandinavia. Many of their clients were artists in search of a lost connectedness. But where serenity and deep healing had ruled before, Stuart's death now created devastation. Kirstin's voice shook as she recounted details of the nightmare that bankrupted her emotionally and financially. The clinic was mired in debt, she said. I asked her why.

"Too few clients had been paying. Our expenses always ran higher than our income. Stuart refused to turn anyone away and simply ignored the disaster forming." Kirstin shook her head and fidgeted with her ring. "It was such a big house to run—three therapists—and the debt escalated. At times I felt alone, so divided. Stuart concentrated on the healing process; the debt was up to me."

Kirstin was forced to sell her car and two valuable paintings, and she began depleting a nest egg left over from a first marriage. In the absence of any life insurance, pension, or bank account, there was no way to resume life as she knew it. But time strengthened her backbone, and she discovered strengths she never knew she had. "One day I received a nasty letter signed by the pompous bank president. He informed me that for the next twenty years I would be held responsible for the debt." She picked at a tiny square of delicious Danish cheese, considering how to express her thoughts. I waited, expecting another attack of remorse. I was wrong.

"I answered that letter in a polite but firm tone. I told the bank president that I would not, either now or later, ever be able to pay off that debt. I told him that my health simply would not permit it." She smiled. "I never heard from them again." I was arrested by her tale. She grew animated. "I found another face of God in that awful situation."

I saw a vision of a woman who loved life and loved herself. Money, as scarce as it had always been for Kirstin, was clearly in her life to support her, not to victimize her.

"Afterward, I gave myself a gift. I was living with my daughter, Mara, whose walls had nothing on them to nourish my eyes. I was starved for beauty. So one day, Mara and I bundled up and cycled four miles to an Oriental rug shop. I had saved a bit of money. I admit it was unreasonable, perhaps even insane, to do what I did then." What Kirstin did was to banish the past in one outrageous, symbolic gesture. At the bottom of her misery, this was the first sign of hope for a better future. Kirstin bought a beautiful, plush Oriental rug for her daughter's bare wall. She makes a magnificent case for abandoning reason.

"No, I didn't *need* that rug! I knew that. Yet my soul was absolutely ravenous." Kirstin ended her account with the best revelation of all: "I felt no guilt. In fact, I felt freer than I had in months." The memory amused her. She grinned and pointed to my feet. "Adele, you are sitting on that very rug!" Fiery reds and hopeful blues, I thought to myself. What a magnificent tribute to her spirit!

"Adele, if you could have seen Mara and me! We giggled like little girls as we raced home barely balancing this rug between us on our bikes. Mara yelled over, 'Mom, are we crazy?' And I yelled right back,

'No! We just found our way back to beauty!'" And maybe back to sanity, I thought.

Kirstin left for America soon afterward. Every six months, for lack of a precious green card, she travels back to Scandinavia. That's not an inexpensive trip, I noted. Yet uncertainty about her status here doesn't faze her; there's little trace of the instability she faced after Stuart's death. "Life and money are elusive," she confided mysteriously. "Life always has other plans for us."

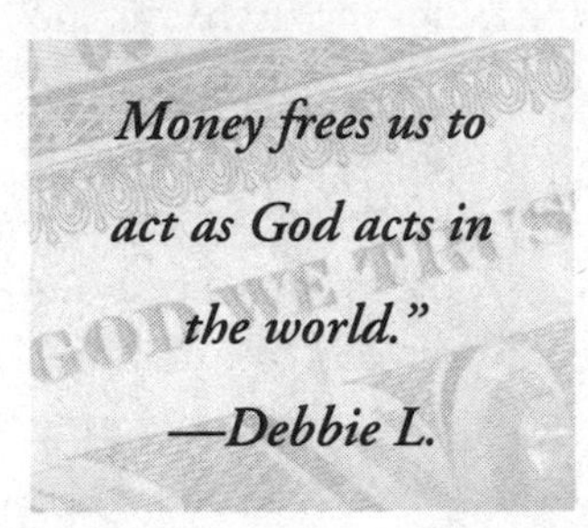
Money frees us to act as God acts in the world."

—Debbie L.

Kirstin revealed that she is financially dependent on her daughter and son-in-law to help make ends meet. Yet the rug under my feet reminded me that Kirstin would prosper with or without them. Her reward, her decoration for bravery, declared a vibrancy for life. Later, we washed the dishes and wiped the counters. As I got my keys out, she announced "I didn't realize how extensive this money subject is. It's easy to say, 'I'm not interested in money,' but that's just talk, isn't it!"

The rain had stopped, and it felt steamy outside her front door. The sun shone on my Cadillac as I backed out of her drive. I felt joy; a bond had been forged between one woman trusting herself to say hard things and another listening to old secrets. I knew that we both were digesting the afternoon's good work. I knew too, that as beauty sustained her, Kirstin was proof that the best things in life are free.

.....

Dear God, we are always nearing the end of the journey. For some of us, it comes later than for others. But all of us are a collection of stories filled with contradictions: rewards and punishments, adventures and stagnation, wealth and poverty, all of it. How You must shake Your head, and yet, I know that we are Your stories and that You do delight in our tales, no matter how tall.

God, this growing old ain't for wimps. There are times I don't like it. Sometimes it comes over me: Everything I've worked for, everything I know, and everything I've loved will go. Yet these years bring me to a new realm of consciousness like nothing I could ever have imagined. I'm seeing everything in a new way, a heartfelt way. Even this money issue that has followed me so much of my life plays differently in my soul. Thank you for this precious time, this sensitivity, this curious awakening, yes, even these unsettling contradictions. Truly, I am in the prime of life.

Chapter Five

Embracing Loss—Resurrected Women

"Adele, I met a man who reads Thomas Merton. I want you to meet him."

How I've held these precious words close to my heart. They have been with me for years, but are as new as yesterday. I delight in repeating them to friends. I feel the magic each time that I say them. Like golden threads, they are deeply woven into the fabric of my life.

It was my unlikely, yet sacred, partnership with this man, Jim Rucquoi, that pushed me to uncover even more money conflicts hidden in my psyche. But more important, Jim was and still is the miracle that God finally delivered to my doorstep.

Initially the challenge was to recognize this miracle. That meant getting past one big obstacle. I revolted at the idea—like any woman of my culture—of marrying a homeless, jobless man, no matter how many fine credentials he possessed. It just wasn't done. And I simply wasn't going to be the one to do such an unspeakable thing, not if I could help it.

After our first meeting, I scrambled to imagine him fitting into my structured world. But no, there was too much that wouldn't conform, try as we might! I was Tevye, dancing around the questions in the classic, *Fiddler on the Roof.* Tevye sought to please God by sticking to the traditions of his faith while absorbed by intolerable changes in the world around him, a struggle to the death, it would seem, between heart and mind. First it was, "On the one hand," and then, "On the other hand." I've come to appreciate the truth of that sort of back and forth encounter. Isn't it God's way of pulling us out of fixed positions so our persistent heart can eventually win over our mind? That's what happened to me.

On the one hand, my father's voice was exploding in my head: "What? He lives on the street? Get rid of him. Now!" Add that to every echo of conventional wisdom about street people: "He's a bum! If he got a job, he wouldn't be on the street." On the other hand, there was my beating heart: "He's compassionate, he's smart, and he makes you laugh. If you pass him up, you might spend your whole life regretting it."

One Saturday night in the confessional, I wept. A calm voice said, "What is beautiful is to continue, as long as you need, to entertain the dilemma, to stay in the flow of doubts about this man." The words were those of a Gesthemani Trappist monk I had sought out for counsel. He continued, "If you close the door on those doubts, you may close the door to the possibilities altogether." Father's words didn't help much, but I left feeling validated. I drove home from that retreat, confident that I wasn't alone, and that somehow, it was okay for this man to stand at the threshold of my world a bit longer. I filled my house with all sorts of spring flowers and pledged to be open to God's possibilities.

Like Tevye, I had prayed for years: "Would it be asking too much for you to find me a kind husband—even if it takes a drastic move, like to Alaska?" Persistent, I presented my case to God: "Other nuns left and found their dream without so much fuss. Why not me?"

I was battling the events of my life, pleading, negotiating, and bargaining with the Divine Being, Who was always there for conversation. Down in my gut, I knew there was no choice but to do it His way.

The day of Lynn's memorable phone message, nature also spoke eloquently. Florida had suffered one of its longest, most brutal, droughts. Every palm and bougainvillea had crinkled dry, and a scorched earth peered between blades of brown grass. The sun glared disparagingly on the dry mess it had created. But on this fateful afternoon, with the odd phone message in my mind, the clouds gathered. Drum-like rolls cut across a purple-streaked sky. Soon the merciful, wet drops began to fall, and rain drenched leaves and branches, pulsing down to the very root of things, cleansing accumulated dust and grime. Joy was everywhere. Squirrels fluffed their tails. Orlando, moist and enchanted and glistening green, was once again the City Beautiful.

How long it had been since I'd mailed postcards to friends, teasingly imploring them to help me locate Mr. Right? I can hardly admit this on paper. The result? Not a single reply! I had honestly looked and come up empty. Close friends knew how lonely I was, always playing third person in a dance of couples and hating it. My friend Sister Toby expressed it this way: "Nobody likes a mystery when it doesn't compute! I believe there is a guy out there for you, Adele. When? I can't say. I can only keep praying." But I'd had enough. Perhaps, in some baffling breakthrough, it was Sister Toby's prayers that led me to declare, finally and firmly, that singles' dances and blind dates were over for me. Staying home, I decided, couldn't be any worse than such indignities.

This new decree was fragile and young, but healthy, a new boundary similar to those I acquired after my Middlebury College debacle. Now, I could be peaceful, and I honored quiet times out by the pool and spent meditative moments in the garden. *Okay, okay, God, I surrender!* I had just celebrated my fifty-ninth birthday and had finally surrendered to life without a partner. I didn't like surrendering. I didn't much care to picture all those lonely years ahead. But eventually, grace took hold and I was able to overcome my sadness. Being single would be part of life's diversity, perhaps my own distinct calling! And then, of course, that is when everything changed.

Lynn had explained, in her message, that she had met this man at a conference in Orlando on race relations. So I simply turned away from her words, ambled back to the kitchen, and stirred my pot of chili. I felt neither a trace of hope nor excitement as I normally would have. "Another member for our Merton group. I'll meet him soon enough."

It was June 4 at ten o'clock in the morning—breakfast at Ronnie's, a downtown restaurant. "I'll pick up Jim," Lynn had promised. "You just show up!"

I waited at a corner table. Time passed. My nervousness grew. Against the backdrop of clanking cutlery and dishes, biases floated to the surface of my thoughts, banging about inside my head. I couldn't stop the inner noise. *He'll be fat. And, of course, sloppy. And yes, smelly too. Weren't all homeless people? Not to mention the enormous psychological problems that would restrict him to the simplest of conversations. And Lynn and I would have to listen to him. But on the other hand, hadn't Lynn been impressed enough with him to invite me to meet him? She was no fool. Sometimes too kind, yes, but no fool. Not the cynic I could be.* I gathered a pile of ready-made negatives as I sipped my coffee. Perhaps those put-downs and stereotypes needed venting, I decided, and allowed them to speak. I admired my new haircut in the mirror opposite me. At least, *I* looked great!

Lynn had reported that he had asked her outright at that race conference, "Is there a Thomas Merton group in Orlando?" And she had replied, "Yes, there's a Merton group in Orlando, and it meets in my home!" *Talk about serendipity! Of all the places to be in Orlando, he finds the woman who hosts the very group he's looking for. There was something divine in that, all right. But on the other hand, he was a homeless man. Lynn, are you kidding?*

Finally, I glimpsed Lynn and a tall figure heading across the restaurant. I sighed audibly. He appeared pretty basic, could pass for normal: no tattered shirt, ripped trousers, or, I noted gratefully as he approached, offensive odor. He was lanky and his blondish gray hair was trimmed neatly. A few strands fell over his eyes. I forgot my anxieties. Eagerly, I stood and extended my hand. "I'm Adele!" My napkin dropped. Jim restored it to the table. I looked into the bluest of eyes. He wasn't supposed to look so good, so happy and bright. His hand covered mine entirely in a hardy grip. I felt pleasantly surprised at his touch. We settled in, read menus, and chatted.

Without dropping his napkin, stammering, or clearing his throat, Jim casually ordered as if he had been in the best restaurants in the world, looking directly at the waitress without a trace of discomfort or flirtation. I noted his clear skin, how the corners of his eyes wrinkled when he smiled. I watched him break open the tiny cream container, how his long fingers peeled open the packet of sugar, how slowly he stirred his coffee. I found every move fascinating, all the details alive. Eggs and bacon and freshly brewed cups of Ronnie's aromatic coffee occupied us and kept the conversation light, easily masking the unanswered questions that lay between us.

By the time the waitress brought second cups of coffee, I was Tevye again. Looking at Jim's hands, it was obvious that no poverty or street life darkened his background. On the one hand, he was ease itself in manners and conversation, refined actually. But, on the other hand, my squawking immigrant parents' voices wouldn't let up: "Hey, we pulled ourselves up with hard work. Tell that guy to get a job!"

Sounds of lively exchange and friendship were the natural way of things at Ronnie's, and no one would know that this man didn't fit, didn't have a single dime to his name. At Lynn's request, Jim recited what he called his signature poem. He spoke in strong, deep tones, a regular James Earl Jones. I was transfixed, the rhymes and cadence ringing in my ears with delight . . . .

I'm just a poet, don't ask for more
Don't look to me for the love of money
or on these words erect more than their sound
I don't try to be funny, tho of late it's true
I do laugh a lot. What's more things strike me that way
This taste of honey grows thicker each day
with more new wrinkles to frame such disposition sunny
than I had seen on a newborn laughing son
More than drain tropical continent's countenance
Runny with mid-day's sudden passionate outbursts.
More than theatrical masks fashioned regardless of money.
I'm just a poet. Don't ask for more!

Suddenly, I felt an overwhelming urge to release every belief that I'd been taught. I wanted to honor this roofless stranger, to surrender to God my harsh condemnation of him for simply being the man he was. I had to get out of there. I stood, brushed the crumbs off my skirt, and strode out ahead of the two of them. Jim reached around me to open the heavy glass door. Sounds of traffic buffeted our words and I didn't know what to do, whether to shake his hand, give him a hug, or just back off and smile politely. Lynn bailed me out: "I hope we'll see you at the next Merton meeting, Jim," she announced gaily, adding, "and don't worry about a ride. We'll find a way to pick you up."

Jim glanced at me, a bit awkwardly. "That would be great!"

Pick him up! Was he Cinderella and we the Prince Charmings appointed to send our chariot to fetch him? What awkward dependence of a man upon a woman! Had Jim been a homeless woman and the roles reversed, perhaps all that baggage would not have weighed so heavily on me; a man makes the living, and the woman keeps the home. Right? But for the woman to possess the greater financial means, please!

So there, under a bright Florida sky, I felt utterly disconcerted about picking him up. For his part, Jim blithely invited me to know more: "Would you like my post office box number? Only three numbers: 612." I nodded and just as casually jotted them on a blank check in my checkbook. But those numbers carved themselves in my memory. Though the sun was shining on us that morning, everything seemed unclear.

I snapped my checkbook shut and stuffed it into my purse. By then Lynn had vanished. What was I still doing there? "Bye!" I called over my shoulder as I dashed to my car and drove away quickly. I rolled the window down, welcoming the rush of clean air. I was glad that I had resisted offering the strange man a ride. I confessed my unease that night to my sister on the phone. She was cool, laughing as if meeting a homeless man was a routine event. "Honey, he sounds okay. After all, you didn't meet him in a bar!"

A Pilgrimage

That Wednesday night, the Merton group gathered just as we had for the past twelve years. Our little assembly included folks of every age, religion, and political predilection. Meetings were a journey, uncovering new ground, unlocking whatever doctrine presented itself. As an older member had once commented, "No one ever left a Merton meeting unaltered or unmoved. You can't if you participate fully." Sure, sparks sometimes flew, but it never got too hot to discourage final hugs. That's the power that Merton's writings held over us, despite the fact that he'd been long dead.

A fresh batch of narcissus blossoming in a glass vase brightened the room; their sweet and citrusy perfume filled the house. So did the scent emanating from the cookie table. I asked our newest member to read aloud the evening's topic, a few lines from a Merton piece about pilgrimage. Like a strong wind, Jim's voice breathed spirit into Merton's words. He nodded and read in that deep, wonderful voice: *What is a pilgrimage? A return to a place where there will be an encounter and a renewal of life. A humble, difficult effort to cross an abyss, to achieve communion with people, who, in such large measure, are deprived of identity and reduced to inarticulate silence.*

A candle flickered. Silence filled the room. I usually tried not to talk too much, to offer my views only after others had spoken, but this night I jumped in, nervously, with my doubts. "Isn't the idea of a pilgrimage scary, always a trip forward or backward, always a move to another place without a roof over our heads?"

Was I trying to justify the presence of our most obvious pilgrim, this strange, impressive man in the worn shoes? A dialogue followed, and while nothing was put to rest, by the time the discussion was finished, Jim was a part of us. As for me, I was a child coming alive that night, wielding a fantasy magnifying glass, checking Jim's every blink, every move, the way his hands laced and unlaced in his lap. Lynn sat comfortably beside her new friend, enjoying his company as he wolfed down a few extra cookies. For a second, I was glad she was so happily married herself. I could hardly believe my thoughts, and I fought them down. *Dear God, I think he does fit in my world!*

The clock struck, and although Jim's ride was waiting outside, he turned and made his way back to me. "How about lunch?" he smiled. The blue eyes again. I looked up, dumbstruck. *God, You joker! A date? A real date? How many years have I prayed for this? But if I say yes, the possibilities are dangerous. There's the money. He might present a problem, but I suppose I could hire an attorney.*

Others turned awkwardly to listen to Jim's offer as an unembarrassed Jim waited for my answer. Later, a friend joked, "You were the character in the E F. Hutton commercial, where everyone stops to listen for her answer!"

"What do you say?" he repeated. Lynn's gaze pressed at me: *Adele, get a grip! All this guy wants is to go to lunch, not Paris!*

"Sure," I replied.

The next day I recorded a dream I had had that night, knowing it surely held a meaning: *A man stood in a fog, not knowing which way to turn, his face burned and scarred, his mouth clamped tight. Only his eyes were clear. His arms flayed about as he started rotating in a circle. He didn't say anything, or if he did, I couldn't hear him. I just watched, and of course, he disappeared, but the fog stayed a long while.*

I had told Jim I would meet him in a downtown park, yet my entire being revolted at the prospect, screaming at me not to go. *Don't put your hopes on a man without a dime in his pocket!* But then my Christianity surfaced. Hadn't I been schooled to live by the truth Jesus taught—that only our spirit life counts? Jim's spirit was kind, funny, and sharp! But here I was a lonely woman, and a lonely person's judgment can be eroded by the sound of a friendly voice.

I planned my words: *Why are you homeless? I would demand. My goodness, you admitted your degrees from Georgetown and Columbia, stints as a naval officer and as a former professor at the City University of New*

York! And that childhood off Park Avenue. What could you have possibly done, or said, or allowed to have done to you, to have landed like this, on Orlando's streets? I want to know! I want to know you."

We met at Lake Eola. I was up to my old tricks, parking the Cadillac blocks away, behind the Greek Orthodox Church where my parents had prayed and dropped rolled bills in the collection basket. I felt safe in that familiar parking lot. Then, shaky, I set off to the lake. I saw Jim's figure coming toward me. I smiled, hoping he wouldn't ask about my car. "Where is your car?" were the first words out of his mouth.

"I didn't bring it," I lied.

Could I confess that I owned a Cadillac to a man who had no means of transport other than the legs God had given him? And so, we strolled. I felt like blurting: *Listen, buster, I hid my car because it's not your style. You're a man without anything, and you're not making it in this world, and you don't deserve to ride in my Cadillac, so there!*

When Jim held up two bags bulging with subs, I was knocked over. "You bought those?" Nothing could have surprised and pleased me more. According to Mama, there was an eleventh commandment that dictated, "Thou shalt be generous with thy money, especially at meal time." My mother kept an eye out for a man's wallet in a restaurant. If he waited, didn't immediately reach for the tab, well, you could pretty much count him unforgiven. If he quickly reached for the bill and paid it, he was a holy man, worthy of adoration. She said she couldn't help it. And it didn't matter who the man was. When a former priest friend of mine was invited to dinner and volunteered to bring dessert, he was forever branded unacceptable for showing up clutching a bag of half a dozen donuts. Mama turned red. She never said a word, but she never looked at him again, railing at me later: "Look, I don't care if he's an ex-priest or the Dalai Llama. Don't have anything more to do with that man!"

So this time, at this strange lunch, seated under an oak, I sat back delighted to be treated to a meal. And Jim was quite the host. He set a fine park bench table: turkey subs, chips, and cold drinks, topped off with two enormous peanut butter cookies. Never had a lunch called up so much reflection. I thought of my earlier ruminations. *Oh, God, which hand am I on now?* Afterward, we strolled down to Greenwood Cemetery, where Mama and Dad lay side by side. It had been months since I'd visited.

Charles Azar, Father 1900–1977 | Adele Azar, Mother 1911–1983

I turned to Jim. "I can hear Mama laughing with us now! She's so glad that you paid for lunch. You've made a real hit with her!" My eyes misted despite the jest. Amid sounds of wind rustling the trees, we walked back to the path. I pushed my hands hard against my temple, against the sensation of what was happening. Suddenly, I was a nun again, standing in front of my sophomore class remembering a lesson from a little gem entitled *We Dare to Say Our Father:* "Those we call 'saved souls' now in heaven, were standing around feeling awfully pompous about their accomplishments. Suddenly they noticed riffraff stationed nearby. Anger mounted. 'Why are *they* here? After all, we have faithfully lived by the rules, gone to Mass every Sunday, dropped money in the collection basket!' They upbraided God and demanded to know, 'How did *they* get here?' In that moment, they found themselves thrown in hell."

I remember him walking beside me to my Cadillac. I still couldn't believe that I had let him see it. "Nice car!" he had beamed. Jim seemed to take everything in stride. Even those affluent wheels. He had said that he didn't consider types of cars that important. I had thought, cynically, *Well, good for you!* I'd driven him back to a friend's tiny downtown house where he was staying for a time. Before he got out of the car, he had leaned over and kissed me lightly on the cheek. I had felt nothing but awkwardness. There had been no lightning. But, after all, it'd been quite a while since I'd been kissed. Outside the car door, he had leaned in to ask, "Can we do this again?" The blue eyes appraised me.

"Let me think about it."

I went into seclusion. I spent hours by the pool, watching a June sun wash over blue and orange ripples. With my skirt above my knees, I sat, catching the rays, my toes swishing in the cool water. I lulled the time away. Inside me, something enormous was clamoring to be birthed. I knew it had to do with my judgments about this strange man and his simple ways.

Sitting by the pool, I picked up my pen and my journal. I traced my money patterns back to earlier times. When I entered the convent I had rejected Dad's love of money. Later, when a spiritual leader spoke at a huge gathering of Sisters aimed at reshaping the rules, I stood up and fought with my fellow nuns when they voted to change the rule that forbade them to carry pocket money. That was going too far. Money had never been and never should be found in our deep pockets! I ranted. It was the devil's coin! Now, meeting a homeless man, my conflict was about blaming him for *not* having any money. Was I nuts? I put down my pen and journal and flung myself in the pool, clothes and all. I swam several laps, got out, and walked over to a patch of dying daisies and pulled every last one of them up. "Sorry, guys! Into the compost pile you go." Old ideas have to be dumped.

"I'm not meeting you again." The phone receiver shook in my hand.

"If that's what you want. But I thought things were going great," he said. The hurt in his voice stung me. *Easy for you to say! My car, my money, my everything.*

Intense gardening and a month of silence followed. In my self-imposed retreat, I planted, watered, weeded, and pruned. I had a sense of what was working for me. Gardening binds us to the earth, which brings new birth, seeds, blossoms, and even death. All I had to do on my retreat was keep my hands in that dirt, feed the plants, and watch the growing drama unfold, blindly hoping that these garden truths might lead me to where I needed to go.

Box 612

One warm morning, after working up a sweat, I showered, dressed, and planted myself near the bay window for some sacred reading. My eye caught sight of a small book that I'd bought months before, *Voice from the Desert,* by the French bishop, Jacques Gaillot. I read the small memoir in one sitting, hating the Vatican for making this man suffer so, ordering him to stop, of all things, assisting the marginal people in his diocese. When he refused, they censured him. One anecdote in particular stood out: "A homeless man was selling a newspaper put out by the unemployed and was interviewed by a TV crew who asked: 'Do you feel that you have regained a certain degree of dignity thanks to this work?' 'Sir,' answered the homeless man, 'I never lost my dignity. It is within me, and it is in you. Let's just say that now people acknowledge it.'" I looked out at Gods' sky. *Jesus! I feel so ashamed.*

My heart exploded and magic filled the entire house. Images of Jim rushed through my mind. I saw the tall figure, the distinguished gray beard, the burning blue eyes. I saw him as a professor standing before his class or, suddenly, standing behind me in my full-length mirror. Our eyes would lock. Then I saw him riding beside me in my Cadillac and at one point taking over the wheel. Without warning, I knew where I was going. The sensation was overpowering. My armor, my masks, my prejudices, the whole panoply of my carefully managed defenses shattered and fell about me. My hand trembled as I fished out a poem that Jim had sent me. It was one of his 'rambling' kinds of poems, but one bit of it seemed especially relevant:

> *a learning, a bringing forth, a going back, depends on how you hear it, use it, what can it teach? the story of us all set in time never to be lived the same, never to appear just that way but always there because certain actions were taken, certain decisions made, certain consequences, certain pieces set to motion, certain weathers, certain people acting with, upon, for, and, against each other, certain expectations, certain sights, certain manifestations, certain insights . . . this certain living it, certain part of it, a certain writing now—let another read the lessons!*

Summer was finished. Another great rain came, leaving the earth exhilarated. A church friend revealed that Jim was now living with a Catholic family, doing odd jobs around their home. I addressed a square envelope: Box 612. I enclosed a greeting card sporting a cartoon, a tall stick figure about to fall over a precipice. It read: "Do anything of interest lately?" I pictured his smile. I hoped that I hadn't hurt him too much.

Jim finally moved into my home. It was easy for both of us, since I had at last been delivered from the quandary of "on the one hand or on the other hand." Totally gracious, Jim was right at home in my house, and I felt great having him there. A former nun, who reads everything from taxes to spiritual pursuits, summed it up beautifully: "Look at Christ! It takes a special kind of chivalry to accept gifts from others. Jesus had that grace and depended on his hosts' generosity for everything!" She looked at me evenly. "If the tables were turned, would *you* have let *Jim* give you clothes, a car, spending money?

Could you have graciously let him share his inheritance with you?" I couldn't answer.

I'd like to say that since then we have lived happily ever after. But, of course, conflicts surged aplenty, including money brawls. We had no choice but to face them, and mostly we did just that.

Lying in bed one night, listening to Jim's deep breathing, mulling over his new life with me, I felt a zap from God. I sat up with an understanding of how glorious a thing it is to have the power to help resurrect a soul. There was no doubt; the gift of my love for Jim had resurrected him. Walking through the house, he would chant, "I was lost, but now I'm found."

Living with Jim is daily nourishment of a kind I've never known, where soulful conversations, startling honesties, and self-discovery all play in our unfolding marriage. Only yesterday we were sitting on the back porch with our morning coffee when Jim, for some reason, was called back to a vivid youthful memory of one summer spent at a farm in Michigan. Details gushed out as if for the first time as he recalled the excitement of early rising, doing chores, assembling for a huge breakfast, along with pungent smells, hay rows, and dairy cows. As he talked, I began smelling and touching his delicious memories for myself. Here was a man never afraid to reveal his whole person. When he left the porch I was again overwhelmed by the miracle of two people so intimately connected, harvesting each other's rich memories. The garden never looked so beautiful.

But I needed a promise that now he was here, he would not leave. I couldn't bear another loss. Jim never held back, "No matter what happens, honey, you've got me here forever." But my future husband had many layers of old hurts; he was a wounded man. At times, I had to contain his anger, distrust, and suspicion. I found that part hard. Yet I came to understand that his wounds were exactly why we were sent to each other, for my growth as well as for his. Living with me, he was able to chart a new course, and it took great courage to start over. His journey—from responsible parenting of two sons in his first marriage of twenty years to the streets—had been long and tortuous and is the subject of his own book, *Letters to Jake,* which he has written over the years for his grandson. It is his own story to tell. As for us, I believe in him more than ever.

December 10, 1993, was Merton's feast day. The wedding bells rang loud! Jewish and Muslim friends gathered with Christian friends to honor us. They brought their own dances and a glass for Jim to stomp that sealed our sacred union. I can't glorify the moment enough.

There stood Jim, handsome in a white tux, waiting at the altar alongside our priests, who were dressed in flowing white chasubles, ritual books in hand. The triumphant third movement of Saint Saens' Organ Symphony broke the chapel silence.

People turned, about to witness the formal end of my singlehood. The pictures later showed me a radiant and smiling bride. Dressed in silky white palomino pants and blouse and a wide rimmed hat, I floated down the aisle, feeling perfectly at one with the universe.

Up that aisle, I walked alone, my head raised high. Everyone there knew how I'd waited for this moment. One by one I made eye contact with my friends, grinning until my face hurt. Never have I seen them from so regal a place!

Jim's blue eyes filled, and I could barely see him for my own tears. An amplified boy's choir of the John Williams recording, "Empire of the Sun," cut loose with soaring alleluias in conquering polyphony. The young voices, grand and strong, filled every corner of the chapel. I locked my arm with my husband's, and we turned to face a world we'd never known before, both of us home at last. The entire assembly held hands, and, holding them high, began to dance in one, joyous circular motion. And why not? Wishes had come true and old prayers had been answered. New prayers were offered, and solemn blessings were given in Hebrew, Arabic, Latin, Gaelic, and even English. We all danced madly around the chapel until the last alleluia. Then Jim and I waved and vanished down the front stairs into our future to even more boisterous applause and whistles.

All the money in the world could not buy the truth of Thomas Merton's words, inscribed on our wedding invitation that captured that golden event: *What we are asked to do at present is not so much to speak of Christ as to let him live in us so that people may find him by feeling how he lives in us.*

Resurrected Women

Our marriage commenced, full of answered prayers, shared abundance, and heartfelt security amid choices unlike many other marital unions. We didn't share nine-to-five careers that could sap our energy and creative spirit. We weren't hooked into a planned future. We owned our house and car and had our pension plans in place. We had enough money to support our dreams, but more important, we were equipped to usher in an entirely new and bright spirituality. For there is no doubt that both of us had risen from a dark place of acute loneliness into a place of sunshine. Friends called us resurrected people, and I couldn't agree more, for God had breathed new life into both of us.

Miracles! God's work often seems slow and is typically camouflaged before revealing its mysterious process. How well the following women know the requirement of patience; it took years for some of them to feel alive again after personal devastation. And it was not so much loneliness, but the anguish of acute poverty and bankruptcy that hurt their spirits.

I hold enormous respect for these ladies. Some spiraled to a living hell as they endured the financial terrors of mortgage officials, bank lawyers, and credit card henchmen. Yet their stories aren't just about money. For years, these women felt a spiritual bankruptcy as well. They and God didn't speak (at least they didn't speak to God). If they did communicate, it was in the form of a raised fist and disparaging tears. But unlike those victims of the stock market crash of '29 who threw themselves from windows, these once-wrecked women somehow managed to survive their ruin and regain their dignity.

Sadly, our society was content to write off these women. Make no mistake; how others see us is firmly entrenched in how well we manage—or fail to manage—our money. As if eyes grow scales at the sight of poverty, most of us are blind to the true character of the struggling poor.

Each of these resurrected women is a joy to know. Sit back and read their stories and glimpse God at work.

Joanna: *A No-Cash, No-Credit Girl*

The doorbell chimed and signaled the arrival of the first workshop participant. Feeling scared and excited, I prayed for God to stay close. I flung open the door and beamed my best smile. Friends, new and old, continued to arrive and poured into our family room's waiting circle of chairs. They were here to talk about a most personal issue—the aspect of money in their lives.

A workshop about money? Nervousness fluttered through the room. Sarah left her car running. John stuttered, "H-hello." Jim dropped the pencil box, scattering yellow markers around everyone's feet. But after a few introductory remarks, a wonderful energy took over and even the shiest tongue was loosened. We were launched. I threw out the first directive: "Let's all count the cash we've got on us right now!" Giggles sounded as eyebrows raised and purses and wallets flipped open and the sound of counting filled the air.

Candy sat close to me on the floor. She didn't reach for her purse. "I know exactly how much I have without looking," she offered. "I've got twenty-one dollars and sixty-five cents." Everyone gasped. She grabbed her purse and rifled through her cash. Creating a fan of her bills and jingling her coins, she showed us, to the penny, $21.65! The rest of us hadn't a clue how much we were carrying, and some were still counting furiously. Then I asked them, "How much money do you *need* to carry on your person?" They looked at me blankly. Joanna raised her hand. She was another stranger attending at a friend's suggestion. Dressed in a trim white suit, honey-colored hair pulled severely back, she was the model businesswoman, all confidence. "I hate cash, and I never carry it." Everyone listened attentively. "I'll tell you why! Living in the Orient, I let my bus card take me everywhere: to grocery stores, the bank, the theater. Also I got into the habit of using my debit card for everything. It's so much easier on the nerves."

Joanna had returned to the States after a ten-year teaching stint in China, and thus provided the only foreign experience in our group. "In

Asia, it's not about cash or a credit card or even making a living. Life there is about a quest for a person's deepest meaning."

"Sign me up!" came a voice from the circle. I urged Joanna to say more. I noted that her pale hands, folded in her lap, sported a large stone ring. Here in the States, she was running a young start-up company. Her meteoric rise in corporate life seemed incredible given her background as a teacher.

"Maybe," Jim suggested, "when you don't seek success, it just comes?"

Like many other resurrected women, Joanna had managed to climb out of grinding poverty and, after several false starts, finally owned her own home—and owned it right off the bat. "It was paradise without mortgage payments," she told us. She had invested her entire teachers' pension in the home.

"I refused to take on a mortgage for the next thirty years of my life. No way! After the poverty I had lived in, and then the freedom of a cashless society, I decided that my new home should be completely paid for." I was puzzled. *Is she against cash, or for it?* I was curious where this would lead.

"Buying that house with cash meant that I could survive on peanut butter sandwiches if it came to that. I'd figure out how to build another savings account."

"You've got guts, Joanna," Alan muttered. Heads nodded in agreement. A friend who knew a great deal about her own cash in hand, clapped wildly.

But Joanna had work to do with us, and she carried us back to her bleak childhood. Hers had been an Appalachian family struggling for survival. Imagine a wooden trailer with a dirt floor. *Not to put too fine a point on it, that family was indeed "dirt poor,"* I thought to myself.

"When I was five," she began, "I remember going to bed hungry. We had to walk two blocks to the public toilets." Joanna grinned, "I treated that walk like an adventure, but not my fifteen-year-old sister. God, how she'd cringe each time she had to go." The group was utterly quiet. I listened, amazed, wondering whether her sister still hated to go to the bathroom.

Joanna's eyes took in everyone. Her well-modulated voice, her educated turn of phrase, and her sleek, tailored clothes belied what we were hearing; we were, I suppose, in shock. How does someone raised in such hardship become so polished? I looked around at her wide-eyed audience.

"Was it daily meditation that helped you through?" Connie asked aloud.

"Perhaps! But there's this, too: mind games saved me. Even though we undoubtedly were the town's 'poor folk,' I felt strangely 'cool,' certainly better off than the migrants. After all, our trailer was wooden and stable; it didn't shake when the wind kicked up. Migrants had to make do under a cardboard roof. I liked them. They were nonthreatening. In the food stamp line, I felt safe chatting with them."

The rest of Joanna's family, however, didn't consider their life "cool" in the least. Her mother despised the food lines and welfare checks and piles of unpaid bills. She complained bitterly to her husband, day and night, as she did the dishes or tended the tiny garden. "After my sister got on Dad's case too, he quietly got out of bed one morning and walked out." Joanna's mother didn't wait a minute to get divorced. Alan pushed his chair in closer. The air was thick with compassion.

Maggie spoke up for all of us: "How on earth did you get through that?"

"Well, now, Mother had her way. I learned a lot about money after Dad left. Money was her topic. Pennies and nickels. Mother never let up. 'You've got to account for every penny you spend.'" Joanna smiled at the memory.

At eight years old, little Joanna learned to tally her expenses in a small spiral book. "A box of cereal was fifty-nine cents, a muffin was twenty cents, and a tootsie roll was a penny," she recalled with disturbing precision.

I studied her. There was no hint of emotion as she retraced those tough memories. Was she at peace with all this? Was it years of inner work that brought her resolution? Joanna appeared opaque.

"Parents in our school forbade their kids to play with us. We were the undesirables, the blacklisted. I remember one kid, in the bathroom, who summed it all up when she said, 'Gosh, you wear the same thing every day.'"

But Joanna's teen years brought a surprise: a virtuoso ability on the flute and high SATs. Suddenly, what she couldn't afford, she was given. Now the country club kids were her academic peers. Joanna won, not one, but three scholarships, including two out of state, from the prestigious Eastman and Boston conservatories.

Even so, the tyranny of scarcity didn't disappear. "My high school teachers scraped up most of the transportation money, but Mother couldn't cover the rest. I finally settled on the state university only a bus stop away," she said. She knitted her brow. "Then for the first time I could remember, I *was* somebody."

"After college, I took off for my ancestors' Ireland, hired as an American teacher for their equivalent of sixth grade. My income swelled. In that Irish hamlet, I was the American queen. It was a time of joy and good experiences, of generous dinners and fun outings. It didn't seem to matter that I didn't own a car; parents sent their cars and drivers for me! I remember them being delighted by the Johnny Walker scotch I brought, like it was really something."

Lunch was served as Joanna's story dissolved into easy sharing all around. I put out the platters, marveling at this woman.

After the workshop, Chris approached me shyly. She had been hesitant to speak earlier. "I'd like to tell you my money story, but in private," she said. We made a date for a picnic lunch the next week.

Chris: *Big Bumps*

There was a light breeze as I sat on a hill in a park outside the city with my new friend, Chris. Below us, school children played, clustering around their teacher as she pointed out Florida foliage surrounding the park's fountain. A lakefront meadow, thick with hibiscus, ginger, and twisted palms, set the scene for our picnic. I provided tuna sandwiches, chips, and deviled eggs. Chris would provide the narrative. A youthful woman with close-cropped hair, she relaxed on a yellow blanket and began a shocking tale of how money and marriage don't mix.

She was the breadwinner in her first marriage. "He wanted everything, and I wanted to please him. I know my story sounds like a corny soap opera. That's what my lawyer called it. 'You've let this man walk all over you,' the lawyer said." As if that weren't enough, a crushing bankruptcy occurred in her second marriage. That trauma left her totally penniless and defeated.

"My second husband, Kyle, stayed at home and kept house and the books while I sweated for a paycheck. I thought he was paying our bills, but it turned out he was just intercepting the mail, doling out what he wanted. The only piece of mail I ever read was lying on my bed one night when I got home—a notice of foreclosure on my dream house, the house I'd scrimped and saved for! Kyle had never paid a cent of our mortgage, but managed instead to run up thousands of dollars on my credit card.

"I grew up in Pittsburgh, and after my father was laid off by the steel mill our family went through some tough times. I've got that here. Here read this." She shoved a journal onto my lap. In her teenage handwriting, she had scrawled:

> *After the fire, which burned Judy [her sister, age thirteen], she has been so severely burned and almost died, I see my family taking a dive. With no insurance to cover our home or car, Dad tries to keep us afloat. He doesn't talk about it and is slipping into just staring out the window. His hair has grayed overnight. He keeps repeating: "Pay every bill you owe, even if it stretches over your entire life."*

"Can you believe Dad was still writing creditor checks in his old age?" Chris despaired. Unlike her father, she had deliberately refused to make good on her debts. Albeit painful, she chose bankruptcy and broke with her father's creed.

"After high school, and finding a job, I could own things! I could write a check, have a credit card. The money rolled in." And she made sure to help fill her mother's cookie jar now that she stood on her own.

"Mom freaked out, called me independent and foolish when I decided I wanted my own home. My journal quotes her very words: 'You want the whole chicken, not just the drumsticks.' I didn't listen. I calculated; it'd be tight, but I could do it. No eating out, no entertaining, no buying clothes, lots of hot dogs, and plenty of sewing for myself."

Within a year, Chris had her house after putting down five thousand of her hard-earned dollars. Wow! "But bankruptcy?" I asked.

She shook her head ruefully. "Can you believe that? I so desperately wanted to save that marriage?" The younger Chris didn't put up a fight, allowing her irresponsible freeloader husband to lose her house, then claim her car, all bought with money she had earned. Here was a woman earning over forty thousand dollars as a management budget analyst for a rural Florida county, who had allowed herself to be run into the ground. Kyle had been an addiction for Chris; the money problems were only the outer symptom of a cancer eroding their union.

After months of bank negotiations, Chris failed to win back her dream house and Kyle succeeded in taking her down with him.

"Finally, sanity! I packed up and walked out with a few boxes and a bed. I still hear his screaming, loud enough for everyone on the block to hear, 'I want the car!' I shrieked back, 'Take it! But leave me alone!'"

Chris had lost a marriage, a home, and a car. In American culture, that spells ruin. Soon she stood at the threshold of another chance: another marriage. This would be her third. She described this new man in glowing terms: "He saw in me what I couldn't see in myself." A psychologist, musician, and model of goodness and generosity, Ben breathed new life into Chris.

"He keeps reminding me that life is good," she said. A beautiful message coming from a man who lives in a wheelchair and had done so all his life. Chris said that at age fourteen, Ben flew to Lourdes in pursuit of a miracle. He told her that he had wheeled himself into the waters, but nothing had happened. At first he had feared that his faith had failed him. But later, he realized that what had healed was his rage at God.

At the time of her first date with Ben, Chris had experienced a return to personhood, self-discovery, and professional achievement. Clothes, a nice car, and the fun of dining in fine restaurants had all been restored. Now she was prepared to give all to another man. And she's never been happier! I asked Chris why she chose to give all that up. It seemed to me that she could enjoy both: Ben *and* a rewarding job. "Adele, it felt more valuable to our marriage that I devote time as Ben's personal assistant."

> ***Yes I pray for money, but God never answers me on my terms but rather on His.***
>
> ***—Pat G.***

Now, no longer a nine-to-fiver herself, Chris has built her life on Ben's sacred earning ground, as a thriving therapist with many clients. "Ben puts the food on our table; he prints a weekly update of our current finances and puts it on my desk. It's all there, every penny accounted for. If I need spending money, out pops a check."

Chris had worked hard to be successful, fallen hard on dark times, bounced back, and now lived a life of total abundance. Both the men and the money in her life had sorted themselves out. These days money is merely an auxiliary issue that surfaces from time to time. Her eyes were bright as she said, "I know others think I struggle with Ben's disability and can't help but notice that I have to feed him, dress him, drive him to work. But given our love, that's a blessing compared to the horror of living with a sociopath who always promised to pay the bills and never did, always lying through his teeth."

Chris chuckled. She stood and stretched, brushing off the crumbs from her plaid shorts. "Ben mailed me a cartoon before we were married. A kid asks her grandmother: 'You married Grandpa, and you're six feet four, and he's only five feet tall. Doesn't it bother you that he was short?' Grandma replies, 'Well, when I met Grandpa, we were sitting down; by the time we stood up, it was too late!'"

We both laughed heartily as we gathered our bags and made our way to her car, chatting. "Dear God," I prayed aloud to the blue sky, "thanks for the day that Chris walked into our classroom, when Jim and I taught *The Artist's Way* class at Rollins College." She laughed, then stopped suddenly. Her eyes met mine.

"Thanks for allowing me to tell my money story at that first workshop. I'll never stew on my bankruptcy the same way." Sunlight slanted through slender pines. I couldn't help but think how nature is always working to achieve health and balance. This resurrected woman was a shining example of wholeness.

Maria: *A Light in the Dark*

Maria was very different from Chris and yet somehow similar. Nails of childhood poverty had fastened Maria to a lifetime cross of financial woes. Working in the fields, picking tomatoes for market, brought little emotional or physical reward in her childhood. Young Maria had no way of knowing about rewards for hard work. She was a victim of poverty, but didn't realize it. It was only a light in the dark times that spurred her toward a different way.

I met pixie-faced Maria when she and her husband joined my choir. Her full soprano voice belied her tiny frame. Her rendition of the hymn *I Have Called You My Friend* carried the musical conviction of Bette Midler. "Music is my salvation," she'd explain. "When I was a kid, I'd go off by myself and belt it out to God in the backyard."

I finally got Maria to talk about money. At my house, I fluffed the pillows on the couch and asked her to sit down. "Do I really have to talk about money?" She sounded like a child.

I laughed, "No, we can sing, if you'd like that better."

She grew serious. "I don't tell this story to many, maybe it's shame, maybe it's a lack of my faith. We were poorer than anybody. As a kid, there was always pressure. We had to pick everything during a short month's harvest, and that income had to last to the next April. My brothers and sisters never finished school because my father pulled them out. It didn't matter because we all felt desperate and lost in a classroom."

Maria's father was a drunkard. He hated work and got out of it whenever he could. "About the only work Dad did was squeeze the last drop from a bottle," she said with lowered eyes.

Money makes me angry. I don't know how it works. And I don't know how to produce it in large quantities.
—Louise M.

"Mom suffered the most. On wash days you'd see her, red eyed and drawn, wrestling water-filled clothes through the old wringer washer. My father wouldn't buy her a washing machine." Maria's father believed that buying on credit would destroy the family and the very suggestion would throw him into a tantrum.

"You sound like you almost believe it yourself," I said.

"I still hate using my Visa, and I won't unless I have to," she confessed. Maria was adamant about keeping her wants in check so she could avoid using her credit card. *After all these years, the ghost of her father still haunted her!*

Like her dad's alcohol, poverty's shame was another secret in Maria's household. Maria cries about it now, but as a girl she never let her friends know how bad things were. To this day Maria has yet to confide to her own children how desperately poor she was as a child.

"We lived near the truck farms in a New Jersey row house. When I was fifteen, I got a job in the city. Sure, I got out of the house for a while, but then, I had to pay Dad twenty-five dollars a month for my room and board. On paydays, no sooner would I walk in the front door than he'd eye me, demanding, 'Where's the money?'" Maria's hard-earned money went, unfortunately, for her father's booze. Slowly, over the years, Maria extricated herself from his grasp.

Maria shared one beautiful memory. "In my sixteenth year, Mother gave me a whole new sense of dignity by secretly planning the most wonderful birthday celebration of my life, maybe even to this day. She baked an Italian cream cake and invited the entire neighborhood while Dad was out. When they shouted 'Happy Birthday!' I cried all over my makeup and so did Mama. I was queen for the night, and the stars sang along with me. In the morning, of course, was Dad's familiar bellow, 'You spent money on her! How dare you!' My mother's black eyes flashed. 'Ignore him!'"

Maria looked regretful. "You can see that with all that fighting and poverty and money talk, I never felt ready for marriage. Who could I trust? There were lots of guys, but I couldn't trust any of them."

When she was thirty-three, a beautiful man walked into Maria's life. Ned was a former book publisher and is now a corporate executive with a thriving company. Marriage brought not only love, but a sense of security that Maria had never known by way of a six-figure paycheck. Yet Maria confessed that even so, scars of "never enough" hobbled her somewhere deep inside and prevented her from being totally free of worry.

"I'd go out shopping, buy my kids underwear, not two or three, but a dozen pairs at a time. I felt compelled to keep their underwear drawers filled. They'd look at me as if I were a kook. But for me, Christmas had meant only three panties in a box. That was it!" Maria rubbed her neck, looking a bit sheepish. "I made damn sure that my kids had more than they knew what to do with." She knew she was over the top and didn't care. Panties and bras and stockings and shoes, and plenty of them, paid tribute to her new status.

"Imagine! We had a maid." Maria sat up straight. "Then we added a two-story glass den that overlooked the golf course. We took fabulous vacations. At times, I'd feel how Cinderella must have felt."

Blessed abundance should have been the final page of this woman's fairy tale. But it was not. God has a way of reminding us of certain old truths in our journey toward Him. Ned was abruptly laid off, given only a few weeks' notice. The event triggered Maria's worst nightmare. "Ned went on to lose one job after another. I was absolutely dislocated: nightmares, hives, severe depression, all my childhood anxieties bubbled up. I considered taking medication."

We fell into silence. Maria twisted her rings. As Ned furiously answered ads, made phone calls, and rewrote résumés, Maria became more and more quiet. She turned inward and attended daily Mass. Whether she felt like going or not, she was there. After communion she would silently scream at God, "Listen! Haven't I been poor long enough? Am I supposed to lose it all? Again?"

And then one day, a glimmer of hope. It was a summer day, and Maria was dusting her beloved grand piano. A line from the twenty-third psalm flew across her mind: "He revives my drooping spirit." Maria beamed at the memory. "That next morning at Mass, God took me by the hand, and like a child, led me to the altar. I knelt for the longest time of my life. I heard something like: 'Look, saints always feel the nails. Why should you be any different?'" From that day on, day by day, Mass by Mass, Maria was awakened to a new and blessed reality.

"Wealth is in the here and now! It lies in whatever is at my fingertips." She held up a pink nail and wiggled it. "I finally got it!" She had begun to keep a journal daily, recording her gratitude at being alive, being healthy, having a loving husband, talented kids, and a beautiful piano. Tomorrow? It would always hold its own surprises, and she stopped thinking about it.

"Just look at me! My kids are in college, I've got a part-time job I love, Ned has kept himself employed, even if not yet steadily. I *do* feel the good times."

"*Bravissimo,* Maria, to all parts of your journey."

Jenny: *A Poverty Vaccine*

Jenny's story is the most stirring of the rags-to-riches sagas I've heard. She took incredible strides to get out of poverty, never losing her faith in God. She deserves a standing ovation.

When we first met, Jenny's aura signaled something deep and firm to me. I couldn't get enough of her. She had learned lessons, had a kind of wisdom that I, as a student, wanted for myself. We'd meet for lunch—my treat—and then for dinner, my treat again because Jenny was always broke. She didn't carry a purse. "No money!" she shrugged. But those lunches and dinners were a wise investment. We talked about God, in fact we called it "God Talk," and our dialogues fed my soul. Jenny was steeped in the wisdom of a recovering addict. What she heard at weekly AA meetings would enrich anyone's life. Often I'd push my chair back and rise from the table replete with Jenny's simple, fascinating, one-day-at-a-time approach to life.

Jenny was in therapy, where she plunged into a past so dreadful I could not imagine how she could face it. Now I listened to her history of those dark, childhood days. She was one of six children in an Irish Catholic family. Her father, once a successful writer, was chronically underemployed; her mother struggled to stay afloat; and two of the children were disabled. Jenny played mother to the whole brood during her teenage years, and she began drinking seriously at twenty. Following soon were the drugs.

"We rarely had milk. Groceries were luxuries. It wasn't unusual that we sat at a foodless table, without my father. We sat as if we were dead. In a way, we were."

I sit back, amazed. How did they survive? Jenny recalled her mother charging groceries at a little market down the street. She would send Jenny and a younger sister. "Mr. Black would put together a few cans for us. I knew that my sister wanted that chocolate bar, but she just stared. Sometimes Mr. Black just sacked up some bread and peanut butter. The sack he put into my arms always felt so heavy. It felt like a boulder of shame and embarrassment. I never looked directly at him, and he didn't check out our bare feet or shabby clothes either."

In Jenny's family, money didn't exist, not even in conversation. You didn't talk about money in her house, though you sometimes yelled about it. "My father didn't have a clue how to support his six kids. So you could say that I was programmed early on to do without, to consider myself a waif and never expect life to be different."

Jenny remembered a horrific scene when her father had finally found a newspaper job and "borrowed" from his office's petty cash to feed the family. "He expected my mother to have the money to pay it back so no one would know. When she didn't have it, he beat her up and ran yelling and screaming through the house." Jenny stopped for a moment. Her eyes fixed on something far away.

"That beating did it for me. It taught me how to feel about money."

Someone once said that when home is unbearable, a child mentally leaves; memories freeze and events blur. But during Jenny's extended vacancy, one loving incident does come to life. It happened before a high school bus trip to Jacksonville, when without proper clothes and little money for food, Jenny knew that she wouldn't be going. Facing his daughter's shame at last, her dad stood at the bottom of the stairs and offered his help. "'This is all I have,' he said, stuffing a ten dollar bill in my hand. It was one of the only times I ever received money from my father. I held the bill as if it were some precious jewel. Even now, there's something about a ten dollar bill that stops me in my tracks."

According to Jenny, her family never had a moment of prosperity. Other families in her small hometown went through bad and good times. "My family knew bad times only, so at twenty, I ran off to marry, mostly because my mother wanted me to. It lasted about five minutes. The only good, and I'm not exaggerating, was my divorce settlement. More money than I'd ever seen in my total life: one thousand dollars in bills. I sat at the edge of the bed and counted and recounted them. My mother watched with a strange look on her face. 'I'm rich, mother,' I announced." Jenny hid the money under a mattress.

"Living with the family after the divorce was a mistake." One day, on a whim, she checked on the hidden cash. "I pulled up that mattress and ran my fingers from corner to corner. The money had vanished, every single dollar. Prosperity vanished with it. I braced myself in utter disbelief. My own mother had stolen that money from me."

Jenny's mother's had only done what any mother does when her children are hungry; she had stolen to feed them. But for Jenny, there was no safety in that house after that day. Besides, in the bigger picture, that robbery represented how money fared in her household—it was stolen, or forgotten, or treated as a silent demon that breathed its foul breath over every decision, poisoning Jenny's childhood and following her into adult life.

Jenny's drinking increased steadily, the pressures of the broken marriage, the miserable family, and her depressed mother completely overwhelming her. "There was no escape. I did what my father did. I just drank until I couldn't take another drop. I had lost all hope.

"Creditors harassed my family, and I could never understand why none of my mother's wealthy relatives came to help us out."

With so much grief and hard luck around, Jenny fell easily into her family's patterns, behaving like a criminal by the time she was an adult. "I'd steal too. I never opened a checking account, never bought insurance, even car insurance, and pooh-poohed using any credit. I refused to take on any responsibility."

Jenny described being hospitalized after taking drugs. She considered taking her own life. She weighed less than ninety-five pounds and looked like a prisoner of war. "One day in the hospital, a caring nurse handed me a mirror. 'Look at yourself,' she said. 'See how very angry you are.' I held that mirror a long while, like a meditation, getting a glimpse of the reality I had created for myself. It was, of course, a wake-up call. When death and life met me there in that reflection, something holy was yanking me back."

If you ask me, money is boring.

—Meg B.

Rabbi Harold Kushner, in his bestseller, *When Bad Things Happen to Good People,* had people like Jenny in mind. She had got off to a rotten start with poverty, drugs, and alcohol, ending in a slow suicide attempt. Things couldn't get much worse. After her wake-up call in the hospital, Jenny felt something was mysteriously alive and possible in her and went looking for professional help. Entering a 12-step program, she began to pick up the broken pieces of her life. Over the years, she not only got back on her feet, but she succeeded in finding her niche. She had inherited her father's journalistic talent—writing. She took her gift seriously and blossomed into a formidable writer and editor who went on to win statewide recognition for her work.

As she progressed, her relationship with money slowly healed. An important step in selling her work was learning how to seek compensatory fees. That was tough. Yet interpreting the twelve steps was clear to Jenny: "Don't sell yourself short! Don't allow clients to walk out without paying you what you deserve."

How had she afforded her weekly therapy fee in the beginning, I wondered? Jenny was inventive. Once, she invited her therapist to hold group sessions in her apartment to waive her fees. With her next therapist, she offered her editing skills and designed a brochure. Sometimes scrimping meant eating breakfast cereal or a peanut butter sandwich for dinner. We joked that it was truly a breakfast of champions; yet her firm commitment to healing was clearly no joke.

Jenny described her next major breakthrough: "I took charge of my painful past. I assumed all responsibility for my once-suppressed crimes by filling my journal pages with stories of self-abuse and betrayals, acts performed under the influence, sneaky times of charging items knowing that I'd never pay them back, and even times of appropriating money from friends. For cigarettes, I once stole from my handicapped sister's welfare allowance." Imposing a brutal thoroughness on herself was like pouring the waters of baptism over herself, Jenny said.

Eventually, her emotional life began to blossom. She felt good again. Talk about a resurrection! Tracking her savings and expenditures became so comfortable that she once led a group of women on this very topic herself. She told the class, "Because I've been in the place where basic survival needs couldn't be met, I discovered a kind of immunity to insecurity, a vaccination of sorts that comes from that place. I call it a blessing of detachment, keeping myself utterly dependent on God."

Jenny said, "When you go down that far into any kind of death, you learn that something inside is waiting to be born. Something beautiful, and sacred, and more real than anything you'd known." Therapy uncovered that beauty for Jenny. For all her self-inflicted wounds, Jenny emerged a beautiful soul.

During the painful purging process of writing down all her transgressions, Jenny recognized something everyone must before finally welcoming abundance. "A Volvo wasn't going to appear in my driveway. I had to interiorly prepare the nest for abundance, practice daily the mental shifts required for change."

"Give your journal to a 'good human being,'" Jenny's counselor had advised. "Let them read your soul, and then you'll be ready for the big part of your journey . . . forgiveness of *yourself.*"

Jenny wrote the final instruction to herself in red ink: "When I'm in a state of grace, I'm not under karmic law, and therefore, I don't have to do anything more to relieve my soul. I don't have to find those whom I robbed to ask forgiveness. I don't have to pay back those whom I deceived."

"You mean I can get off scot-free?" she asked her therapist with disbelief. But there it was.

"With God you *are* scot-free."

Jenny's abundance grew. She met and married an attorney, and together they purchased a fine four-bedroom home. Out of that home, Jenny directs and counsels other young writers.

The last time that Jenny and I met was at a small Middle Eastern family restaurant. I asked her again about resurrection.

"Well, let me treat this time," she answered.

Deborah: *Blowing a Fortune*

"Let me tell you how my fortune disappeared, how it just slipped through my fingers like water. Five hundred thousand dollars evaporated in just a few years." Deborah, knowing that I'd inherited a similar amount, pointed to me and exclaimed, "Don't you follow in my footsteps!"

Her journey began in London in the early forties. "Dad had made a fortune, but just as quickly, he lost it, plunging himself and us into bankruptcy. Oh, what gloom he spilled over onto everything; I mean everything. When I was eight years old, he put me to work steaming the stamps off envelopes to save money. I tried to pry them loose and burned a few. It was as if I'd burned the house.

"In a few years, Dad was back to making plenty of money and enjoying the prestige of arranging finances for our synagogue. A war hero, he also used his money to rescue Jewish refugees, and so was a bulwark of the Jewish community in London. In many ways I had a dad I could be proud of."

Deborah and I were headed for Daytona Beach. It was a blessed day, the sun high and beaming. "Dad's a good place to start."

She pitched her bag onto the backseat as she said, "Dad's energy was always locked into making money, whether rolling in it or bemoaning its loss. His distress and irascibility cramped our whole household. When a client rang the doorbell, we were swiftly ushered out of sight as if we didn't exist. I hated it." Deborah talked on while we sped to the beach.

The Atlantic was beautiful as always, giant waves pounding the beach, seagulls playing on the bouncing surf. Our feet crunched over sand to a perfect spot. Strangely, this Tuesday we had the beach to ourselves. I pulled a couple of orange drinks out of the cooler and after two long swigs, Deborah began again in her clipped English.

"As a teenager, I hated money. Maybe that hatred flowed from Dad's love of money. Whatever the case, I found myself identifying more with my nanny and

> ***We produce goods and services, then buy goods and services using the medium we call money. We idolize this medium.***
> ***—Dorothy P.***

other house servants and street vendors than those considered my peers. I questioned my identity as a rich daughter. Could those people like me just for me? Could I ever fit into an ordinary world?"

I felt deeply connected to Deborah. "Hey, Deborah," I touched her arm, "you're echoing my own doubts after I got the inheritance! I wondered whether the money would separate me from everybody I knew and loved."

She nodded and went on. "Thinking I could get a better handle on what I really was feeling, I enrolled in a psychology course, the first time I surrounded myself with ordinary working men and women.

"One young guy questioned my work-free lifestyle one day after class in the pub. I lied and told him I had a bit of savings. A few beers later, I blurted the truth. Honestly, I felt as if he'd knocked me down because he stood up and waved a frothy mug in my face, signaling to everyone. 'Here, here!' The group grew quiet. 'We have with us a Rich Bitch!'"

Soon after, Deborah took off for America, hoping to leave class division behind. She felt pure joy in America, hobnobbing with anybody and everybody, eating hamburgers, and waiting at bus stops. In Los Angeles, the rich and famous drove little Beetles. Amazed, she couldn't tell who had what. To an observer, she fit right in.

"Then Steve came along, a simple carpenter. I loved his long hair, suspenders, and easy manners, his playful blue eyes. I fell for him immediately." She took a deep breath. "That fall spelled the beginning of good-bye to my father's inheritance."

After their marriage, Deborah's money paid for their home. She signed the title in both their names. Slowly, somehow, whether she willingly gave him control or he wrested it from her, he took charge of the money and played the stock market with her assets. In a wild escapade that lasted only a few years, her half-million dollar bank account vanished completely.

"How could you let that happen?" I cried out loud, grabbing a handful of sand and heaving it hard behind me.

"Don't be so quick to judge," she fired back. "You can be sure that I carry enormous shame about it.

"Let me tell you something about those years with Steve. This man taught me something much more valuable than holding on to money, something my parents had never grasped. It was about simple things. With Steve, I could "waste" time. I could wear plain clothes, go to movies and sit in the middle, eat hot dogs, and take in county fairs and ride roller coasters. Steve taught me to laugh, to live in the freedom of the ordinary."

She giggled like a kid after that litany. I sat back in awe. Deborah had received the commonplace as a gift. Experiences that were uneventful to us were extraordinary events to her.

She added, "For the record, I didn't *like* losing the money. I still wonder at that part of my past. Maybe how we think about ourselves is connected to how much or how little money events have shaped our lives, don't you think?"

To her infinite credit, given her financial tragedy and despite her ingrained view that money creates separation, Deborah's inner journey had little to do with money—it was to find her real self. Yet, I wondered later, whether finding herself had everything to do with money. Didn't Deborah's issues with wealth direct her path?

Molly: *The Sting of Bankruptcy*

Molly is the unfortunate victim of Depression Era parents who hated to spend a dime if they didn't have to. Money in this family was less the *cause* of than a handy *target* for a family's distress. Regardless, Molly felt insecure from her earliest days. "No, no, no! We can't afford it!" was the background noise against which every situation was gauged. Every family decision no matter how small passed through this daunting filter, a barrier that shortchanged Molly's ability to think about money.

When I mentioned wanting to talk to her about her history with money, Molly looked astonished. "*Money* talk? Are you kidding?" I wrote her off. Her particular tale of financial woe would have added immeasurably to my collection, but she wouldn't be budged. You can imagine my surprise one winter afternoon when the phone rang. "I'm in the neighborhood and ready to talk to you. Are you busy?" Delighted and apprehensive, I lit my interview candle and grabbed my tape recorder.

Molly, pink faced, appeared at the door, bundled against an unusually bitter blast of mid-winter cold. Her eyes avoided mine. I took her coat, noticing that she trembled. I offered hot tea and settled her in front of the fire. The room was cheery, firelight dancing on the walls mocking the gray overcast outside. Molly jumped up and paced in front of the hearth. I tried to appear calm and pulled my cat onto my lap.

"Bear with me," she said, her voice uncharacteristically tight. The first anecdote began. "I thought we were always so poor. So I tried an experiment when I grew up, like a jump-start out of my 'poor me' self, and hired a personal shopper. It was a crazy kind of luxury, but I thought that maybe I could shock myself, like a sort of money lobotomy," she laughed. "I didn't tell anyone.

"Emma Newburn got thirty dollars an hour to jazz up my image. *Thirty dollars an hour!* But Emma did her thing and yanked me into Bloomingdales and Bergdorf Goodman's, a far cry from my usual bargain basements. I followed like a kid forced into a dentist's chair. Through the labyrinth of sweet-smelling, gold-dripping displays and racks of elegant gowns, I tried desperately to absorb some of this woman's sense for posh. My stomach took a dive at the price tags: three hundred dollars for a jumpsuit and two hundred dollars for shoes! Emma was teaching me all right; she was teaching me that I didn't belong there!"

As it turned out, that leap into luxury was too far for Molly; you can't go from Kmart to Saks before walking through Sears. At the time, Molly was still dropping pennies into her piggy bank. Emma ignored that and just kept on pushing, insisting next on streamlining Molly's closet. Friction grew between the two women. "Get rid of these Molly," Emma instructed her, holding up various items. "I must have been drugged to hire this woman," Molly growled. "As soon as I got her out of the apartment, I headed for the Advil."

Molly's parents had taught her to be stingy with money. "We bought the poorest meat cuts and wore new clothes only after old ones ragged out. I heard it in my sleep, 'Don't waste food! Buy the cheapest gas. Save everything.'" Molly never knew what an allowance was. No tooth fairy surprises appeared under her pillow. There were no extras of any kind. And how could she forget her eighteenth birthday, alone in New York, when she dared to call home collect. Her parents refused the call.

Molly was warming up to her subject. "Here's the really bad part. Shortly after I settled in Orlando, I was run into by a hit-and-run driver who totaled my new Toyota. The guy never paid a penny for his crime. Medical bills flew at me like a jet stream. I had no insurance. I needed physical therapy, but how to manage that without coverage? My recovery was solely up to me. I just couldn't do it." Molly's voice rose. "No money, no car, and no boss to count on. I lost my new job.

In a few weeks, my savings dried up. It was the end. I had to declare bankruptcy."

By now Molly's story had escalated into an uninterrupted howl. And money was to blame. But was it? Something else was in motion here, something deeper than this dreary account of losses. What about her parents and their unresolved issues? Was Molly reflecting their despair? Aside from what she received from them, or didn't, what responsibility did Molly bear for her succession of disasters? Could she afford to write it all off to bad luck, that's that?

"Molly, was the problem really money?" I asked. She watched the burning logs. Finally, she mused in a whisper, "I always thought so. What else could it be? The *bankruptcy* was real!" She took a long swig from her cup.

"Tell me about that, Molly."

"I signed away my dignity. Sure, it saved me from my creditors, but then it followed me, constantly gnawing at me. I was so ashamed. I couldn't let anyone know, not my friends, certainly not my family. I didn't have a credit card so I blew my secret every time I laid bills and coins on the counter." I wasn't sure why St. Paul's terse confession came to mind just then, but it did: "I do, not the good that I would, but the evil I would not." How often I'd felt the weight of that experience. Our choices end up attacking us, and we often cannot fathom why.

"Bankruptcy means giving up, taking the easy way out," she said, looking ashamed.

"But wasn't it easier after that?"

"Noooo! The bills didn't stop. I worked a bunch of jobs, did the Kelly girl routine. I delivered phone books by night, worked as a convenience store clerk. Life sucked!" She turned to me, her eyes flashing. "I'm a journalist, not a store clerk!

"I want you to know how I survived," she said. I perked up. She declared, "It was my Buddhism that saved me."

I sat back and stretched my feet to the hearth. Molly had finally taken her pain to a place where it eventually could make sense, the place most of us go when the tears won't stop. I asked about her conversion to the Buddhist way of life.

> ***Money is a metaphysical relationship. It can buy trouble or buy security. Attitude is the key.***
> ***—Virginia A.***

"Well, it paved the way to finding Josh," she laughed. Josh and Molly had been married for six months, the first time for both and neither had ever known such deep closeness. Three months after their marriage, Molly had grabbed the initiative and quit all her menial jobs. Her husband's generous income freed her to write. Today Molly and Josh live comfortably in northwest Daytona Beach.

"Look," she said, holding her open purse toward me. "I've got dollars and cents inside! And not one creditor hounding me."

No amount of management or frantic effort can make something work that wasn't meant to. Without a doubt, personal bankruptcy *is* devastating. Yet there is a good in bankruptcy: it *can* bring relief from long-term stress, and it sets the stage for opportunity. It can't be said often enough that bankruptcy may be the necessary surrender before that prayed-for breakthrough.

And what a breakthrough for Molly. A few months later, I ran into her at a bookstore, stuffing her new monthly business newsletter into a mail slot in the front of the store. Her newsletter is a mouthpiece for the spirit of wholeness now sweeping corporate life. This was the premiere issue, and Molly is the founding editor. I marveled at the change in her, she looked directly at me, her voice was sure. She grinned. "The pity party's over."

.....

How many times, after a desperate winter, have I given up on a bloom or been ready to pull up a withered stalk. It was dead, damn it. And then, on a warm day, I would see a bit of green looking up at me.

Oh God, You are the eternal gardener of souls. You coax us daily to live more fantastically than we ever imagined possible. Help us accept that sometimes something must die before we can reap our harvest.

Chapter Six

Sharing the Bounty—Couples

No matter how deep our love and no matter how the world might have viewed my marriage to Jim in a mature light, money easily could have shattered our new union. As a newlywed, I was utterly naive about how money can shake the foundations of the best relationship. When a married friend picked up clues that I might be headed for disaster, she invited me for a private dinner. That night, a crack formed in the thick wall of denial I had constructed around my relationship with money, my husband, and God.

Mary and I met at our favorite Chinese restaurant. Over egg rolls and white wine, Mary got right to the point: "The best advice I can throw your way, Adele, is to be prepared for just about anything. You and Jim carry explosive differences. I mean, you married a man off the street, and you've never been married yourself. Plus you've got the money."

Mary was enjoying a happy ten-year marriage, her second go-round, and I listened closely. I had felt increasingly concerned about Jim's and my money quarrels. The negativity threatened us, escalating to periods of sullen silence, and I was at a loss as to what to do. I felt a bit strange talking about my new husband, whom I loved dearly, but Mary didn't blink an eye. It was obvious that my friend wasn't going to choose sides, and when I complained about Jim's lavish spending, she looked at me evenly.

"The purchases Jim considers important might freak you out. I know; it happens to me. Jules came home a few weeks ago with some outrageous contraption, raving that it was the greatest invention since the wheel and that we needed it, though it cost a fortune! I tried to keep my eyes in their sockets and not allow my tongue to lash out, but my stomach took a spin."

We lifted our wineglasses and laughed. Mary frowned and played with her napkin. "I know that Jules and I will always stumble over money issues because, as I see it, money plays close, very close, to our cognitive and emotional lives, and there just isn't any end to that."

"You mean I'm going to have to learn to live with some of this?" I asked incredulously. I couldn't imagine dropping my righteous stance about my husband's "bad" habits.

"I mean just that," she said. "And you need to learn some things about yourself. This money thing isn't just about Jim. It's about you, too."

Our talk unmasked issue after issue—which I had never named aloud—pertaining to money. I confessed to Mary that, even before our marriage, Jim and I had a blowup that took us into the ring: his love of music versus my bank account. He delighted in paging through music catalogues, one after another, ordering CDs to his heart's content and charging them on my card. It was as though he couldn't fill his thirst for music: New Age bongo drums, orchestrated classics, ballet suites, you name it. We were stacking up enough CDs, it seemed, to last us the rest of our listening lives. My tongue formed a welt from my biting it each time a new CD arrived in our mailbox. After a while, I couldn't even look, I told Mary, covering my eyes for emphasis.

"I lifted my eyes to heaven and pleaded, 'Is this worth a fight?' Eventually, blessed relief did come; Jim simply stopped ordering them. Maybe he had enough CDs for a while. Or maybe he read my face. The lesson was clear: pick my battles well because, if we stay alert, and with a little grace—maybe a lot of grace—some issues, especially money ones, can simply go away, vanishing like mist."

"Well, that's a good start, Adele," Mary laughed, "but I want to assure you, most money issues don't 'vanish like mist,' despite all the grace of the moment."

That night, I couldn't shake my friend's warnings. Her words whirled through my head as I lay wide awake by my sleeping husband, considering our diverse taste, habits, and temperaments.

Soon after that dinner, I saw clearly that Jim and I needed help. Try as we might to ignore them, the money struggles kept popping up. While one was being resolved, another was brewing just behind it. First there was the Colorado trip out to the Thomas Merton conference. My

Cadillac, unaccustomed to mountain climbing or pulling a pop-up tent was unhappy at being dragged over dirt and rocky roads. I complained to my "know better" husband, who answered, "Relax. This car is a big six cylinder." I shut up. *Adele, you're too attached to this car. Maybe, but what about the repair bills waiting when we got home?* Sure it was a money issue, but more than that, this sedan had befriended me, had exemplified one earlier breakthrough: God had no problem with my driving a Cadillac. So you can imagine my tears later at the mechanic's directive: "Get rid of this car. There is nothing I can do." Jim felt awful. I felt murderous. It was a death in my family. I'd had "Carlisle" for more than eight years.

Then another long-term relationship had to be dealt with: the backyard botanical garden. It was *my* enchanted plot. Jim, thinking teamwork, completely reorganized my arranged green grouping. *Dear God, those are my plants.* When his shears mercilessly pruned the azaleas, I was surprised at the sharpness of my tone. This time, he came back, "What am I, just your beast of burden out here? Don't you want me to think?" Honestly, I didn't know what I wanted. Surely I didn't want a slave to just follow me around and do as I directed. Or did I?

We reached an angry silence when he, unaccustomed to the ways of Florida citrus, harvested all the navel oranges off the tree at once, even breaking some of the branches. I blew my cool. "Jim, oranges stay on the tree until we're ready to eat them. Now I'll have to juice all of them and freeze them." I wanted to cry. It was not a money issue, but it felt like one. And so, we had entered the trickiest and perhaps most wonderful part of partnering: speaking up, standing up for oneself, testing each other's dogmas, and, of course, praying the rough edges would smooth out. But how long would it take?

Prayer is good, but so is useful dialogue. I asked my friend Rachel, a marriage therapist, to meet me for coffee at a local bistro. It was a sunny, cool afternoon when I spotted her tall figure walking briskly toward me from across the street. We found a table in the back of the restaurant.

"And what, my friend, can I help you with?" she smiled generously. We had ordered, and she settled back in her chair.

"Rachel, sometimes I think God steps aside when couples plunge into marriage and decrees: 'You're on your own, kids.'" She laughed. I went on. "Tell me how couples do money, what gets them into trouble or even into divorce," I blurted. Jim and I had just fought over cutting down the ancient laurel tree outside our bedroom window. Sure, it would grant the garden more sun, which he considered a priority. But I balked at the eight or nine hundred dollars for a tree surgeon.

Rachel smiled again. "And so you and Jim went toe to toe over the tree," she summarized.

An articulate and brilliant woman, Rachel warmed to the subject, plunging to the heart of it while I took notes and sipped tea. "Divorce isn't about money at all, Adele. Never was! It's just an excuse for not getting intimate, for not looking at the interior life, or the lack of one. I get distressed at how young newlyweds drag their unresolved emotional issues to the altar. Until they address them, get real, something's sure to go amiss beyond their garden of romantic delicacies." She sipped her coffee thoughtfully. "Count on it! Money's the hairy scapegoat posing as the feared mortgage or car payment or the accumulated Visa debt. I'm seeing a couple right now. He bought a boat without any discussion. He wanted it because as a kid he didn't get what he wanted, and he thought that he was entitled. She didn't want the boat because as a kid she got everything she wanted and felt freer about having and not having things. Each was convinced their argument was about the boat, and, of course, it never was." Rachel smoothed her bright multigreen scarf, running her fingers down its length as if noticing the colors for the first time. I was fascinated yet disturbed by her words.

"So what you're telling me is, when Jim and I fight about money, we're just creating obstacles that keep us from getting close?" I stared at her.

"Yes," she smiled. "That's exactly what I'm saying."

We chatted a bit more and then paid the bill. I felt distracted. Given all the strikes against me, a real marriage with a real soul mate was looking like it could last only one short inning! My mind whirled as I bade Rachel good-bye.

I scrambled to understand. Let go of judgments! What judgments? I was right about Jim's irresponsible spending! Yet, as the day wore on, a persistent, small voice whispered, "Jim will decide who he is and how he should save or spend the money too!" That night I had no illusions that I would never again bite my tongue, but maybe it didn't have to be so often. As I saw it, that part was up to me. The transformation that I was about to undergo regarding money probably saved my marriage. Together we faced some painful moments, the price that had to be paid for the gift of intimacy. Like all couples, we had to learn how to cook together, eat at one table, garden as a team, pay the bills, bank the money—the "fundamentals of newlywed suffering," as one friend called it. And like many couples, we came into the marriage with unequal funds. In this case I had all the money, and Jim had none.

We can laugh now at some of our early squabbling, some of which had to do with money, some didn't. "Let's give up meat," Jim suggested one night after I had served up one delicious porterhouse. But here again we found ourselves on opposite sides.

"Listen," I came back, "how can I serve a traditional Arabic meal without meat?" That was followed next week by a shattering quiet surrounding the discovery of a check Jim had bounced. He was mortified. I search to find the words for my reaction.

In the first days of our marriage I had thought carefully about how to share the inheritance. Should I gather all accounts under both names? Would that be an expression of generous sharing? It was for me a huge decision. I consulted my beloved stockbroker, Bob, who reminded me of women he'd seen turn over their accounts only to watch the bulk of them disappear. That confirmed my worst nightmare. What's more, if, in any way, Jim depleted my nest egg, I could only blame myself. I felt the force of prayer led me to keep the boundary. To my surprise, Jim agreed without any fuss.

We established a separate account at another bank where each month I deposited a given sum that Jim used for whatever expenses arose. For the first time in a long time, my husband had his own checkbook. Within the year he did what I consider the unthinkable! He bounced a check.

As bad as not having enough money in the bank to cover expenses can be, I discovered something worse: spending with no regard to an object's value. On a shopping spree in a Deland bookstore, Jim casually laid a beautifully bound antique book on the checkout counter then wandered to the back of the store. I picked up the aged collection of poems. The tag read seventy dollars. *Seventy dollars for a bunch of poems?* I felt sick; my partner hadn't even thought to consider the price! I said nothing, and forked over "our" Visa while Jim continued to browse. I tried to hide how horrified I was, but the pressure kept building. Finally, on the ride home, I let loose and filled Jim's ears with my diatribe. He listened patiently right up to our driveway. I parked and he got out. He leaned over and solemnly declared, as if his life depended on it, "Honey, I promise, I'll never buy anything again without first checking the price." That promise was exactly what I needed to hear. And he was as good as his word.

The first time we checked into a hotel, in Las Vegas, I didn't know my role. Was I supposed to stand back and let him do all the negotiating at the front desk? What did he know of good rates? He was just off the streets. And besides, it was my money. All that chatter and hubris inside me created incredible anxiety. As it happened, Jim was in a very different place. "I may be off the streets, but I did have a life before you. I don't need a wife to be meddling in something that I'm confident with." We now laugh at how bellboys stood back as we heaved verbal grenades at one another.

Eventually, I dropped the confrontational, mean-spirited approach, but it didn't happen overnight. When Jim, feeding a developing photography hobby, dumped dozens of rolls of Kodak film into our grocery basket one day, I didn't flinch. I sensed no problem, just dozens of photos to look forward to. But I was horrified to discover that he was trashing upwards of 80 percent of the developed pictures. I felt rage. Hurt and depressed, I retreated to the greenhouse and poured water over every desolate leaf, muttering affirmations I couldn't mean: *I will change. I will be better about this. I will change. I will be better.* But I am learning that the kind of will required in marriage is a constant good will, and lots of it. Jim's behavior has been a testing ground for me. Later, I relaxed when I learned that photographers routinely shoot hundreds of pictures to get one prized image. That's the price of this particular artistic endeavor.

The gender issue raised its ugly head as I kept stuffing bills into Jim's pocket so he could pay when we were out. My journal endlessly recorded this cultural bias. *Who says the man is always supposed to pay for the things of the house, or the movie tickets, or the restaurant tab? I swear this is a worn-out cultural bias, and I'm playing into it. I noticed that he didn't mind taking it. It was his cultural bias too.*

Dear God, whose money is it anyway? When I think about it, it's been You all along stuffing my own pockets. So after all, do I want to stop stuffing his while snubbing the damn culture or should I continue and suffer this show of dishonesty? Besides, what does gender have to do with it anyway? When You instructed us the way You did, did You ever specify man or woman? Wasn't it directed to all of us: "Here, take these accounts and do good with them. Increase them, make them fertile, so that when you depart, you leave behind my Goods.

Your Tree—Your Place—Your Money

Every money behavior we stumbled over evoked another cultural attitude. As for these bumps in the marriage, I began to see that each one presented an opportunity. Ever since I converted to Catholicism, a fruitful line in the Christian scriptures lay deep in my heart: "To them who love God, all things work together unto good." Jim and I were always better after the bumps. It's as if we had entered a new place, and I felt a surge of love for God and usually charged over to my mate to shower him with kisses. The strange and surprising part of this struggle was Jim's prophecy: "You know how I hate arguments, but this money thing will help deepen our understanding of each other." Awesome! I loved Jim saying that, but the words were still his. It took a long time for that truth to reach me. I was still learning so much about the soul of my beloved.

One day we walked into Orange Cycle and purchased a pair of top-of-the-line bikes. Jim had an old garage-sale Schwinn that he had brilliantly restored, but he decided to give it to someone more needy. Each morning, he pedaled it downtown and offered it to the people he met there. Most of the homeless men were suspicious and shook their heads no. Jim weakened and wondered whether he *should sell it after all.* That had been my suggestion all along. But then he saw a young guy wearing a hospital emergency shirt, hunched over on the park bench, his face in his hands. "You on the street?" Jim asked.

"Yeah," the man looked up, "a couple of weeks now."

"Could you use a bike?"

"Could I!" My formerly homeless mate came home filled with, as he said, "a spiritual goodie. Honey, to give someone wheels when they walk miles to everything, when they carry backpacks and their legs buckle, is to them a gift from heaven. I wish I'd had one when I lived out there." And that was that. Jim, in all his complexity, was a simple soul. And I thanked God for that.

Our back porch, like a cozy chapel, had become the place for honest leveling with each other. Sunlight and grace streamed through grandfather oaks onto our open books. We read to each other, questing, sharing old memories of hurt and resurrection, not trying to make up for the lost years, but simply being present to the miracle of finding each other when we did.

"For one year we've been at it. And it's taken the house painter, the carpenter, and the tree man in the last two weeks to show me how far we still have to go around this money thing. What right do I have, after all, to exert myself in an issue about your tree, your place, your money?" A robin sang to us as Jim continued, "Could a man really live this way, play second fiddle to his woman, and come out a man? Looks good in theory. And God knows I've got my own comfortable reasons for it to work out!

"I feel that you blame me for it. Like all this wouldn't be happening if it weren't for me. Maybe you're right. God knows if there is any guilt lying around, I'll pick it up. But, honey, if the roles were reversed, that I could squire you, that you could lean on me, that *you* for a change could taste vulnerability and all the rest, how would you feel?"

Listening to him was critical to this marriage. I knew in my bones that it was true that I'd hurt him, and I didn't know where to go with that. My tight money beliefs, particularly since this marriage, show up daily. Jim could see them much more clearly than I. *God, how our mates expose us to ourselves!*

Recently we had planned and held a neighborhood garage sale. What happened in that garage sale deepened my approach to money, gave it my present vision. One of my lamps attracted an antiques dealer. I had marked its price at twenty dollars. He said, "I'll give you fifteen." "Eighteen," I replied, and he said, "Sixteen." That was the old money dance of my father of which Jim would have no part, and he soon disappeared. His discomfort telegraphed itself to me when he opened the door a crack. The bargaining ended with the difference being a dollar in my favor. The man handed me the bills and jested, "Tell me, ma'am, what earthly difference did those few dollars make to either of us?" *What earthly difference did a few dollars make?* What a wake-up call! The bargaining had nothing to do with the money. Call it ego, competition, the need to win, or even the hidden desire to lord it over another . . . all of it made me cringe.

I sought refuge in my journal that night. *Was it the pulse of my beating heart that had to get in the last word, the best shot, with a good win? Let me vow to You, dear God, never again to hassle foolishly like that. Honestly, how You must laugh. Thanks for the enlightenment, and thank you, Jim, for seeing it first.*

That was nine years ago. Now, dawn was breaking and the pale new light brought promise with it. I could see our swimming pool glistening, surrounded by clay pots overflowing with red geraniums, pink impatiens, and dozens of jewel-toned verbena. It was spring, and the flowers showed me what they could do with a bit of coaxing.

Couples

ON MY LAP WERE THE THOUGHTS AND REFLECTIONS OF DOZENS OF married women that I had interviewed. I sorted through the pages of testimonies about the shifting forces of love. Each story was precious to me. These women's insights reminded me of my own early days of wedded life. How Jim and I, in love and blithely unaware, had been seized very quickly by, as one interviewee put it, "the money monster." I chuckled, reading another woman's words. She had been married for twenty-one years and framed the money dilemma this way: "We're still learning not to come up with a winner and a loser. We had both better win!"

I smiled to myself. How amazing are the ways that couples work things out. One wife had rattled on to me, obviously delighted at a chance to express herself, "Look, here's this culture that promises, once we shun the briefcases, a long unexplored expanse of time where we'll do the things we'd always dreamed of. But how much of each other can we take?"

The women I talked to were honest, owning up to the complex feelings underlying their marriages and friendships and their relationships with money. Each woman sensed that sweeping money issues under the rug would threaten the best of marriages or relationships. But not all of them were so forthcoming with their partners, and they admitted that to me. Their openness to finding out how to handle money in a close relationship points the way for the rest of us.

Martina and Jacob: *Toe-to-Toe Combat*

Martina and Jacob's marriage is a stunning example of just how rough going it is when a couple can barely utter the "M word." Jacob liked being rich. For him, money had a luxurious feel. Martina hated riches.

Money was an embarrassment to her. Before every purchase, whether it was a house, a car, or a pair of shoes, these two went through bruising battles that left them feeling hopeless and drained.

Nothing could have prepared me for the morning I interviewed Martina about her financial life. It was one of my first talks about money with a married woman. We sipped raspberry tea in her living room. The spacious and tasteful space reflected Martina's thoughtful, orderly nature. That day, she opened up as she never had before in our years of friendship, exposing a desperately cluttered closet brimming with money anxieties and resentments. To my utter surprise, she burst into tears as soon as we sat down. I sat quietly, not attempting to stop her. Through the window, I could see a sleek, gray Mercedes parked by the manicured garden. Martina, a slight, tanned woman, finally picked up a tissue box, pulled out a wad, and began to mop her face.

"This sounds strange, but I don't like having money. I want to budget it. Like normal people. Money parameters, believe it or not, make me happy, give me a sense of control. If the sky is the limit, as it seems to be with my husband, I lose it." Martina smiled weakly.

"As for him, his childhood insecurities surface in terrible spending sprees. His lawyering skills and the endless moonlighting, produce a generous income, but more often, our debts outstrip our income." She dabbed her swollen eyes. "Forgive me. This is just, just such a relief. I mean to talk about this stuff. I never do." Martina explained that her father, a law book publisher, was loudly critical of lawyers' lifestyles. They're all selfish, driven, and rich, he scoffed to his daughter. Consequently, Martina has always felt that she betrayed her father by marrying into the law profession and living a lavish, no-holds-barred lifestyle. At a dinner party one night, Jacob announced, loud enough for his wife to hear, "My wife wishes to live poor. Me? I've been poor and I've been rich, and I prefer rich."

As I sat watching Martina, I asked myself something that would come up many times during my research: why do men and women sometimes marry people with a totally different persuasion? One view, according to marriage therapists, is that we choose partners to help us overcome childhood wounds. Perhaps Martina married Jacob to overcome her wealth prejudice, for her father definitely trained her to distrust all rich men, especially lawyers.

I wanted to exclaim, "If you and your husband only knew the magnificent possibilities that spring from acknowledging your very different money personalities." Our partners hold a mirror to our strongly held beliefs, and we can learn so much from those differences. But at this point Martina simply needed to vent. Watching her misery, I wondered what could have happened if Jim and I had not sought help. There by the grace of God go I.

Martina admitted that discomfort with money is her major personal issue. She goes to great lengths to mask the fact that she is affluent. "When our elegant home in Oregon sat on valuable acreage and wouldn't sell, I wondered whether potential owners were turned off because the exterior looked too natural, too pristine. I don't mow lawns. I don't believe in manicured lawns," she said. "But I couldn't hide the facts of our wealth. When my son celebrated his fifteenth birthday, a friend at the party shouted, 'Wow, Colin, I didn't know you lived on this big ranch!' My face did a slow burn. Now is that silly or what?"

I think we women are far more savvy about money than we think we are.
—Patricia T.

Abruptly, Martina stood. "Let's have some lemonade," she said, and left for the kitchen. The sun slanted on the silver frames on her coffee table. Two younger faces smiled back at me from one photograph: a happier version of Martina and Jacob snapped at their wedding before money mattered so much. Martina returned with two frosty glasses.

"Somehow I've got to work this out," she blurted. "I can't go on like this about money. It's always the same. We just can't come together about it."

We sat quietly while delicious cooking smells wafted through the house. It was hard to believe that, in the midst of this abundance, there could be such despair. But finally expressing honesty as clean and raw as this, Martina was on her way to change. My friend and I sat quietly. We chatted a bit more before I left, but clearly Martina didn't need my advice this day; she was simply acknowledging her private struggle. I drove away, thoroughly shaken by the encounter. How many women would confess to such dysfunction? I couldn't imagine.

Meg and Ruddy: *Overabundance*

I thought a lot about Martina on my way to visit another couple who were also wrestling with wealth. Meg and Ruddy were both in their early thirties. While traveling to South Carolina, the land of rolling hills, fabulous low-country food, and Southern hospitality, my husband and I dropped in on them. We relaxed in their beachfront home, a weathered gray clapboard affair on a barrier island. The place was a Southern paradise.

The couple had lived in Central Florida, but Meg's career had taken them to South Carolina and a new life. Meg is the administrator at one of the largest banks in the East. Today Ruddy and Jim meandered down the sandy beach while Meg and I made peanut butter sandwiches. I smiled at the two peanut butter jars—one chunky, one smooth—the result of marriage compromise.

We propped up our feet, munched our sandwiches, and sipped iced tea. Meg was anxious to talk about money. Like other women, she complained of its complexities, and particularly how difficult it was to marry someone with a different monetary style.

"Ruddy and I came into marriage having totally opposite money orientations," she said. "I never realized how deeply our personal orientations would shape the way we would stumble through money decisions!"

The evening before, Meg had listened quietly as her husband talked of his family's background. She confided that it was the first time she had really taken it in. Ruddy's childhood was full of deprivation, poverty, and lack, and the contrast to Meg's rich childhood embarrassed her.

"As a kid, I had everything," she said, acknowledging that she was uncomfortable hearing the details of her husband's experiences. "Dad, in his early thirties, was elevated to pastor at the largest First Church of Christ in our town. His salary was extremely generous and was managed by a church administrator who deposited much of it into mutual funds. He'll earn more after retirement than his current salary," Meg blushed. (I smiled. Another stereotype gone, that of the poor, sacrificial minister.)

"When I was in kindergarten, Dad hired a contractor to erect a *Gone With the Wind* house on a hill," she said. "Friends oohed and ahhed at our house; it always looked like more than we actually had."

Meg's mother loved living in the house, and like her role model, Jackie Kennedy Onassis, she shopped endlessly for fine china, lace tablecloths, and good silver. Despite the fact that her mother was a top-notch seamstress, she dressed Meg in Lord & Taylor fashions and paraded her in front of guests. Overabundance left young Meg feeling incomplete, dissatisfied, and oddly out of touch with the world.

Accustomed to servants, Meg never had to clean up after herself, and recalled with amusement the first time she cleaned a toilet. "One Saturday night, I spent the night with my friend, Gail, who couldn't play until her chores were done. She let me help, and it blew my mind that she was responsible for household duties! I had never, ever picked up a broom or a mop or cleaned a toilet! But I liked doing it. Do you believe me?"

Meg perked up and leaned forward in her chair, enjoying the memory.

Meg's blue eyes looked faraway when I asked her, "If you could change anything about your parents, what would that be?" The question hung for several minutes. Out the window, I noticed a tiny trawler on the horizon. A pair of pelicans skimmed just inches off the water, right behind the breaking waves.

"I'd say, 'Mom, stop depositing more money in my savings than what I saved. Just deposit what's in my piggy bank. It's my savings, not yours! You embarrass me, and I'm not grateful.'"

Suddenly Meg stood up, yawning, obviously spent. She ambled into the other room, and I heard kitchen sounds. "Want anything else?" she called.

She returned, an apple in hand, and took a bite.

"Maybe this is God's way of getting this stuff out of me," she said. "But now, the money still hasn't stopped pouring in. Both our jobs find us flush. I save, hoard away. Working clothes are my only extravagance." Her hands made a church under her chin. "I've never seriously thought about what I wanted from money. I never planned."

"Even as a banker?"

"Money is boring," she retorted.

Our husbands traipsed up the stairs toward us, and I rose to hug her. I had to bend down to accommodate her five-foot stature. I said in her ear, "You've kept your value system straight. Maybe your parents overwhelmed you, but someone showered you with integrity."

Her eyes filled. We didn't speak of money again. We were all hungry. I eyed Ruddy with a new perspective. His role as Meg's husband had to be a difficult one, I thought. I wondered what sort of unspoken things lay dormant in this house. A low bank of clouds swept the horizon, dark rain clouds signaling a storm on the horizon.

Ellen and Ray: *Better the Second Time Around*

I wondered about Ruddy and Meg a year later as I drove to Mount Dora to chat with Ellen. I had just heard that Ruddy and Meg had separated, and I wasn't completely surprised. Their money issues were overwhelming, and despite a bit of therapy, they eventually swallowed the couple. I looked forward to talking with Ellen, whose marriage had taken a new and positive direction after years of conflict. I followed Ellen to her garden, where she brushed off a bench and invited me to sit. Every bloom sang with perfection. I surveyed the Florida yard, as polished and well appointed as its creator.

Ellen is a Ph.D., a published author, and, like so many other brilliant women, deplores her money fears. In her outspoken manner, she gets right to the point. "What I really want to say about money is that it makes me very angry. I don't know how to make it. I don't know how it works. I just don't understand where it comes from, or how one would go about producing large quantities of it." Ellen frowned deeply.

What makes life tricky for her is a belief that money is the key to getting things done in this world. As the director of a spiritual retreat center, Ellen is charged with raising money, a prickly issue for her. From my experience at her presentations to corporate executives, Ellen tends to be an action-oriented person. She keeps numerous projects in the works, she admitted, but doesn't get to them all because they require money, and she doesn't know how to acquire it. She feels childish and naive about it. I listened to her accounts of money conflicts, articulated with humor and frustration. "I feel locked out of some secret money society and feel powerless to do anything about it." She shook her head furiously.

Despite her self-doubts around money, Ellen realized that, after a disastrous first marriage, where she abdicated power to a controlling husband, money would play a central part in her second marriage. She intuited that if she didn't take control of her financial life, she'd lose control of her spiritual one, a concept that many women do not yet realize, she said.

Creating a life where money matters profoundly, but not profanely, is the hallmark of a self-actualized woman like Ellen. So in this second go-around with a partner, Ellen went about making the changes she needed. "Since marrying Ray, I've established a private account where I put excess family funds or extra money that I may make from teaching an extra course or doing a workshop. This money is not available to Ray. He feels relieved! Can you believe it? I use it for two purposes: clothes and the house. I cannot even begin to tell you what a liberating experience this has been. Following on that success, now, in terms of the actual handling of money, he is happy to let me handle all of our financial business: banking, paying our home loans, investing our savings."

As I sat with Ellen, I realized that money energy can bring us to a new place, widen our vision, restore our divine power. What Ellen accomplished may appear easy, but the changes were wrenching for someone steeped in rigid habits. Our lives cannot be changed without vision, and the vision cannot come without a deep desire for a different kind of life. Ellen, who confessed that she still has much to learn, took charge of her financial life, as many others have done, and can attest to rewards she never thought possible.

Anna and Bill: *A Splendid Current of Money*

One morning, my husband and I met Anna, a 30ish woman whose expressed beliefs about money were, to me, like savoring soul food. Her story revealed that she's never been hooked on it, despite having made lots of it. "I don't think I really grasp this thing called money, but it has always been there when I needed it," she said.

As soon as Anna entered our home, I felt her spark of power. A very small ad, tucked into the corner of a page, had caught my eye a week before: "We come into your home and organize your disaster spaces. We'll make your home clutter free. Satisfaction guaranteed." We needed her! When I told Jim I had hired her, he raised his thumb in victory.

Anna Dickson, the clutter buster, arrived at our home two weeks later in blue jeans and a yellow shirt. Wasting no time, she flung open doors to brimming closets and inspected messy shelves. She pulled boxes out of dark corners. Dust flew. Embarrassment crawled up my spine. Anna, impervious to my shame, surveyed the growing junk pile. She held up items, some long forgotten, one by one.

"When did you use this last?" she inquired like an army general, or, "Do you really want this?" I got the feeling that she thought some of my possessions were not worthy of discussion, and I was aware of a stream of anxiety about letting go of them. My visceral reaction to moving useless material out of my life mirrored my parents' money fears. For the first time in my life, I realized how much embarrassment issues from hoarding.

Anna supplied kindly support as I let go of memories, treasures, and trash. It all went. Mama's cracked floor lamp, her old never-used picture frames, and finally, ancient photographs whose inhabitants I could no longer identify. Surprisingly, I began to feel lighter. We spent two dusty days saying countless good-byes to junk boxes that had languished in our space for years; Jim and I were undergoing a spiritual cleansing at Anna's scrubbing hands!

On the last day, I determined to know more about her. "Could we get together for a lunch? You've got some healthy thinking that I want for myself."

We met a few weeks later, in a hip little restaurant, and Anna launched into an enthusiastic update of her recent business successes.

"A couple recently asked me to create two offices, one for him, another for his wife, and we worked nonstop for two days and gave them top work. They were happy, and we walked away with a generous fee. Another client, a woman grieving the loss of her daughter, asked us to help her stop hoarding. I cleaned out her closet and stuffed our car with four hundred outfits bound for the Salvation Army. They were thrilled, of course, but we were very pleased to have helped her through her a grieving time while earning money. Now that my business is prospering, I find that I am wanting more. I'd like an upgraded car. I want to take some wonderful trips."

> ***As a couple, we decided never to discuss money in the bedroom.***
>
> ***—Regina C.***

"Anna, how about your money relationship with Bill? How different is it from your first marriage?" Anna sipped her tea.

"Well, Bill has his own business, and I save a lot of our earnings. He insists on taking a draw out of his business of only six hundred dollars a week. We use it for bills; expenses for his son, Kirk; and for savings. I save a lot of my paycheck, and I use it for bills too. I employ a cleaning lady bimonthly." She saw my raised eyebrows.

Anna rummaged in her purse for some notes about their finances that she had brought with her. "You see, I'm well prepared," she laughed. Referring to her notes, Anna rattled off her financial strategy. She saves a third of her earnings each week. Any large purchase that affects both of them brings them to the discussion table. Bill had a home office built, and they had talked about it a lot beforehand. They decided how to pay off the expenses and how much they needed to save, and they did it.

"If Bill needs something for his business, he'll buy it and he doesn't have to consult me. And the same is true for me."

Despite their ability to talk it out, it became evident that the two, just like in every other couple I'd interviewed, exhibited different personalities around money.

Anna continued. "Bill and I both feel rich. But, unlike me, Bill is a 'lack' thinker. He gets into a depression if he thinks his business is doing badly. He saves lots of money for the 'What ifs.' As for me, I buy things for luxury and convenience. He just never allows himself that kind of prosperity. As for cooking, I like to skip it and buy takeout food. Be queen for a day. And when Bill doesn't see why we need a cleaning lady, I insist on help around the house." She chuckled without rancor.

So far in their eight-year marriage, the Dicksons haven't had any major money conflicts. Once when they were offered a chance to go to an expensive marriage therapy workshop, she overrode his veto and off they went.

"Tell me about your youth," I encouraged her over a rum plum dessert, delighting in a young woman fueled by such enthusiasm.

"I grew up in a blended family of ten; four were mom's, five were my dad's, and one was theirs. My parents struggled to send us to the good Catholic school down the street. There, I learned about tithing, and thoughts about the goodness of money jelled."

Catholic schools! Teaching the goodness of money! I could hardly believe my ears. More than that, I marveled at her self-assurance. Young Anna was way ahead of most of us. She propped her chin in her hands, relishing the conversation. Did she ever crave costly luxuries?

"For the longest time, I wished for diamond earrings and finally bought a pair for two thousand dollars. Beautiful, but with one flaw: they hurt. I discovered I couldn't fly and wear them, I couldn't go river rafting and wear them. Only to work, and there, I lost one. It was found, and I had more secure backings made, but they hurt even more." She threw up her hands in mock despair. "Finally, I sold the diamonds. It was a Zen lesson: Sometimes what we want is not worth the effort!"

Anna's stepfather was a kind man and always told the children how lucky he was to have married her mother, how smart her mother was to make their dollars stretch. When Anna's mother tried to buy him an expensive sweater, he resisted. "Use the money for the girls," he told her. He died at thirty-nine with Anna holding his hand. We sat in silence for a moment. Anna spooned her dessert, then continued.

"At nineteen, I moved to England for six years. Sometimes I had money and sometimes I didn't, but I always had all I needed. I trusted it would come. And when the cash dried up, Mom would send a check or I'd find a temporary job, and the money would flow in. In 1988, I traveled to India, armed with one carry-on bag. I simply don't get attached to things."

I shook my head in amazement. She laughed. "Look at me. I am forty-two years old and have moved about thirty times in my life. For whatever blessed reason, I have little attachment to material things. Recently, a neighbor remarked that our house is too empty. She doesn't understand why Bill and I won't buy more furniture." She shook her head.

We finished our coffee and I delighted in reaching for the tab. Anna had preached a better sermon than the one I had heard at last Sunday's Mass. An unexpected downpour greeted us at the restaurant door. I watched her slight figure disappear into the parking lot, a newspaper over her head for protection.

Anna is not afraid of success. And she's blessed with an abiding faith and a supportive husband. If every couple put as much energy into examining and living their lives as Anna and Bill do, there would be a lot less unrest prompted by the alleged evils of money.

Natalie and Neal: *Spiritual Bread at Work*

A silver-haired fifty-four-year-old beauty, Natalie Alton had launched a brand-new career as a corporate executive when others her age were downsizing. Prior to her new job, she had been directing a small but successful Center for Successful Aging outside of Deland. "Lots more money," she admitted with a wry smile. I got the idea that it was a bittersweet situation for Natalie, this new lifestyle of having money. Natalie ran her hands through her cropped hair, her legs pulled up on the park bench where we had agreed to meet.

I told Natalie that I wondered whether the huge spike in income, coming from the wife, had stressed her marriage. She was silent a moment, biting her lower lip, then she looked at me and admitted, "You know, I've always thought that I acted pretty cavalier around money, but now it's a whole new level of thinking and acting. I've evolved beyond my parents because I've learned at last to have fun with money. Also, this lovely salary has diminished that gender role I've played all my life. I'm the primary breadwinner now, and I'm so proud of that. When I want to spend seven hundred dollars on something, I don't have say to Neal, 'Now you go out and break your back and earn that seven hundred dollars.'"

I was surprised to learn how well their marriage had adapted to the change. Natalie told me that her husband is content with the way things are and doesn't mind a bit if she earns more than him. When they make buying decisions, they talk them over carefully until they are resolved. To her delight, Neal took on the management of the money, a job she despised. He now paid the bills and balanced the checkbooks.

"At first, it was difficult for him. He didn't juggle money like I do. That made him crazy." As a bachelor, her husband had prided himself on just staying current, and then Natalie burst on his scene. The months when they couldn't meet their bills, he was frantic: "My God, what will we do about the lawyer's bill?"

Right after Natalie took her executive position, she sat down with Neal and worked through their financial issues together. "That effort actually brought us closer," she said, smiling in remembrance.

The career change, as it turns out, empowered Natalie and Neal to do what each does best, despite the dictates of conventional gender roles. "When we refinanced our house for the new addition, I did all the brokering and the trading, a perfect balance." She negotiates with contractors and handymen; he does the paperwork.

Despite her sizable salary and the smoothness of her marriage, she admits to a distrust of money. "I'm afraid that I won't have enough or that I'll spend too much or that I can't provide for our future or I'll be remiss with life insurance and investments, and so on."

I noted a slight tremor in Natalie's hand as she plucked a leaf from a nearby bush. "My childhood was filled with money troubles. My parents were immigrants. I inherited lots of their fear. Sure, money is freedom but it's bondage as well. I've got to financially prepare for the next five or ten years. That scares the hell out of me." She gazed at the calm surface of the lake below our perch. Given her new lifestyle, complete with higher mortgage payments and dozens of other commitments, she felt slightly out of sorts, she said.

"I finally understand how men find themselves in bondage, glued to high-stress jobs that carry fat mortgage payments, grand car payments, children's college tuitions," she said, making a face. "Thank God, Neal's not materially minded. Sure, he gets a kick out of our upgraded lifestyle. But if I disappeared from his life tomorrow, forcing him to live on his salary alone, he wouldn't feel a bit deprived."

She stood and stretched. She was a tall woman. Her eyes were pale blue in the light. "I'm fifty-four years old, and something in me has shifted, like a new self-esteem. For the first time, my worth in the marketplace is valued. It makes me behave differently. I take myself more seriously."

I waved to Natalie as she drove off. Here was a supposedly liberated woman, but she still carried her immigrant parents' fears about money. From the complexities of her story, her worrisome habits were evident. It takes a lot of soul work to get completely free of old money fears. I walked to my car reflecting on the corporate culture, that male tribe that was stretching Natalie, forcing her to create a new identity for herself. All of her childhood teachings were being overridden, I mused; a microcosmic example of the deep changes rippling through womankind at the turn of the century.

Sheena and Mark: *Poor and Counting*

Sheena Mayes, a statuesque woman with closely cropped salt-and-pepper hair, appears younger than her forty-five years. Perhaps it's due to her extraordinary drive to do good. When there is need, Sheena is there, whether it's to feed the homeless, lend possessions, or help her students. A professor of music at a large state college, Sheena is a tremendously competent woman and teacher. Try naming a book that she hasn't read; impossible! Name a class that hasn't thought her their best teacher. Also impossible! Yet when it comes to money empowerment, fear paralyzes her. "Money issues blow me away. I'm afraid, shy, and, yes, ignorant. I don't balance a checkbook well. It's that part of me that hasn't grown up," Sheena admits. "I just don't know whether I can talk about this stuff," she stammered.

I find it amazing, though not that uncommon, that this bright professor and published composer is nearly crippled when it comes to things financial. When she is shelling out money for others, tens and twenties fly out of her purse. Sheena and her husband launched a scholarship fund for underprivileged students at a local college. Several times, she has slipped gas money into a young secretary's purse. And she once handled a student's water bill at city hall. Unquestionably,

Sheena considers her money a gift from God to be used in the service of the poor.

"Sheena," I broke the silence. "Tell me where all this giving began!"

"Once, in the middle of the fourth grade, I came to understand that when you see someone in need and you help, *you move closer toward them.* It seemed so natural."

"What do you mean natural?"

"Well, if necessary, I would leave right now and chase down to the Orlando Homeless Coalition to arrange pot roast suppers every night."

Sheena is not the least bit aware that most people don't feel the same way.

That mystic mandate, saintly as it is, isn't always easy for her husband, Mark. Sheena's lavishness for the down-and-out has the potential to jeopardize an otherwise happy marriage. In the early years of their marriage, Mark found her penchant for writing checks to strangers difficult. Now, friends laugh that this ten-year marriage wouldn't recognize a problem if it had one. Sheena and Mark found each other at just the right time. Both were late bloomers to marriage; both were in their forties and had never married. Both had been written up in the local paper, and both were fervent, but not fanatic, Catholics. But Sheena's "Mother Theresa" role, as one friend put it, can be awkward for Mark. He once said to me, "What's a husband to do with this undoubtedly saintly-and-ready-for-canonization wife? Join her or shut up?" Mark continued, "I'm not going to change her, and I don't want to. Doesn't that go with the love?"

Sheena appreciates his patient devotion. "Mark understands that I'm still emerging. I've got an old mode of believing that I'm a burden to him. I overreact or am overly concerned about his reactions to things connected to money. But I know that he's got wide vision on our accounts. Someday I want to repay my husband for his unbelievable generosity toward me."

"Just the other day, if you want to know, I scanned a shopping catalog and thought about buying a blouse. But my gut sent up this thought: *Someone in Nepal needs a cataract operation. That blouse money, thirty dollars, would pay the expense.*" She shrugged. "I just can't help making the comparison."

Painful divisions exist between rich and poor and will always be there, but to Sheena, the reality of that division is paramount. She shivered. "Jesus had so much to say about it that sometimes I think the poor are the only humans that matter."

I leaned back. We listened to a mockingbird's song as the socially conscious Sheena played with her watch bracelet, a Christmas gift from Mark that she would never have bought for herself. Sheena's drive to feed the hungry and clothe the cold must be tempered with her commitment to honor her husband's needs as well. For Sheena, it's not an easy balance, but I didn't doubt she would rise to the challenge.

After I left Sheena, I drove in the country for a while, needing to sort things out. All of the wives I had interviewed, except Anna, a bright exception, struggled with a degree of torture about money. Money, it seems, is the most divisive element, perhaps more than sex, in a marriage. Sheena's childhood images brought forth many of my own. Are most of us still teenagers scrambling to make adult financial decisions? Just how much do those early money impressions influence us now? That night I hardly slept. My own childhood flashed through my mind, one scene after another, filled with memories about money. I thought of my mother and father. My sister and my brothers. Money had been the core of our life together; it was the language, the vocabulary, the very essence of my youth.

.....

Dear God, You alone know our vanity, selfishness, and arrogance. You know how we must be unrelentingly vigilant to resist using money's power against each other. Surely, when spouses have honest good relationships with money, I know the world turns as it should.

Chapter Seven

Celebrating the Treasures—In God We Trust

From the corner of a small Greek café, Jim and I watched strangers pass by outside. A soft rain misted, but we felt cozy inside. Heaps of antipasto salad, pita bread, and a decanter of wine sat before us. At some point before the check arrived, I was still stuffing several bills into Jim's wallet lying on the table. I wanted it to appear that he paid for the meal, just another continuing episode in our role playing the money game. Taking a final sip of chardonnay, Jim jammed the full wallet into his back pocket and laughed. "Marrying you and your money was a whiplash experience!"

The past years of watching this new Jim reacclimate to a money-fed society left me in awe; would God's miracles never stop? I had found a man for whom money was of little consequence, never had been—and I loved that about him. He stood up, tall and lanky, and left an extra bill on the table. I joined him and we walked out of the restaurant, hand in hand, into the soft Florida shower. He was still smiling. "Yep, nothing less than six years of whiplash! I'm still scratching my head."

I was scratching my own. What a match! What had I done to enjoy the blessings of this partnership? Looking at us that day nobody would have believed that this man, only a few years earlier, had walked the downtown streets without a roof to call his own. But Jim had adjusted easily to my way of life, and here we were, comfortable together. We fought sometimes, just as we prayed and laughed ourselves silly other times. Jim and I worked and reworked our marriage and money contract as needed. Somehow we endured and found friends who supported us and a therapist who guided us where we wanted to go. And from all that shifting and changing and loving, watching the money come and go mysteriously guided me to my avocation as author and workshop leader on money.

I liked what I was learning and I am still learning, daily adding, it seems, new chapters to my impossible, miraculous story. Tales of other women coalesced with my own, each revealing how painfully, yet beautifully, money can be a spiritual tool for self-discovery.

Just Buy It

I READ THAT THE PROPER USE OF MONEY CAN BE A RELIGIOUS experience. Like the spiritual life, money longs for expansion and further expression; it is a live medium. It is never finished with us, prodding, provoking, and even uplifting us if we allow it to.

Accepting God's material extravagance has required me to stretch and grow. I recall, following my inheritance, the anguish of buying my first home, a lovely three-bedroom place with a backyard garden overlooking a narrow valley. It was ideal for me. Yet when it came to closing the deal, I felt paralyzed. It took my brother's verbal shaking down for me to be able to let go of the down payment. "Listen! Stop being silly. You like to watch your assets snowball then you refuse to touch the money. You didn't inherit this money for it to sit in the bank! Buy the damn house!" I signed the papers.

I cautiously accepted God's abundance by taking small steps, one at a time. The cars I drove over the years reflected my various states of wealth—and indecision. Recently an old friend called and asked whether I would like to buy his Volkswagen Cabrio. Jim and I were a one-car family. I'd eye two-car families with suspicion, always wondering why they didn't share driving and save money! Andy's shiny Volkswagen, a gorgeous red plaything that smelled brand-new, suddenly seemed irresistible. He had bought it only the year before. I glanced over at my husband who tossed my look right back; he knew the question well, and he was having none of it. Was this God calling? Another stretch? My voice was strong as I said, "Sure, Andy, why not?" My brother's influence rang in my head: "Just buy the damn car!"

I handed Andy a check and moved into foreign territory that day, an untested world that seemed outrageously daring and youthful. I sat in the red dream car, caressed the leather seats, and sorted out the various dials and buttons. Then I took off. Fire in the wind! Friends gushed that the racy Cabrio convertible was all me. Glancing in the rearview mirror one day, all the cars of my previous lives appeared; I saw the pattern. My cars were, I realized, metaphors of my soul's struggle with bounty and material goodness.

Early vehicles were chosen according to gas efficiency and low maintenance, period. In convent life, we shared driving and wheeled from point A to point B without much thought. Weren't we about higher things? I don't remember the make of a single one of those cars. Then, I bought a car of my own, a cream Toyota. That burned-out baby gave way to a rust-colored Datsun. After therapy, I splurged on a gas-guzzling black-and-beige Buick, and not long after the inheritance, I was zipping around in the stately Cadillac Sedan de Ville, though not without suffering waves of embarrassment. When Jim arrived, the Caddy went, and we chose a boxy Dodge van that lugged us and our things, including bikes, on long drives. Jim affectionately dubbed it Rocky. And now, the most colorful and bodacious of them all; I was free as the wind and at ease with Lady Abundance at last.

I must say that the first years of our union were hugely blessed by the general economic conditions prevailing in America, the booming nineties. They allowed us to live off the explosive growth of my modest nest egg, a fund that amounted to a good deal less than seven figures; I was no millionaire. But rarely did we have to dip into our capital. Nonetheless, money issues still knocked us out of joint. Jim hadn't been reared like me, and I was tripping over what I took to be his childhood silver spoon. Jim could spend money without flinching, leaving me in disbelief and, to be perfectly honest, a bit green with envy. After all, hadn't *my* father's way been the *right* way? This man, sauntering into my life from the street, completely shattered what remained of any comfortable money beliefs I could still claim.

For example, there was the case of my faithful twenty-year-old Frigidaire oven. It had to be replaced shortly after we were married. We stood silently at the Sears counter and ogled the latest top-of-the-line glass-top stainless range, with a price tag around $2,500. I was paralyzed. My father's voice, "Buy the best, honey. Always the best. It's cheaper in the long run," warred against, "Over two grand for a silly stove?!"

Jim saw my grim face. "Don't we want this cooker?" he asked. His face was serene, unconcerned.

"Give me a minute," I gulped. My mind felt scrambled. I was back in my crazy not-enough place, the old emotional lack knotting up my gut, nearly knocking me over. We let the silence take us where it would, the wise saleswoman having correctly gauged that we needed time.

Finally Jim said, "Look at it this way, sweetheart. My role may be to help you spend your inheritance, not recklessly, but maybe help you get freer about these things." When I said nothing, he looked at the woman. "Let's buy the damn oven!"

Jim, too, was becoming freer about these things. One day, right out of the blue, as we were replanting two palm bushes near the front lawn, he suddenly announced, "God help me, I'm beginning to feel responsible again." He stood back and let the sun play on his face.

I laughed. "Prove it!" I retorted.

He looked at me directly. "I'd like to take over paying the bills."

Hold on! Control the bill paying? I was floored. Suppose he misses a payment, putting my credit rating at stake? As it happened, bill paying became an expression of Jim's love; every month, he happily relieves me of this burdensome task. His growing comfort with taking on responsibility after his long hiatus from a workaday world meshed beautifully with my crusade to throw the dice and run with him. Doubts about his sense of responsibility receded. I knew in my bones how right we were for each other. And like the quiet peace that takes over when one is least aware, I felt, for the first time in my life, the warmth of right living. Jim and I were nesting in an Eden of abundance, a holy horn of plenty, always replenishing itself to accommodate our needs. Truly, this was a radical new world. Each night, my heart's prayer was: *What return can I make to the Lord for all He has done for me?*

I have been on a long voyage, discovering patterns of spending completely foreign to me. Another early storm erupted in our favorite bookstore. As usual, Jim lugged a stack of poetry books up to the checkout counter. He opened one and began to read. "Listen to this," he said enthusiastically. Seeing the stacks, I shut down. I was in no mood to listen to any lofty words and felt that such extravagant expenses surely signaled imminent bankruptcy. "But you haven't even read the poetry books on your own bookshelves!" I blurted. He looked at me, almost with pity. A little girl behind me stood wide eyed. I couldn't bear her look and burned with shame. I looked at Jim for a long time. *Face it, Adele. Jim's buying sprees aren't sending us anywhere that you can't handle.*

You're jealous. You envy his freedom. Could you, just once, find a book yourself and buy it for the simple delight of a single picture in its pages? I looked down at the book in my arms, having never intended to buy it, only wanting to give it a look; it was a *House and Garden* coffee table number splashed with hundreds of gorgeous photos. Could I bring myself to part with thirty-five dollars for such a splurge? I caressed the cover. I noticed that Jim was watching me. His eyes were narrow, and I heard the familiar testiness in his voice when he's heard enough. *"Just buy the damn book!"* A wave of joy poured over me as I joined the cash register line. Armed with my Visa, I once again slayed the dragon that belched admonitions like "If you buy a book, by God, you read every page." I felt the weight of the lovely book and held it to my chest. Would I read it all? Possibly. But probably not. So did reading it all really matter? Maybe just having this kind of printed beauty close at hand was worth the price. What a concept!

"Sweetheart," Jim said without a trace of I-told-you-so as we walked to the car, "remember the slogan on the front page of the *New York Times*? 'You don't have to read it all, but it's nice to know it's all there.' " With Jim, life was growing into one big you-mean-I-can-have-it-all? experience. Still, having it *all* isn't always what it's cracked up to be. I'd heard the point made long ago in the dim light of a convent chapel. The words belonged to Jesuit paleontologist Teilhard de Chardin: "Do not forget that the value and interest of life is to do ordinary things with the perception of their enormous value." Simple abundance?

Sacramental Abundance

One morning I read Deepak Chopra's thoughts on abundance from his book *Creating Affluence*: "Why not acknowledge that God is a perfect model for abundance? He has surrounded himself with the most glorious material creation of all: planets, stars, cosmic energies, and forces that defy our wildest imagination."

For me, abundance is many things. It's little things, like visiting my orchid collection, sipping coffee under my gazebo, petting my cat, or watching movies with my husband. What life could be richer?

I discovered early in my research that a feeling of abundance means different things to each awakening human—whether monk or soccer mom or homeless person. One woman testified, "For me, I didn't feel abundant until I mailed the last mortgage payment." Another swore it was a single trip to a beloved region of Italy. A dress designer smiled when she said, "My husband and I no longer quarrel over money. That's our version of abundance!"

Money is, I've learned, a sacrament, a holy symbol if we let ourselves see it that way. In its reflection, I have peered at my lack of faith, my narrow view, my disbelief in love. I have seen not how much I own, but what I think I still need. I begin to see desires born of emotional insecurity and buried grief. Oddly, this spiritual anorexia, this lack of willingness to nurture myself with proferred material goods didn't show up when I approached the stock market; there, almost compulsively, I took giant leaps of faith. I gambled as my father had before me, freely spending for all kinds of opportunities.

Along the way, I also have discovered a much-welcomed thread of generosity, a willingness to be fair with those who needed help. At lunch one day, a friend mused, "I know you. You'd avoid money making if it jeopardized a friendship." She'd heard of a long-outstanding business loan I'd made to a good friend and how that friend and I never battled despite her repeated tardiness with payments. Eventually my friend did pay off her debt, affirming for me that friends can indeed enter into contractual arrangements and still enjoy intimacy.

Abundance has no end. One gift I hold particularly dear is an addition to our living space where Jim or I gather our wits or write in deep quiet. We'd talked about the idea for months, after having made a habit of sliding by each other in our narrow hallway and refraining from opening the refrigerator door for fear of colliding. It was time to get the hell out of each other's way. I could hardly believe I was even thinking about it; a second car is one thing, but a *second house?* Surely that kind of lavishness was for the rich and famous, certainly not for us.

One warm afternoon, I dragged my poolside chair close to a blooming white hibiscus. It was the feast of St. John Climacus. Jim said "Let's do it," but I had to think things over. We had found exactly the kind of spot we were looking for, and the price was right. A second-floor condo getaway, a perfect eight-mile bike ride from our home, with just one bedroom, but with a bright and new kitchen, and it was a quiet place. An enormous, green-carpeted living room had a welcoming feel. A more whitewashed, austere, crisp workspace could not be imagined. Its previous owner, of all things, had been a young poet! But it just seemed too much! Who did we think we were anyway? I stared at the white flower. *For heaven's sake, Adele, this time give the idea some faith, your best thinking.* It was good to be outside. Florida knows how to do sunsets that lift my spirits. I thought of Henry Nouwen's spiritual classic, *Clowning in Rome,* and how it affirmed a couple's need for solitude in marriage: "When we pray alone, study, read, write, or simply spend quiet time away from the places where we interact with each other directly, we enter into a deeper intimacy with each other. It is a fallacy to think that we grow closer to each other only when we talk, play, or work together." In the growing dark by the pool, I knew I had to decide. I laughed out loud. *Buy the damn condo!*

We baptized our new space The Loft. Jim summed it up, "When I walk in there, it's like a holy place filled with the promise that something is about to happen." Except for our old computers, we allowed no other technology to disturb the peace: no television, no phone, no Internet. After one or the other of us—usually Jim—has been gone for a day or a day and night at The Loft, there's a grand falling into each other's arms upon return. Then we sit and share inner adventures. The Loft is teaching us an entirely new language of intimacy.

One early afternoon, sweeping dead leaves from the drive, I found myself opening to nature in a new way. I looked up at a cloudless blue sky, and I realized that there is a deep intelligence holding everything together that was speaking to me. This new broom that I pushed and pulled over the cement I had bought at the supermarket that morning *without checking its price.* I stared down at the crisp leaves. Suddenly, they were metaphors for so many dead assurances that had cluttered my life. The old dictums that had dominated my thinking, kept me prisoner, were being swept out. I stopped. It was a clear visionary moment. I felt clean, responsible, mature. I danced up the entire walkway to Robert Frost's lyrical words:

> "Never ask of money spent—where the spender thinks it went.
> Nobody was ever meant—to remember or invent what he did
> with every cent."

Three years after our wedding, another miracle materialized in our boundless field of possibilities. Jim got the surprise of his life when the mail arrived one bright afternoon. My ex-hobo husband came running onto the porch, breathless, waving a letter. I put my book down. "You're not going to believe this, honey, but I've come into some money." He stammered, his hand was shaking. I stared at him. No, I didn't believe it.

"Let me guess the amount," I said, doubting it was anything to shout about. I joked, "Ten thousand? Twenty?" We played back and forth until I couldn't stand it any longer. "Don't just stand there! Tell me!"

Jim whispered in my ear: *"One hundred and fifty four thousand dollars, sweetheart!"*

Jim had entirely forgotten about a retirement account he had set up when he was teaching. The college trustees hadn't forgotten him, though, and they tracked him down. The hair stood up on my arms. I sank in my chair and stared at the faithful grandfather oak shading our porch. Neither of us spoke. Money materialized, from nowhere it seemed, for a man with once-empty pockets.

Now, with his own money lining his pockets, Jim could spend as he wished, with accountability only to God. My stomach suffered. It would be hard for me to let go of this. The prospect of Jim blowing every dime danced in my head. It wasn't going to be easy, but here it was: Jim's opportunity to make his own peace with money.

Only a few weeks later, it happened. My husband announced cheerfully, "I need a new computer."

My heart sank. Before I could catch my words, out they flew. They were Dad's words, not mine. "What's wrong with your old computer?"

Jim looked at me evenly. "It can't do graphics. Listen, I need a new one, and now I can buy it on my own."

I felt the ground shifting. *Adele, it's his money.* But I had bigger worries than Jim's buying his own computer. *Will he still love me? Was it simply, as he had frequently joked, because I had the house that he married me?* Our counselor saw the windfall as breathtakingly rich and beautiful, something that would fertilize our lives with new possibilities. "Don't be afraid of it," she urged. It was the same message all over again: *Claim the abundance and be grateful enough to enjoy every moment. Give us this day our daily bread.*

That Sunday at Mass we both sang lustily. Jim leaned over to whisper, "I'm so full of thanks for this. For the first time, I feel special. That's new for me." He looked at the statue of the risen Christ high above the altar and then back at me. He whispered, "Look at God's smile." When the basket passed, Jim glanced my way as he slid in a check.

We sat close; I held my hymnal with one hand, my husband's hand with the other. You could hear my voice rising above the others: "Take our bread, we ask You, take our hearts, we love You, take our lives, Oh, Father we are Yours, we are Yours." Take our bread. How appropriate, I thought. Money, this great gift of Yours! Never had money seemed so much a part of God's life. A shiver ran through my body. My eyes misted. How had I been so blessed to even glimpse such a reality?

I marveled at how quickly Jim, once a homeless man, made peace with his money. It had taken me years. He reminded me of my brother, who handled windfalls and losses with little trace of emotion. Once, my brother and I held a winning raffle ticket for a five thousand-dollar jackpot at the crowded Syrian-American Club. I felt the blood rise to my face, wanting to hide as the room filled with applause. Someone else should have won. We didn't need that jackpot. But not my brother! He stood tall to accept the check. He didn't even mind when the emcee cracked, "My God, the rich get richer!" He only laughed, waving the check in the air: "Let the money come!" Both my brother and my husband handled abundance as naturally as boys trading baseball cards. They have been my best tutors.

If I've learned nothing else in all this, I've learned that there is no end to learning. The issues are always alive. A day doesn't go by when I'm not thrust into some sort of passage. One day, long before Jim, it had taken heaps of strawberry ice cream to fling me toward freedom. I've cherished the story ever since. A Native American nun related it in a conference entitled "The Greening of the Spirit." She said, "It was my family's bleakest time. We were down to speculating what would be for supper that evening, wondering whether there was to be supper at all. We had only change in the blue pitcher. Mother told me to take all the money and go to the grocery store. 'Buy all the strawberry ice cream you can with every penny.' I was horrified. I searched my father's face, but he only said, 'Do as your mother tells you.'

"I plunked down every penny on the counter, trotting home with several cartons of strawberry ice cream. A table was set with bowls and spoons. 'Go, invite all our neighbors. Tell them we're going to have a party,' Mother said, her voice firm. As the ice cream with chunks of sensuous strawberries filled and refilled each dish, the night grew festive. Neighbors spun stories that allowed us to forget, for those few moments, the desolate hours. You must know that, in Native American tradition, the strawberry symbolizes prosperity and abundance." Sister smiled. "Curiously, I remember never having gone hungry any day of my childhood, but I'll never forget that radiant night, when we mocked and danced and sang away every demon, the night my mother introduced us to pure celebration!"

That story played out in a recent stock market nosedive beginning the end of our Wall Street joyride. Oh, the unexplainable jitters. Shopping one day, Jim and I let ourselves be drawn into a home design store, attracted by a handsome blonde recliner that sold for about two thousand dollars. Jim had been wishing for a recliner large enough for his long frame. But now? I was definitely not in a spending mood. But as he experimented, moving from one chair to another, I noticed how much he was enjoying himself. I simply stared ahead, knowing what was coming. He sighed as I finally turned on my heel, but something in me wouldn't let me move. *Let the money go! Buy the strawberry ice cream.* Now I love seeing my tall husband, book in hand, sprawled in his leather recliner.

For all the tough lessons that have come my way, I often want to kiss the very ground, and sometimes do, when it counts, before morning prayer as I'd been taught to do so long ago in the convent chapel before slipping into my pew. I think about my past. I don't know why things—life and death and money—had to be so dark, why my parents' Great Depression scars pressed so hard into my soul. I don't know why I had to fight my inheritance—my gift—long and hard before I could say that I loved the money. Nor do I know why I had to get poor to get rich before I could get smart. Whatever may come, I am daily grateful for it all, and for this wondrous sacrament called money.

. . . . .

Blessings flood me from the first blush of dawn. My heart sings and thanks You for this intense fulfillment and longing. I leave my sleeping husband. I retreat to the porch where I groom and feed my African violets, and take in the mystery of my blooming purple cattleya. I go outside for the newspaper. Rich colors flood through the garden window. Dear God, my cup runneth over! I am one with the unhurried quiet vitality of everything. You say it best in the Talmud, "The richest man alive is the one most content with what he has."

Appendix

Money Aerobics—Seven Stretches for Your Money Muscles

Honor the Energy

Celebrate your income and all it represents. Designate a special object in your home that will remind you of your income sources and the blessings each brings you. Make sure the object is something you can see every day, such as a small statue or piece of art. Thank God at every turn for material blessings. Learn to love and appreciate the beauty of money in your life. Trust money as you would other forces that come and go in your life with whatever constancy and regularity.

Compose your own money prayers. Make the prayers part of your daily dialogue with God, remembering that nothing is too small or too unimportant. Keep the prayers short and, if possible, commit them to memory. Like a mantra, voice these money prayers while in your car, on a bus, in the park, or whenever you enter into the arena of commerce. Each prayer is a stepping-stone, and uttered often can take you beyond financial fear, transporting you to where God lives and keeping you in touch with the divine hand.

When you suffer a material loss, let the painful feelings find expression; cry or shout out the pain, fully honoring the loss. Talk to God about it. Get angry! God can take it! Financial loss is, ultimately, always about recovery and creating openings for things new, different, and needed in your life. You'll soon learn to let go quickly.

Release the Energy

Light a scented candle when you pay your bills. Put on soft music. You are not alone as you dispense your money; the candlelight is a powerful symbol of God's presence. Pray over each bill, thanking God for the electricity that cooks your dinner and runs your dishwasher, the water that bathes your body and your lawn, and the movies that entertain you month after month. Use a lovely pen. Keep your checks and bills neatly organized, perhaps using colorful clips. After you write each check, jot "thank you" on it. Stuff the envelopes, seal them, and pop Love stamps in the corners. You'll feel that the energy released for your money allows you to participate in something grand and mystical: the very functioning of human commerce on a planetary scale.

Be generous with yourself. Buy yourself a small luxury every few days. It might be a slice of double-fudge cake, a nice pair of hose, a lipstick, or a copy of the *New York Times.* Spend without anxiety. Then thank God lavishly for each gift.

Make a habit of often spending a small amount on someone else. Slip money into a charity box or buy someone's lunch. Spending money on deserving people and causes makes life better. If you believe you're struggling to get by, reduce your giving, but always practice generosity, toward yourself and others, to feel abundant. It's a law of nature: you're richest when you give it away.

Catch Your Breath

When you're about to hand over money or a credit card to a clerk, even for something small, take a minute to catch your breath. Within that monetary pause, reflect on your motive and invite God into the transaction.

What's really behind this exchange of currency, and what societal pressures are involved? Ask yourself, "Am I acting freely? Am I acting most like the me I know? What feeling can I identify with possessing and using this product?"

Avoid Running

Do you shop because something else in you isn't engaged? Are you keeping a tough emotional issue at bay? Are you putting off real work that's calling you? Are you trying to fill one basket with goodies that clearly belong in another? Many women load up on new blouses and shoes and furniture rather than facing emotional woes. Others stifle real creativity with shopping. They think a new lamp brings the same satisfaction as painting a landscape. It doesn't. Others use shopping like food, stuffing themselves to feel better, to camouflage a craving for love they're not getting. Overspending brings no genuine solace, and often leaves a terrible aftertaste.

Exercise a one-day "cash fast"; don't indulge in any money exchange at all. Do this, not for self-denial, but for the boost in self-confidence. Feel the personal power associated with the resistance to spending. Spending can be nothing more than indulgence. The strength you'll feel emanates from a place of abundance and not a place of lack. A wholesome abstinence from spending can be spiritually fulfilling and, like prayer, can guide us to a new awareness in our lives.

Be gentle with yourself. Don't put yourself down for overspending, and do not attempt to change your patterns all at once. If you overspend and can't figure out where it all goes, carry a small pad with you and write down everything you buy. Track each purchase, no matter how small, even that dollar you spent on a toll. Maintain this practice for several months and discover a new appreciation for money. Chances are, you'll have more money. Why? Because you'll spend less on inconsequential items.

Flex Your Limits

Practice taking risks. Regularly stand at the edge of your limits and take a leap. Buy a lottery ticket. If you have a little extra, play a stock on the Dow Jones, bet on a horse or a basketball game, or invest in a small business. Break the old, rigid thinking that says: "I'd never do that with my money!"

Are you a spender or a hoarder? Every behavior is a signpost along your particular spiritual path, and you alone know what it means. Try to consciously counteract any undesired money pattern that holds you hostage. If you feel poor, begin to act and think rich. If you desire an unattainable luxury for your home, imagine it already there. If your habit is to fearfully check price tags before you admire an object, next time, don't look at the price tag, let an object's beauty and function speak to your heart unimpeded.

These risks will help stretch your money muscles. Ask yourself: What does this feel like? Why am I anxious? Do I live in faith? Or fear? What do my behaviors tell me about my larger self?

Maintain a Journal

Fill your journal with thoughts and perspectives as they occur to you. Take out your journal after you've shopped. Note the streams of fears or delights you felt during your purchases. Do the same with your savings, your investments. Did you become anxious when you wrote that last check? Later, reread your entries. What new awareness emerges?

Keep a money scrapbook, collecting the receipts for all the goods coming into your life. Paste in pictures from ads of the things you bought that delight you. Do the same for things you wish to acquire, but can't at the present time. Make a treasure map of future material goods, with clipped pictures. Stop being afraid to dream.

Copy money quotes in your journal, such as: "Worrying about money truly makes me poor." Then record your impressions of these quotes.

Keep in Touch

Women like knowing they can take care of themselves and each other. So gather with others in a money support group. You can openly examine the values that lie behind your acquisitions, contributions, and savings. Money talk doesn't have to be about strategizing for the future, watching the stock market, or bemoaning what's gone, but can be simply about increasing clarity. Your group can share childhood stories about the hidden parental, cultural, and spiritual influences that have shaped your money ideas.

Experiment with group exercises to animate the process. Take out your bills and coins. Share the feelings that the symbols on them evoke. Chances are it's not the buffalo or the former president facing you that matter, but the faces of people who, through their money beliefs or your dealings with them, have influenced you negatively or positively.

While enjoying their company, don't look to the group to approve of your unique money pathway. Spending according to how other people think, buying what they buy, measuring yourself against the accomplishments and defeats of others may be your problem. Remember, your money adventure is your own special pathway to God. The point of the group is to have a safe place to speak your truth and to grow more comfortable with your financial life.

Trust someone who handles money well and who can offer you clarity on your tough money issues. This may be a friend or a counselor. Keep an ongoing conversation with this money coach, checking in with her or him from time to time, making sure you are completely honest when revealing your financial worries.

Again, always remember to thank God.

Further Conversations

Money as Sacrament invites us to look deeply at ourselves, to look at what motivates us, what attitudes we hold, and how we align our attitudes with our pathway to God. Money is a common symbol for perceiving our intimacy with ourselves, a mirror of our soul's intention. Seen this way, we can no longer take lightly any exchange of currency as we prepare to break out of crippling and crusty beliefs around money to a world of bright and joyful relating.*

1. Spiritual Integrity
   Walking along your particular spiritual path, how are you honoring the gift of money?

2. Deepest Longing
   What is the deepest calling you can hear about the sacred potential of money in your life? Where is that call taking you?

3. Money as Blessing
   Something as ubiquitous as money must be a divinely ordained blessing. How does your own experience support this? What would it be like to understand money as blessing in all your economic agreements?

4. Divine Purpose
   Are you able to see a divine purpose in all the currency flowing in and out of your hands? What is that purpose telling you? Can you see money's power to reshape your very soul?

5. Parents' Patterns
In what ways do you feel that your parents' financial habits have crippled you? Have helped you? How could you be freer of their influence? Are there ways you can honor your parents' money patterns?

6. Feelings of Scarcity
Is scarcity always a bad thing? Have feelings of scarcity played a major role in your life? If yes, are you dealing honestly with those feelings?

7. Having Enough
Can you say what it would take for you to feel you had enough? Can you imagine an existence where you didn't need more? What exactly is enough?

8. Detachment
It has been said that the only way to maintain true power over wealth—as with any other gift—is to live detached from it. How does this truth play in your own life?

9. Money Bias
Think about your money biases. Do poorer people merit your scorn? Do you ever find yourself fawning over people who have more money than you? What do such behaviors tell you about yourself? About others? About God?

10. Stories Abound
Consider a story of someone you know who is an example of having had a positive money experience. What part of their story connects to your story? How do these stories bring you into a greater oneness with others and with God?

Adele Azar-Rucquoi obtained her B.A. from Manhattanville College in New York and earned her Master's degree in Religious Education at Barry College in Miami, Florida. She has taught courses on creativity at Rollins College and, with her husband, Jim, led a popular seminar entitled *The Money Thing*. Azar-Rucquoi is a founding member of the Foundation for Mideast Communication, a group that offers peace-making workshops between Arabs and Jews, as well as the director of the Central Florida chapter of the International Thomas Merton Society. She is active in the Central Florida Interfaith Community, Elderhostel, and Jewish-Christian relations, and has conducted workshops on prejudice reduction, conflict resolution, and leadership training. She resides with her husband in Maitland, Florida.

For information regarding *Money as Sacrament* workshops, please email: Adele@MoneyAsSacrament.com